The Hidden Power™
of Photoshop® CS:
Advanced Techniques for Smarter, Faster Image Processing

RICHARD LYNCH

SAN FRANCISCO | LONDON

SYBEX®

Associate Publisher: Dan Brodnitz
Acquisitions Editor: Bonnie Bills
Developmental Editor: James A. Compton
Copy Editor: Liz Welch
Production Editor: Lori Newman
Technical Editor: Doug Nelson
Compositor: Chris Gillespie, Happenstance Type-O-Rama
CD Coordinator: Dan Mummert
CD Technician: Kevin Ly
Proofreaders: Laurie O'Connell, Nancy Riddiough
Indexer: Ted Laux
Interior Design: Caryl Gorska
Icon Illustrator: Tina Healey Illustrations
Cover Design: Ingalls + Associates
Cover Photograph: Øivind Sandum

LIBRARY OF CONGRESS CARD NUMBER: 2003115581

ISBN: 0-7821-4255-9

Dear Reader,

Thank you for choosing *The Hidden Power of Photoshop CS*. This book is part of a new wave of Sybex graphics books, all written by outstanding authors—artists and teachers who really know their stuff and have a clear vision of the audience they're writing for. It's also part of our growing library of truly unique digital imaging books.

Founded in 1976, Sybex is the oldest independent computer book publisher. More than twenty-five years later, we're committed to producing a full line of consistently exceptional graphics books. With each title, we're working hard to set a new standard for the industry. From the paper we print on, to the writers and photographers we work with, our goal is to bring you the best graphics books available.

I hope you see all that is reflected in these pages. I'd be very interested to hear your comments and get your feedback on how we're doing. To let us know what you think about this, or any other Sybex book, please visit us at www.sybex.com. Once there, go to the product page, click on Submit a Review, and fill out the questionnaire. Your input is greatly appreciated.

Please also visit www.sybex.com to learn more about the rest of our graphics line.

Best regards,

Dan Brodnitz
Associate Publisher
Sybex Inc.

Software License Agreement: Terms and Conditions

Dedication

To Sam for making sure I got up in time to write, Murphy for keeping Sam in line. Lisa for not finding too many things to do so I could, and Julia and Isabel for much-needed distractions.

Acknowledgments

A huge thanks to Sybex for helping me get the Hidden Power series under way. Special thanks to Bonnie Bills for the ability to see what other acquisitions people did not and for understanding the concepts and direction behind my proposals. Thanks as well to all the pleasant and enthusiastic staff at Sybex, who proved to me that pain is not an essential element to writing a book, especially Jim Compton, Dan Brodnitz, Lori Newman, and Senoria Bilbo-Brown. ■Unqualified thanks to Al Ward (http://actionfx.com) whose enthusiasm, generously open ear, and patience helped me form ideas, concepts, and tools used in both Hidden Power books. Additional thanks to Gregory Georges (http://www.reallyusefulpage.com), Fred Showker (http://www.graphic-design.com/), Doug Nelson (http://retouchpro.com/), each for enthusiasm, interest, and support, and tool testers Susan Stewart, David Bookbinder, and Danny Raphael. ■Thanks to Photosphere (http://www.photosphere.com) and the Seattle Support Group (http://www.ssgrp.com) for generously providing selected images for use in the book. Thanks as well to Color-Vision (http://www.colorvision.com) for use of the Spyder colorimeter. ■Continuing thanks to Stephanie Wall, Mitch Waite, and Beth Millett, who helped get me started, and whom I can't thank enough. Those unusual and (I hope) not betrayed: Kevin Harvey, Alan Weeks, Larry Woiwode, mom, and other vowels and consonants: VT, AT, VL, VN, TZ, LD, SL, etc.

About the Author

Richard Lynch has written three books on Photoshop and digital imaging, including *The Hidden Power of Photoshop Elements 2*. He writes as a columnist for *Digital Photography Techniques*, teaches digital art classes, spent years as senior editor for a how-to photography book publisher, and currently works in communications, information management, and web development.

CONTENTS AT A GLANCE

Contents

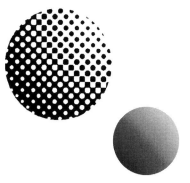

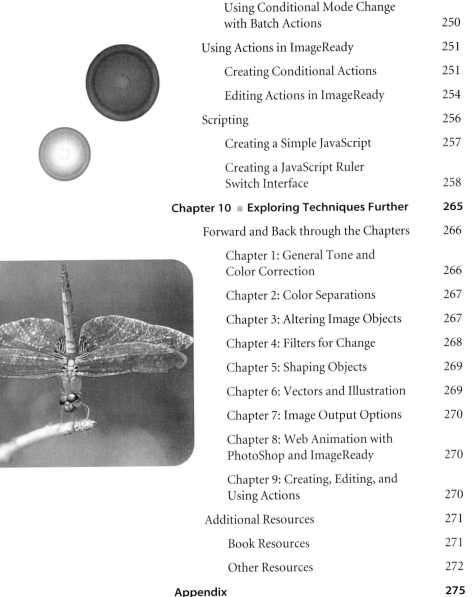

Introduction

Although I wasn't really thinking about it at the time, in a way, I really started writing this book in 1992 when I first started using Photoshop professionally (with Photoshop 2). At the time I wasn't planning to write a book, but I had already been involved with scanning and editing digital artwork for several years. I had become enthralled with the possibilities offered by digital image editing and admittedly somewhat obsessed by Photoshop. Even in those early versions, the program seemed more limited by the systems it was run on than the other way around.

Over those first few years, I was learning, reading everything available about the program and digital imaging and trying to digest the program, make sense of it, and create easier ways to get things done while maintaining the quality of my work, and improving my style every day. One of the most disturbing things I read was that it would take five to seven years to become proficient in Photoshop—the program had barely been around for that long, and no one would have that kind of time to devote to learning a program. The claim seemed impractical, but at the same time there seemed no end to what I had left to learn.

Over the 10+ years since, both the program and systems have become more sophisticated and powerful, further expanding the boundaries of what could be done with Photoshop and digital images. The Internet and digital printing have blossomed, leading to the development of different ways to deploy images and to a need for a broader understanding of how to use digital images in different media. During that same period, more sophisticated and demanding users have had the opportunity to develop their skills and have input into how the program was built and what it could do. As there were more things to look at in the program, books became bigger, broader…and regretfully often filled with piffle and fluff perhaps in an effort to look like they had more to say.

I have written three books on Photoshop. With each, the goal has been to do something unique to help users understand how to *really* use Photoshop—not just to rehash the tools and functions as so many books do, and as the manual already does. Each book has been geared toward looking at what users need as a Photoshop user, as use of the program evolves, as user sophistication evolves, as technology evolves, and as my own understanding evolves. The hope has been that I can distill my experience and help users understand the program more quickly and completely.

In understanding Photoshop, one of my most pivotal and enlightening experiences was taking time to discover Photoshop Elements. The limited tool set in Elements encouraged me to look at processing images differently, simplifying and distilling the logistics of how I approached images. Many of these changes in perspective gained through working with Elements changed the way I work in Photoshop, and at the same time helped me develop a new appreciation of the tools unique to Photoshop and available for the Photoshop user. This book looks at Photoshop from that distilled perspective and explores the hidden power that lies beneath the surface in the tools you have in Photoshop.

When that author wrote that it takes five to seven years to become proficient with Photoshop, it was in the early days of the program when even those writing about it didn't have the opportunity to develop and enhance their style. Now, with a mature program, a mature approach to learning about digital images can help speed up the learning. While I agree that it takes a long time to get good with the program, perhaps a better perception of the learning curve is that you never really stop learning Photoshop. There is always room to improve your understanding adjust and enhance your technique, streamline your workflow, and improve your image results. The goal of this book is to help move you briskly along that path.

Who Needs This Book?

This book isn't for everyone. People come to Photoshop from all different directions and with different interests. Some are photographers making the switch to digital, some are graphic artists moving into digital rendering, some are prepress or printing professionals, some are migrating from some other software like Elements or Paint Shop Pro, and some are just serious hobbyists or people interested in digital images. Some are tossed in front of Photoshop at their job (perhaps against their will!) and are told to learn to use it. Some don't fit into any of these categories, but most of us can read that list and identify ourselves. Each potential user brings a broad range of understanding and interests to Photoshop and digital imaging. Most of us have unique reasons for coming to Photoshop. Some folks eventually become Photoshop Users, and some merely fiddle with the controls. This book is for those who want to be Photoshop *Users*.

One thing all people who use Photoshop have in common is that at some point they open the program for the first time and start to crack the shell. They locate the program icon after the install and double-click to open the most broadly used image editor on the planet, and are faced with hundreds of options from which to choose—so many options, in fact, that the experience may often be overwhelming. They may have no idea what to do next.

Some may have been hoping that the program would be more intuitive and would just do more things for them. Some may be lucky and have an idea of what they want to do and where to start, and they may have some relevant photographic or art experience that will help them move forward to overcome the initial learning curve.

Some folks use Photoshop for a long time, and yet don't ever use it to its potential or understand what they are doing to get a result. Just because they open the program and can slug their way through some of the tools, they don't necessarily end up becoming Photoshop Users—although they use Photoshop. They never even begin to approach the tools or a level of understanding about digital images that really sets apart a Photoshop User from Photoshop dabblers, or users of other image-editing programs.

This book is all about looking at the tools and techniques that you need to know to be a real Photoshop User. It isn't a beginner book that will spoon-feed you lots of detail about how to use the basic tools that you should already know, or can become familiar with by consulting the manual. It *is* a book for those people who really want to understand Photoshop and get the most from it. It covers important features and concepts that you need to get results in print and on the Web. This doesn't mean you have to be an advanced user to enjoy and learn from the book, and it doesn't mean that every step will be an adventure for every user. It does mean you have to have an interest in exercising the production and power tools that make Photoshop elite.

So who needs this book? You do—if you have purchased Photoshop because you need the unprecedented degree of control it provides.

Who Needs Photoshop?

People sometimes ask me questions, or apologize for being beginners or for asking obvious questions or for not having my book, "yet." The questions are welcomed because it helps me remember what it was like to have to climb the learning curve—back in Photoshop's infancy when there were fewer resources, and many fewer ways to get help. It helps me keep in sight the idea of what people really need to learn.

Photoshop is now a mature program with many mature users who need mature information. It is primarily a photographic tool, and the text of this book approaches it from that direction. Photoshop isn't for the casual user who just needs to download and print images from the digital camera—there are plenty of programs that can do that, and often one will come with your digital camera. The most frustrating thing about questions I hear about using Photoshop is not so much the levels of the questions, but the misconception about Photoshop and what it is and does. Sometimes people are convinced that they need to use Photoshop either because the program is "the best," or because someone told them they needed it, or because it is the most popular image-editing program, or because it is the only program they've heard of that helps them edit images, or because they think it performs magic. Not everyone needs it—they just think they do. Basic tasks like converting TIFF files to JPEG or rotating the orientation of an image don't require Photoshop; they can be handled by Adobe's own Photoshop Elements, a program that's easier to use and less expensive.

Questions from beginners who have a serious desire to learn is all well and good; those aren't frustrating questions. Everyone starts at the beginning and they will have beginning questions. It is frustrating when people —who don't have the true need for Photoshop, or the real desire to learn it—are nudged into buying an expensive program when they can certainly get away with something else.

So who needs Photoshop? Those who are doing or plan to do professional, volume production work on images. This includes *volume* CMYK, *volume* image processing, program workflow customization, and *volume* complex image processing (e.g., animation, graphic website creation). If the drive to purchase Photoshop is just that it has bigger, badder tools, and that it can get better results, the hope is not a realistic one. There are big bad tools, but these tools enable you do it yourself—they won't be doing it for you.

Not everyone needs Photoshop. But if you need Photoshop, you want to know all the hidden power that can be found in the tools discussed in this book. If you don't have to do the things discussed in this book, you probably don't really need Photoshop at all.

What's in the Book?

If you are a Photoshop user, you must be wondering what could possibly be in this book, and where those "hidden" tools must be hiding. You might be thinking that those tools must be exotic and odd, or unnecessary. Nothing could be further from the truth.

This book is not just a freak show of obscure three-eyed tools and frog-lady functions that will weigh on your patience by long, boring descriptions. What tends to hide more in Photoshop than the tools is their purpose. This book is partly an exploration into lesser-known and less-discussed tools that serve a unique purpose in Photoshop. It is also a look at tools I use every day, and that I wonder how other users get by without discovering. It is, in part, a look at how to use features that have been staring you in the face for years that you've not been using to their potential, never bothered to learn, can't find in other books, and don't know what to do with. Once you really look at these functions and tools—most of which are hidden in plain sight—you'll see what they were designed to do, and they won't seem nearly so strange. In this way, they can easily become part of your everyday repertoire, and give you a better understanding of processing images and more of what you paid for in Photoshop.

What we won't look at are the hidden tools that are simply obscure, or those that you will find little purpose for. There are tools hiding all around in the interface; a few have uses that aren't obvious and a few are hidden gems. Some tools in the program fall into the "What would I ever use *that* for?" category. Others fall into closely related categories like "Oh, sure, I get it, but what's it good for?" or "Ho! That thing? It's useless!" category. These are the areas where you might be most surprised. By the end of this book, even some things you use every day, like layers, can have a different, creative purpose. After reading this book, you'll group such tools into categories like these: "I don't know how I did without this!" or "I had no idea this tool could do that!" or "I've been using this wrong the whole time!"

The "Hidden Power" tradition started in *The Hidden Power of Photoshop Elements 2* (Sybex, 2003) brings with it unique tools created just for this book and its readers. These tools are meant to help you become more productive. They put into motion the discussions and step-by-steps presented in the book by providing actions that play back many of the procedures to help walk you through when you have difficulty, or provide an automated solution to multistep procedures. This is the other half of the Hidden Power concept. You'll get tools on the CD that help you quickly set up image scenarios that you can use to make better corrections that work with every image. You learn the theory in the book and don't just apply the tools blindly—you apply them to help you do what you know how, and to see what you expect in your images.

Depending on how you already use Photoshop, discovering the hidden power in the tools can mean different things. For some, it requires learning to use tools that hide in plain sight, perhaps using the tools you already use more effectively, and perhaps discovering new uses or features in tools you already thought you knew and used to their potential. Sometimes it means taking a different approach, and often it means experimenting. In more ways than one, it is meant to launch you from using Photoshop to being a Photoshop User.

This sideshow isn't held in an alleyway off the main concourse; it is held right in the big top. What you'll find there are not freaks and abnormalities in the procedures and functions, but powerful tools that extend what you can do in Photoshop that I use all the time, and that you'll use to improve your results every day.

Organizing the Book

One of my favorite things about this book is that I don't have to sit back and start with an overlong description of basics. Anything of that sort has been relegated to the Appendix at the back of the book where you can reference it if you need to. If you can't find a particular topic in the Appendix, you can find out more about by asking me questions directly. You'll see more about how to get help with your questions in the "More Help with Hidden Power" section.

The book is broken into six parts: Image Color; Altering Image Objects; Creating Objects, Photo-realism, and Illustration; Implementing Images; Automating Photoshop and Expanding Horizons; and Appendix.

Part I: Image Color starts you looking at the source of your images: the tone and color breakdown that makes up what you see. The goal is to help you understand how an image comes together from its roots. It isn't just a discussion of meaningless theory that tells you the history of RGB and then says "OK, apply *that* to your images." You will learn to physically and manually take apart the elements of your image so that you know what your images are made of. You'll learn useful techniques like working with channels in the layer stack and manually separating CMYK that are good for color-correcting every image—techniques that don't depend on an automated setting or magic behind the scenes. This allows you to understand the images and work with image color and tone in a way that brings channels and layers together as a more intuitive set of tools. You should emerge from this part of the book with a hands-on knowledge of color and tone, and you will have techniques that work in applications for every image.

Part II: Altering Image Objects focuses on making selective changes to the composition of your images. The greater emphasis is on using advanced features to separate out problems, and target changes using the right tools for the job. My favorite of these tools, Blend If, will be revealed in several ways, and is the catalyst for other advanced techniques. Filters for Correction looks at the useful filters that aren't just effects, but those filters that you'll be using every day to improve (rather than stylize) images. Selecting image objects, isolating image areas, and making intelligent masks based on image tone (which you learned to manipulate in the previous part) as well as intelligent use of filters, gives you ultimate control over the color and shape of your result.

Part III: Creating Objects, Photo-realism, and Illustration looks at creating image elements and using them to enhance existing images. The chapters look at using shadow and highlight to shape objects, how to create patterns—and not-so-patterned patterns—to give your objects texture, and give an example of creating an object. Creating objects from scratch can sometimes also involve using Photoshop's powerful and flexible vectors, both for shaping results and making infinitely scalable results.

Part IV: Implementing Images covers a few ways to look at getting results from your images in print and on the Web. Creating webpages with Image Ready—one of Photoshop's most notorious hidden powers—will uncover a wealth of buried features such as tweening, controlling animation, and implementing slices. The explanation of printing will help you get results whether or not you embed image profiles.

Part V: Automating Photoshop and Expanding Horizons begins with a more in-depth look at automating Photoshop functionality for your own needs. We'll look at some of the newer, perhaps often underutilized features for controlling your individual preferences with a click, and we'll delve into recording complex actions that you can use to create functionality and image setups. You'll learn to work with bulk processing of images as well as automating process and techniques you use all the time. If just recording an action doesn't do what you need, you'll learn the basics of creating new interface components to actually add different functionality to Photoshop. The last chapter offers suggestions for further explorations you might make, extending projects from previous chapters, and lists some further information resources.

Appendix. This useful appendix is a sneaky way for me to plunge right into the fun stuff at the beginning of the book. It is a catch-all for things that need to be discussed for more background, but which may be a little out of line with the advanced focus of the book. This section helps fill in some theory that is left out elsewhere. This includes necessary ground-level building-block information that usually bogs down the beginning of a book that readers at this level will not always need. It also ties in some fringe concepts that are perhaps a little too odd to use every day, but that shouldn't necessarily be ignored. Some is the stuff that over the years people have both complained about and thanked me for when I put it in books, but that doesn't always get immediately applied in Photoshop.

The CD

The CD contains a few things that you will want to have when working through the book. First, it contains images for all of the exercises so that you can work along with what is going on and experience getting the results discussed in the book. It includes sample images and any other content (such as JavaScript code) that works better as files than as pictured on a page. It has actions you can install that both demonstrate discussion and work for you to help produce results, and other add-on tools that help you work like I describe in the book. It is your resource for the parts of the book that you wonder why they aren't done in color—they don't need to be, because they are more effective as images you can work with on the CD.

Shortcuts

Standard shortcuts between Mac and Windows use are really the same in Photoshop—the only thing that happens is a few keys are swapped. The table here shows Mac/Windows equivalents. The text will show the shortcuts as a composite of both (as illustrated in the Example in Text column). The hope is to make the book both Windows and Mac user friendly. I side with neither and use both.

Mac	Windows	Example Mac	Example Windows	Example in Text
Shift	Shift	Shift+P	Shift+P	Shift+P
Option	Alt	Option+M	Alt+M	Option/Alt+M
⌘	Ctrl	⌘+V	Ctrl+V	⌘/Ctrl+V
Control	Right-click	Control-click	right-click	Control/right-click

More Help with Hidden Power

I didn't write this book just to retire to a comfortable chair somewhere never to look back at the readers while they remain stranded in a sea of information—as can often happen with Photoshop books. I can be reached in several different ways for questions, comments and support, including e-mail, my website, newsletter, and forum. I hope to help users not only learn the techniques in the book, but have the opportunity to flesh out and broaden uses of the techniques and examples, discuss new ideas, and tie together loose ends. We can work out the logistics of developing new tools and methods of applying them to enhance the experience of learning for everyone who reads the book, and to make more information available even after the book has been published.

E-mail

Use thebookdoc@aol.com to contact the author directly. Depending on volume, email will be addressed as possible, and not necessarily in the order received. Frequently asked questions will be answered in the *Hidden Power of Photoshop* newsletter. Additional information can be found on the website for the book.

Website

Websites with more information about the book are available at http://photoshopcs.com/, http://photoshopx.com, or PS6.com. The site will include information for readers, including links to the newsletter, additional tools, tutorials and a contact page where you can enter comments, questions, and so forth.

Hidden Power of Photoshop Newsletter

To keep readers up-to-date on any changes, and to answer frequently asked questions, a newsletter will be sent to all subscribers several times a month. To subscribe to the *Hidden Power of Photoshop* newsletter, just send a blank email to: hpps-subscribe@yahoogroups.com. Subscription is free and the newsletter is open to anyone that wants to join. You can also visit the site and archives here: http://groups.yahoo.com/group/hpps. If this service changes for any reason, updates will be made available on the website. An alternative means of subscribing is also available if you don't want to use the Yahoo! service.

Part I
Image Color

Color and tone give an image its shape and dynamics. You need to orchestrate color and tone to produce the best images—not just for the screen, but for print, the Web, or however the images might be used. To get the best results, it is crucial that you have a solid understanding of how to tinker with color and tone in images (and sometimes how to manhandle those values). This part of the book takes an intimate look at making image color changes and corrections, starting with general theory, corrections, and some workhorse tools, then moving on to making targeted changes. Along the way, we'll look at dissecting an image in separations to isolate different qualities with accurate selection based on tone and color.

Chapter 1

General Tone and Color Correction

When making image corrections of any kind, you'll tend to make broad, global corrections first before moving on to tackle isolated problems. If you have no plan of attack and try to correct an image by just going at it willy-nilly, chances are you'll end up with random results—sometimes good, and other times not. Starting with a basic plan of attack can help you get better results consistently.

The first thing you'll want to do when approaching any image is to evaluate and then adjust the general tone or color. A good general correction of your image balances the color and lighting and assures that the image you are starting with is the best and most dynamic it can be. These corrections should become automatic, but not *automated*.

Before making any corrections, you'll need to know what you are looking at on screen and understand some key concepts so your results and the process make sense.

Looking at what you see on the screen

What makes an image

Dynamic tone and color with levels

Snapping image tone and color with curves

Curves for color correction

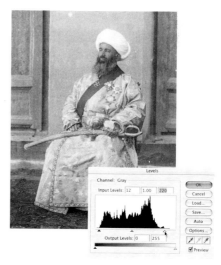

Looking at What You See on the Screen

With digital images, what you see on screen is only an approximation of the digital information that is stored—and is only a best guess as to what you will see when the image is used. There are a number of reasons for this, aside from the fact that your eyes will play tricks on you by adjusting to the lighting in the room or the monitor, or that you might have varying levels of colorblindness. You'll get the best images by intelligently hedging your bets using smart correction techniques and trusting only *part* of what you see.

Even people who know better often take for granted that what you see on screen is a good general representation: a representation of the digital information *and* of what your result will be in print—or even what you will see on other monitors. Making the image look on screen like it will in all these cases is actually a tall order, and sometimes more like a dice roll, depending on how you handle it. If you haven't made some effort to understand color theory and work within the limitations, your expectations may be a little unrealistic.

Monitor Color and Print Color

The biggest hurdle for many people is that color on a monitor doesn't translate one-to-one into the same color in print. That's because the two media use entirely different methods of producing the color we see.

When looking at a computer monitor, you see RGB color in action: color essentially created with red, green, and blue lights projected on the monitor screen. Projected light is an *additive* color scheme: Colors are created by combining various levels of those three primary colors. The more color, the brighter the result. Full strength of all RGB colors adds up to white. A lack of any color becomes black (or as near to black as your monitor screen will get).

When looking at a printed page, you see reflected color: Color is created by combining different amounts of ink or pigment to absorb and reflect light. Usually these inks or pigments are cyan, magenta, yellow, and black (described by the acronym CMYK), but somewhat different color models can be used. The light that is left over (not absorbed) reflects from the page and results in the color you see. This is a *subtractive* color scheme; the more color added to the printed image as a combination of the inks, the more light is absorbed, and the darker the overall result. With less ink, the color is lighter until reduced to the color of the page—assumed to be white.

Note: If you are printing on a nonwhite object (e.g., black paper), you may need to add white as a spot color to get images to print correctly.

In both cases, your eyes receive light, either as projected or from the reflection. The color schemes are actually very much related: CMY (without the K) and RGB are complementary, cyan being the opposite of red, magenta the opposite of green, and yellow the opposite of blue on the color wheel (see the ColorWheel.psd file on the CD). Red, green, and blue channels can be separated and stacked in layers to mimic the additive light result. To do this, you would split out the color information for each of the color components (we will step through this process in Chapter 2), then specify Screen mode so that the component acts as projected light (using Screen mode). If you invert the colors that the layers represent (each RGB color for the CMY complement), invert the mode (Multiply for Screen), and invert the background (white for black), these same component layers can represent the subtractive color scheme. In theory, the same tone can be used in opposite schemes to represent the equivalent RGB and CMY result. You can see this in Figure 1.1, and in RGBlayers.psd and CMYlayers.psd on the CD.

Figure 1.1

Information for the color components in a CMY and RGB image can be identical.

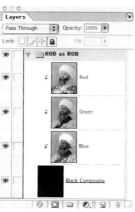

RGB in layers using Screen mode

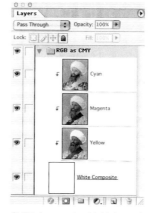

CMY in layers using Multiply mode

Blue channel in RGB, yellow in CMY

Green channel in RGB, magenta in CMY

Red channel in RGB, cyan in CMY

While there is a theoretical relationship between CMY and RGB color, in practice other issues muck up that relationship. The foremost of these issues is that the reflected light scheme is not as efficient as the projected light scheme. Other issues have to do with media being inefficient; the reflectivity and color of the paper; and the reflectivity and color of the ink. In other words, in a perfect world CMY could be interchanged with RGB and you wouldn't need any K, but because of inefficiencies the result degrades. Black ink is added to the CMY scheme to compensate for the deficiency in practice. But while it helps, the conversion from RGB to CMYK will still not produce a perfect representation of every color.

Every conversion that isn't perfectly efficient causes a change in the image whether it is a digital conversion (for example, converting RGB to CMYK) or a physical one (for example, projected light reflecting from ink). Previews attempt to compensate and make the conversions appear correctly on screen, but they can't account for every variable with complete accuracy. Considering what the odds are, Photoshop previews do a fair job. However, this all adds up to the fact that you can't trust what you see 100 percent.

Other Problems at the Capture Stage

Assuming that what we see on screen is the right thing is not all we may take for granted. It is easy to assume that the image was captured accurately. This suggests faith in the equipment and lighting. Any number of issues—from the quality of light (for example, lighting color), to distortion by the lens or scanner, to errors in processing, to incorrect monitor settings—can impart their personality on the result. For instance, when an image (taken with poorly color-balanced light and scanned from time-yellowed photographic paper using an uncalibrated scanner) appears on your monitor (which your child not-so-secretly adjusted so that the standard program palette grays are a more exciting purple), the images you painstakingly adjust to perfection on screen project an affinity for Martian culture by the green tint that appears in the skin tone of the prints. When you print out to laser paper—not meant for your photo-quality printer—even that green fades to a duller cast.

As odd as that might be, the result is actually mostly predictable, but it will sure look like an accident. If you fall into the category of having purple-y grays, and have never visited the Color Settings dialog box, you should have a look at setup instructions for Photoshop and several areas of the Appendix to this book, including information on calibration and handling profiles. However, these deviations may not be so broad as the scenario described here: You may have a slight tint to your shadows or a hue in highlights that can cause you to consistently over- or under-adjust areas of your image if all you do is look at the screen. You want to have the greatest chance of seeing the right thing on screen, not just something that will get you by. Calibrating your monitor can help reduce the appearance of deviations on most monitors, and will help you achieve more consistent results. If you haven't calibrated, do it now. Refer to the Appendix for more information.

What Makes an Image

Digital images are usually assembled for you: Your scanner or digital camera gets the digital information by sampling the scene or scanned area, and provides the information neatly in a digital file format. The image information is most often captured using RGB theory: Light is measured as the red, green, and blue components, and the sampling is mapped to create color for individual pixels. These three light components can be combined to re-create an RGB rendering of the image.

An extraordinary example of how light theory really works are the images taken by Russian photographer Sergei Mikhailovich Prokudin-Gorskii in the early 1900s. Prokudin-Gorskii took what were essentially color images before color film was invented. He did this by using a special camera that had three lenses, which allowed him to expose a scene to three glass plates simultaneously, resulting in three black-and-white images. Each of the lenses was filtered, one with a red filter, one with a green filter, and one with a blue filter.

The result was an RGB separation of the scene onto those three glass plates, which essentially represents the RGB channels in Photoshop (see Figure 1.2).

Figure 1.2

Prokudin-Gorskii's images came out exposed to a glass plate. His images are archived on the Library of Congress website here: `http://lcweb2 .loc.gov/pp /prokquery.html`. **Search the collection for Kush-Beggi to find this image.**

The only way Prokudin-Gorskii had to reproduce the images was by projecting the glass plates using red, green, and blue filters over the lenses of a special projector. Using the projector, the scene was re-created—more or less in full color—by re-introducing color to the filtered information that was stored. Prokudin-Gorskii only had a fancy projector; you, on the other hand, have Photoshop. Using it, you can re-create these scenes from scans of those plates, adjust the color, and fix damage, distortion, and exposure problems.

I've included an interesting and rather colorful shot on the CD of the Minister of the Interior, Kush-Beggi, for the first exercise. It was taken by Prokudin-Gorskii sometime between 1905 and 1915. I've taken the liberty of adjusting for most of the lens distortion between the plates and cut the plate scan up into the separate channels. I'll show you two ways to assemble this image and make color from the black and white, and quickly discuss a third as well.

While these step-by-step discussions may have some details (mostly shortcuts) that you already know, such detail will not be maintained throughout the book. Our goal is to cover the basics once and move on quickly.

Re-creating Color from a Separation (the Quick Way)

For this exercise, you'll need to get some images off the CD, so if you haven't taken the CD out yet, do it now. The three images are kb-red.psd, kb-green.psd, and kb-blue.psd. Don't have other images open when attempting this exercise to avoid confusion.

1. Open kb-red.psd, kb-green.psd, and kb-blue.psd in Photoshop using File → Open (or ⌘/Ctrl+O). You will be able to select multiple files in the Open dialog box by holding down the ⌘/Ctrl key.

2. Open the Channels palette if it is not already visible. Do this by selecting Window → Channels.

3. Choose Merge Channels from the Channels palette. See Figure 1.3.

4. Choosing Merge Channels opens the Merge Channels dialog box. Choose RGB from the Mode drop-down menu, as shown here. Be sure the number in the Channels field is 3, and click OK. The Merge RGB Channels dialog box will open.

5. Under Specify Channels, choose kb-red.psd as Red, kb-green.psd as Green, and kb-blue.psd as Blue, as shown here, and then click OK.

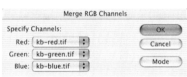

These five steps will create a color image from the three black-and-white images you opened in step 1. This is an uncorrected color depiction of the original plates. Save this image as kushbeggi.psd. You may want to come back to this image to fix some of the other problems later.

Re-creating Color from a Separation (the Harder Way)

To do this task a little more like Prokudin-Gorskii did, this set of steps shows a somewhat more difficult, but perhaps easier to understand, method. The idea here is to combine the separated colors using layer properties rather than channels:

1. Open the three images (kb-red.psd, kb-green.psd, and kb-blue.psd).

2. Copy the kb-blue.psd image. To do that, select the whole image, copy it, and create a new image. In the New window, set these options:

   - Select White as the Background.
   - The size will be automatically selected.
   - Select RGB as the Mode.
   - Type **RGB Layers** in the Name field.

Click OK, and paste (⌘/Ctrl +V). Pasting creates a new layer.

3. Rename the layer **Blue**. To do this, double-click the layer name in the Layers palette and type **Blue** when the layer name is highlighted. (See Figure 1.4.)

4. Copy and paste the kb-green.psd into the RGB Layers document. For the most part, this process will resemble step 2, except that you will use the document already created rather than creating a new one. Name the layer **Green**.

5. Copy and paste the kb-red.psd into the RGB Layers document. Name the layer **Red**. These steps get all the necessary image information into the RGB Layers document and stack the layers in RGB order.

6. Activate the background by clicking on it in the Layers palette (or press Option/Alt+Shift+[). Fill the layer with black. To do this, either use the Fill function (Edit → Fill → Black) or the Paint Bucket tool. You can choose the Paint Bucket tool by pressing G (or Shift+G to toggle from the Gradient tool); press D to change the colors on the toolbar to the defaults, and fill in the background with black by clicking the tool anywhere in the image. Be sure the tool options are set as follows:

   • Set Fill to the Foreground color.

   • Set Opacity to 100%.

   • Deselect Use All Layers (if necessary).

   These settings will create a black background (a dark projection screen) for you to add your color.

7. Change the mode of the Red, Green, and Blue layers to Screen. Pressing Option/Alt+] will help you navigate up the layers in the palette if you feel it is easier than clicking them. When you are done, leave the Red layer active.

8. Create a new Fill layer. You can hold the Option/Alt key and either choose Layer → New Fill Layer → Solid Color, or choose Solid Color from the New Fill or Adjustment Layer button on the Layers palette  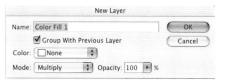. Holding Option/Alt with the second option will make sure the New Layer dialog box appears. In this dialog box, click the Use Previous Layer To Create Clipping Mask option, and set the Mode option to Multiply in the Layer Options palette (see Figure 1.5). Set the color to red (255, 0, 0 in RGB) in the Color Picker.

   Using Multiply mode will darken all the grays in the Red layer to red. This represents how the red light information will look. (You can shut off the Green and Blue layers to preview.)

Figure 1.3

The Channels palette has a pop-up menu that you access at the upper right of the palette; the menu allows you to choose channel-specific tasks.

Figure 1.4

When you finish step 3, you'll have the background and a new layer named Blue.

Figure 1.5

You can name the layer, set its mode, and choose Group With Previous Layer in this dialog box.

9. Create a Fill layer for the Green layer. Activate the Green layer, and then create the fill layer as you did in step 8, using green (0, 255, 0 in RGB).

10. Create a Fill layer for the Blue layer, using blue (0, 0, 255). This will complete the setup. The layers should look like they do in Figure 1.6.

At this point, save the image as kushbeggi-filterlayers.psd. What these steps show is essentially what Prokudin-Gorskii did to re-color his grayscale separations: he applied the red, green, and blue colors to the separated information using filters and projected them onto a screen.

Multiply mode works just like a filter would, darkening the brightest area of a channel to the pure representation of the filter color. All Photoshop channels really do is create this representation for you.

Yet another, more advanced way to accomplish this same result is to throw out the color fill layers and use the RGB check boxes in Layer Styles to modify the color. To open the Layer Styles palette, double-click on one of the layer thumbnails. With the palette open, leave only the box checked for the color channel the layer should affect: R for Red, G for Green, and B for Blue. Figure 1.7 shows how the palette looks when affecting blue only.

Selecting the check box targets the layer so that it only affects the information in the channel(s) you specify. To merge the layers back together, you can just flatten the image. We'll look at how to make separations from full color in Chapter 2.

I have included a copy of a scan from the original glass plate on the CD, called gorskii-original.psd. As an advanced project, you may want to take the image and attempt to adjust for the lens distortion. You may need to use Transform, as well as other distortion tools and filters, since the glass for each lens and the incident angle on the scene are slightly different. If you'd like, you can download the 68MB original scan in 16-bit form from the Library of Congress website to indulge in 16-bit editing as well.

Figure 1.6

Be sure the layers are in this order. Fill layers should be Multiply mode, and color layers should be Screen mode.

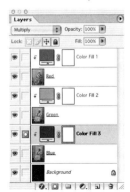

This process, 100 years in the making, actually shows how a digital image is stored. Your camera or scanner will follow just about the same steps as Prokudin-Gorskii did so long ago, by separating the color information in the scene into RGB components (red, green, and blue). The separation is stored as grayscale information; in this digital era, it is stored in a digital file rather than on film. The image is re-created on the monitor by projecting that stored information as red, green, and blue light—in this case, by tiny phosphors on your screen.

In a certain sense, the color is always affected by limitations in color sensing and the ability to store information. 8-bit-per-channel images can store "only" about 16 million colors; 16-bit per channel images can store more than 30 trillion colors. The latter is arguably only a very good approximation of actual tone and color.

The quality of what you see on screen depends on the quality of what is captured, but it also depends on limitations in the display. If the filter colors (or light color) are wrong when input or when displayed, the image will appear "out of color" as opposed to out of focus. We can make the best of

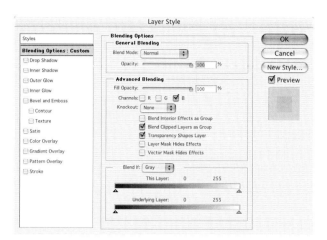

Figure 1.7

Deselecting the R and G check boxes under Advanced Blending will make the layer information affect only the blue light component in the image.

what we have captured by making intelligent color corrections. We'll look at color corrections in the next few sections. Now that we have the Prokudin-Gorskii image back together, we can use that image and make general corrections and work more in-depth with the hidden power of tone in your color images.

Dynamic Tone and Color with Levels

The Levels tool can be used for a variety of things, but one of the most useful is extending the dynamic range of tones and colors already in an image. Say, for example, you were using black-and-white film to take a picture and you underexposed the image. This means enough light won't get in, so the whites in the image will be a little dull. It will make the whole image a little flat because the image won't use the entire dynamic of possible color and tone. The compressed range will sap some of the life from it.

Using the Levels tool, you can redistribute the image information that was captured by redefining what should be the dynamic range of the image. All you have to do is look at the Levels graph, and it will show you where the image is missing tone (open the Levels graph by pressing ⌘/Ctrl+L). Figure 1.8 shows the blue channel (kb-blue.psd) from the Prokudin-Gorskii image before and after adjustment.

To make this adjustment, take these steps:

1. Open the kb-blue.psd image.

2. Open the Levels Adjustment Layer dialog box (Layer → New Adjustment Layer → Levels). Looking at the graph ("before" in Figure 1.8), you can see that the grayscale values in the image don't extend to the full width of the range; the graph is flat at the black and white ends.

Figure 1.8

The blue channel for the Prokudin-Gorskii image used in the previous exercise can be adjusted to balance color by using levels to redistribute the tone.

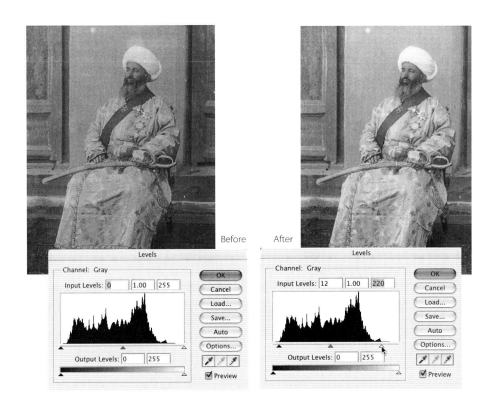

3. Using the Input sliders, correct the shortened tonal range by adjusting the slider positions. Drag the black slider to where the graph begins to climb and the white slider to where it ends ("after" in Figure 1.8).

You can use this technique for any grayscale tone adjustment; simply move the black and white sliders in to where the information in the graph begins and ends. Doing this redefines the tonal range for the image. The correction takes the information and redistributes it from black to white (rather than black to gray, gray to gray, or gray to white). The result is that the dynamic potential of the image is expanded.

The Input and Output numbers you see on the Levels palette represent levels of tone. Tonality is captured in 256 levels of gray (between 0 and 255). Each level is a distinct tone ranging from white (255) to black (0). The number 256 reflects the number of possible tones in one channel of an 8-bit image (for more on bits, see the Appendix).

The Levels tool should be one of the first tools you reach for when doing color and tone correction. It can help you correct underexposure, overexposure, and many other related problems in a few simple steps. It can also correct for general color shifts due to lighting or filtering or related general color problems. Correcting color is almost identical to correcting tone. The only difference is that you want to correct the tone in each of the color channels for a color image, rather than just the composite.

To correct the color using Levels:

1. Open kushbeggi.psd. This image is on the CD, but you can use the one you saved earlier when you compiled the RGB channels.

2. Create a new Levels adjustment layer.

3. Select Red from the Channels drop-down list.

4. Adjust the tonal range for the red channel by moving in the black and white sliders directly below the graph where it just begins to climb to redistribute the tone.

5. Repeat steps 3 and 4 for the green and blue channels.

6. Switch to RGB and move the center (gray) slider to adjust image brightness.

The result after these changes should be a brighter, more dynamic image for our example. The same technique will work on many images to improve them—especially faded images and those lit by a single light source, or those that have a predictable, linear shift. For more complicated shifts, this type of correction may need to be used in conjunction with a curve (or other) correction to better control the result.

Save your image as kushbeggi-L.psd. You can compare the before and after by clicking Open on the History palette and then clicking the final step.

Using the Levels tool in this way is based on solid science and works as a general correction technique for almost any image. The reason has to do with visible light and the way we perceive light. A scene will usually appear to your eye to have a full dynamic range in tone from white and black. If the scene is lit with pure white light, it also has the potential for every color in between, because white light contains the full potential of the red, green, and blue light components. The light interacts with the scene and is reflected, then captured on film or digitally. What is captured should reflect the potential of what should be in the scene. In other words, a perfect world will reflect the full potential of the light in it, and some of each component will be captured.

For the image to properly reflect full potential dynamic for color and tone, each channel has to have a full range. Making the levels change corrects for aberrations in capture.

There are often differences because the science of capture is less forgiving than our perception. While our eye might adjust to a scene automatically, digital and film capture will not adjust—they just grab what's there. A scene lit with impure or colored lighting or captured with poor exposure reflects what the camera sees—which is not necessarily the potential of the scene. Levels give us the opportunity to easily see what failed to be recorded and restore the potential and dynamic range. The upshot is color and tone balanced for white light.

If individual color channels don't have full dynamic range, it cuts down not only on the potential tones (black to white), but the potential colors. For example, if the green channel has a graph that shows only 50 percent of the potential range, the image can't have the color created by mixing with that range of green. In fact, each level missing from the range cuts down the potential colors by more than 65,000 possibilities. Restoring the range restores the potential and is effectively a safe (rather than destructive) color correction.

If any Levels graph shows a shortened range, it suggests one of the following:

- The light source was not pure.
- The capture wasn't balanced.
- Filtering was used.
- Exposure was not optimal.
- The light in the scene was otherwise influenced.

Extending the dynamic range in the color channels helps correct for and restore the color imbalance by reestablishing a balanced source based on white light and the potential for all colors.

The only instances where the levels correction of this sort fails or does not improve an image are cases where a color shift is desired or where there is a nonlinear influence. The desired color shift can be exemplified by a scene where you used a color filter on purpose, or if a scene has an intentional or inherent light cast (as in a sunset), or where the color and tonality in the scene is very limited. (Correcting to create the full range of color levels could have a bad influence on the image.) Nonlinear influence might be exemplified by an incandescent light in a blue room: The color might shift red in highlights due to the reddish color of the direct source, but blue in shadows because of reflected light from the walls.

Of course, Levels is not your only tool for image color correction, but it does offer a good starting point. You will need to learn to understand histograms and work with curves for more versatile corrections.

Understanding and Reading Histograms

Histograms appear in several different places in Photoshop, including the Histogram palette and the Levels dialog box. The width of the histogram graph represents the range of potential tonal values. The height of a given line in the graph represents the number of pixels in the image with a particular tone. Aberrations in the graph, such as steep peaks and valleys, gaps in information, and/or clipping (spikes in information that run off the chart), may represent some form of image damage, limitation, or loss of image information. The graph can also describe high-key, low-key, high-contrast, and low-contrast images. Evaluating a histogram is as easy as looking at it and understanding a few basic properties. Figure 1.9 shows examples of how histograms look with different image types.

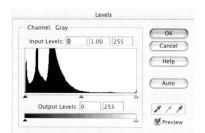

When weighted toward the blacks or dark end of the graph, the histogram represents a low-key (dark) image.

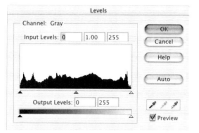

A histogram that is skewed to the light (right) end of the graph represents a high-key (bright) image.

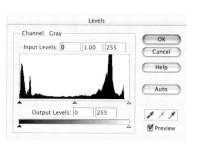

A histogram that peaks in the dark and light areas while having lower pixel density in the middle of the graph represents a high-contrast image.

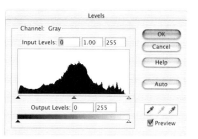

A histogram that shows a peak in the center is low-contrast.

An image with a mix of global and local contrast displays as a flattened graph in the histograms with few peaks and valleys.

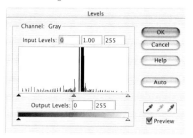

Gaps between tones on the histogram or sparse information suggest the image has limitations or damage, such as poor scanning.

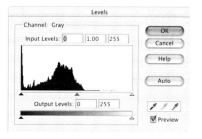

Graphs that show clipping (information that runs off the chart) suggest a concentration in the tonal range. Concentrations often occur in the extreme highlights or shadows of an image and may also suggest damage.

Figure 1.9

The look of a histogram graph can tell you about the content of an image.

It is possible to evaluate a section of an image by selecting it with the selection tools. The histogram charts the results only for the active or selected portion of an image.

Apparent anomalies can be the result of capture, such as bad scanning (faulty techniques or equipment), incorrect image exposure, filter use, or unusual lighting conditions. Anomalies can also easily be the result of image processing: mode conversions, corrections, poorly applied filters, and so forth. Any abnormalities might not always represent problems, but they are certainly good indications of unusual conditions.

Do not be overzealous in accepting the appearance of the histogram as an absolute judge of the image; be sure to make the visual assessment as well and use the two assessments in tandem. Your visual assessment should override the digital one, especially if you get good results in tests and have reason to trust the view of your monitor. Your primary goal should be a good image, not a good histogram.

Sometimes shifting the range using levels—even radically removing information in the image—can work to the benefit of the image by improving contrast and dynamic range. When the histogram presents a "tail" toward the shadows or highlights (see Figure 1.10), it can often be clipped in part or whole. Tails on the histogram often represent highlight or shadow noise, rather than actual image detail. Snipping the information turns it to absolute white for a highlight (or absolute black for a shadow).

It is sometimes desirable to eliminate none, some, or all of a tail, depending on the image and the length of the tail. As a general rule, the longer the tail, the less—proportionally—you should cut off. For example, you may completely remove a tail that covers 15 levels, you might trim half or less of a tail that covers 50 levels, or 33 percent of one that covers 100 levels. This will help retain image integrity and character.

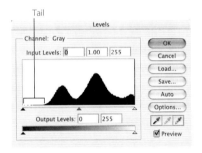

Figure 1.10

A "tail" in a histogram usually represents nothing more than image noise.

Don't feel that you have to crop a tail in the image just because it's there. If the results seem too drastic after cutting a tail, they are. Put simply: Crop a tail if doing so improves the image; don't crop a tail if it compromises the image.

Images that appear too dark or light can be corrected by using the middle slider in the Levels tool. Moving the slider to the left lightens midtones, whereas moving it to the right darkens them. This may seem slightly counterintuitive; however, it makes a lot of sense. The idea is that you are moving the median so that more levels of tone fall within the lighter or darker half of the tonal range.

As a general guide, try not to move the midtone slider more than 25 levels (10 percent of the image tonality) in any direction when making corrections with the middle slider. This keeps the redistribution small and more forgiving. You can always come back and lighten or darken an image later in additional steps and adjustment layers, or adjust using other tools like curves, which we'll look at in the next section.

Snapping Image Tone and Color with Curves

Curves are the ideal tool to help fine-tune and reshape the tone of an image. Whereas levels have only three control points that you can change, curves can have many (up to 16), and this can help you work in different tonal ranges with targeted results. Curves are both a more versatile correction tool and a more volatile one than levels because of their power. You'll find that using curves for corrections can reduce the steps involved because you can apply one curve and make numerous corrections to various parts of image—often without selection. While levels are a good tool for evaluating and adjusting dynamic range in an image, curves are a good tool for adjusting image contrast and dynamic range in small chunks of the tonal range.

Because curves are powerful, applying them requires a little more savvy than applying levels. Before we begin, let's take a brief look at the interface and how to manipulate the curve.

Using the Curves Function

You access the Curves function by creating a Curves adjustment layer (Layer → New Adjustment Layer → Curves) or by selecting Curves from the Image menu (Image → Adjustments → Curves). You can also access a similar interface when working with duotones and assigning transfer functions.

> The difference between using curves (or any other adjustment, for that matter) in adjustment layers is that the adjustments can be revisited without making a permanent impact on the image and layers to which they are applied. Applying an adjustment directly will make a permanent change that cannot be revoked without retreating in the image History.

Curves can be used in two modes: one based on percentage and the other based on levels. The line that runs from lower left to upper right of the graph represents tonal response. When you first open the dialog box, the graph will read out an even tonal response if the Input value (the original tones) is equal to the Output value (the result). Changes that you make to the graph by adding and moving points modifies the relationship between the original image tones and the result. So, say you add a point to the graph at 128, 128 and move it to 128, 64; all of the midtones will become 50 percent darker (going from 50 percent black to 75 percent). The shape of the curve that results shows how moving this one point affects the rest of the image tones. Moving any point on the curve can affect that entire image in different proportions based on the shape of the tonal response curve.

Depending on the mode, the initial points either represent levels (0 = black, to 255 = white) or percentage (0 percent black—or white—to 100 percent black). You control the mode using the button on the gradient bar directly below the graph (see Figure 1.11). Levels may be thought of as referring to RGB measurements, pertaining to 8-bit grays (and 256 possible levels of gray per tone); percentage may be more appropriate for CMYK, referring to percentage of ink coverage. Either can be used, depending on what you find more intuitive.

Figure 1.11

The Curve mode button in the center of the lower gradient bar switches between percentage black and levels when clicked.

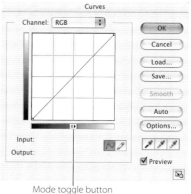

Mode toggle button

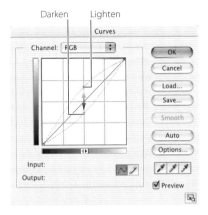

Figure 1.12

Moving points on the curve (pictured here in tone levels mode) will darken the image with less volume under the curve and brighten it with greater volume.

If you roll your cursor over the graph, the Input and Output numbers below the graph change as per the position of the cursor. These numbers represent the vertical (Output) and horizontal (Input) positions on the graph.

If you click on the graph and drag (holding down the mouse button), you can move the point and the curve. As you move the curve, the tonality of the image shifts according to the change in the curve. When you're viewing in tone levels, the image will get lighter as you shift the arc of the curve up, and it will become darker as you shift the arc of the curve down (see Figure 1.12). When you're viewing percentage, the relationship is reversed.

You can manipulate the position of points that you have placed on the graph that are active (highlighted in black) by typing numbers into the Input and Output fields. If you roll your cursor over the image with the Curves dialog box open, your cursor will become an Eyedropper. This will allow you to sample color and tone directly from the image. To transfer a sample to the curve, hold down the ⌘/Ctrl key and click the mouse. Photoshop creates a new point on the curve representing the tone sampled in the image.

Though the Curves dialog box includes other options, the ones listed will be all you'll need to make specific adjustments.

WORKING WITH POINTS ON A CURVE

To add a point:

- Hold ⌘/Ctrl and click to sample the image.

- Roll the cursor over the curve and click.

To move a point:

- Click on the point and drag.

- Highlight the point (by clicking it) and change the Input/Output values.

- Highlight the point (by clicking it) and press the keyboard arrows in the direction you want to move the point. Hold the Shift key to move 10 levels in the arrow direction.

To remove a point:

- Roll over the point, hold ⌘/Ctrl, and click.

- Highlight the point (by clicking it) and press Delete.

- Click on a point and drag it off the graph.

Manipulating Curves

If Levels is a tool that affects *dynamic range*, the Curves feature can be considered a tool for affecting *contrast*. You can make sweeping changes to an image or fine-tune delicate areas of tone with curve adjustments depending on how you handle them.

A simple way to look at curves and curve adjustments is that contrast *increases* in the tonal range between points where the curve is steeper and contrast *decreases* in the tonal range where the curve flattens out. The curve in Figure 1.13 will increase contrast in the image midtones (between 25 and 75 percent black).

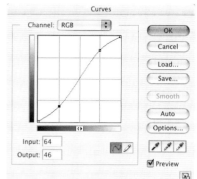

Figure 1.13

A steeper rise in the curve between Input values of 64 and 191 tone levels make contrast more intense through the midtones.

The curve in Figure 1.14 will decrease contrast in the midtones over the same range. Note that the increase in contrast over the midtones in Figure 1.13 decreases the contrast in the highlights and shadows. In Figure 1.14, decreasing the contrast in the midtones increases the contrast in the highlights and shadows.

You'll work with this type of trade-off (somewhat like equal and opposite reactions) when you're manipulating curves.

When you add points to a curve, you won't always do so to move the curve. At times it will be useful to place anchors on the curve to keep the tone in that area of the image from changing, or to act as a pivot for adjustments. For example, anchors set in the highlight and midtone can keep the tone in the highlight from changing while you adjust shadows (see Figure 1.15).

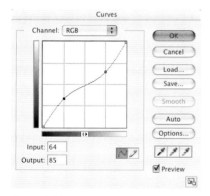

Figure 1.14

Decreasing the grade of the curve slope in the midtones increases contrast in shadows and highlights.

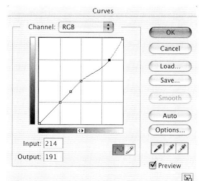

Figure 1.15

Anchoring the curve with extra points that just hold the curve in place can reduce the effect of an equal and opposite reaction in your changes.

The Eyedropper can help you measure the actual range you want to affect. The Eyedropper appears as you drag your cursor over your image when the Curves dialog box is open. In Figure 1.16, the original image was taken in direct sunlight, resulting in a high-contrast exposure. Curves can help reduce the quick transition from highlight to shadow. In this image (included as contrast.psd on the CD), measure the brightest and darkest areas of the tonal range you want to include. To do this, drag the Eyedropper on the image and ⌘/Ctrl+click to make sample points. You can also note the sample value and enter it in the input field manually.

To make an image correction using Curves:

1. Open the image you want to correct (contrast.psd is included on the CD).

2. Set the options for the Eyedropper and Info palette. For the example, we chose a sample of 3 by 3 for the Eyedropper and changed one of the Info palette colors to K (Grayscale).

3. Open the Curves dialog box by choosing Curves from the New Adjustment Layer submenu (Layer → New Adjustment Layer → Curves).

4. Sample the bright end of the range you want to correct (see Figure 1.17) and create a curve point.

Figure 1.16

This image was taken in direct sunlight and shows harsh shadows.

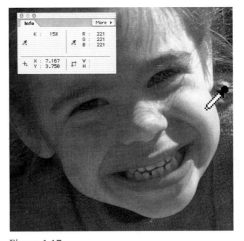

Figure 1.17

The highlight area of the cheek is the lightest portion of the area that will be changed.

EVALUATING COLOR AND TONE WITH EYEDROPPERS

The Eyedropper samples image information and displays the result on the Info palette. All you have to do is put the cursor over the image area you want to measure, and the Eyedropper will sample the composite of the visible layers. It can be helpful in evaluating an image throughout the correction process. For example, comparing grayscale values for sample and target areas before cloning can tell you whether those areas are a good match before you make the clone.

The Sample Size setting for the Eyedropper tool affects the result of samples used with curves. Tool options include only Point Sample (samples the pixel at the tip of the tool icon), 3 By 3 Average, and 5 By 5 Average. The Average options look at a square of pixels (the tip of the tool icon as the center pixel) using the selected dimensions and average those to determine the result. In certain cases where tone is noisy, such as skin tones, you should use a broader sample size to get a better average reading of the tones you want to measure. Using too small a sample size might only make confusing samples; values between one pixel and the next might change too rapidly to make sense. Control+clicking/right-clicking brings up the Sample Size menu when you're using the Curves dialog box.

To use the Eyedropper, follow this general procedure:

1. Select the Eyedropper tool (press I).

2. Choose the radius for the sampling area on the options bar.

3. Bring the Info palette to the front by selecting it from the Window menu, or by clicking the tab in the palette well.

4. Spot-check with the Eyedropper by passing the cursor over various areas of the image that you want to check while noting the values in the Info palette.

Samplers can also be placed (using the Sampler mode for the Eyedropper Tool) in the image to provide a constant readout of a particular spot in an image. You can place them with the Sampler tool , which you access by scrolling the Eyedropper tool (press Shift+I to scroll the tool), or by holding the Shift key with the Eyedropper tool selected. Up to four samplers can be placed in each image. These samplers will not move until they are removed from the image (press Option/Alt with the Sampler tool active, roll the cursor directly over the sampler to be removed, and then click). Each sampler will have its own readout in the Info palette.

Figure 1.18

The image moves pretty abruptly from light to dark. The second sample should be somewhere in the area where the image tone makes the transition to shadow.

5. Sample the dark end of the range you want to correct (see Figure 1.18) and create a curve point.

6. Use the input fields to adjust the position of the curve points to effect the desired change. In Figure 1.19, the 51 percent (134 levels) point was changed to an output of 33 percent (171 levels).

7. Continue adding points and adjusting for other tonal relationships by repeating steps 5 through 8.

8. Accept the changes in the curve by clicking OK.

It is possible in some cases that you will want to include additional curves using steps 3 through 8 to make further modifications to the tone. See Figure 1.20, for example. Such modifications may be the exception rather than the rule in fine-tuning delicate areas.

Keeping a curve smooth rather than choppy or abrupt is more likely to render good results. Jagged curves tend to be unpredictable and will more likely produce special effects than corrections. If changes seem extreme or become difficult, make them over the course of several applications of curves rather than just in one shot. This approach will allow you to compare adjustments by toggling layer views, as well as allowing you to fine-tune.

Controlling color with curves works somewhat in the same way as making contrast adjustments. Results can actually be calculated to make exacting corrections that would otherwise be impossible.

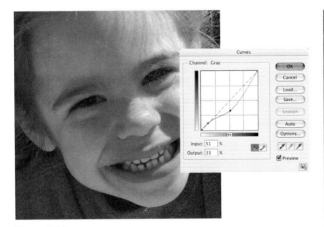

Figure 1.19

The changes in the curve lighten the image and reduce contrast in the midtones while improving contrast in the highlight and shadow detail.

Figure 1.20

The result of several curve applications has improved the tonality of the image by lessening the harsh contrast between light and dark while enhancing contrast in selected areas.

Curves for Color Correction

Color casts in images can result in flatness and unnatural or plain old bad color. Basic color correction with levels often eliminates most of this problem, but color casts and shifts between the lightest and darkest parts of an image are often a little more complex than looking at a histogram or doing a general color correction in levels. If a color shift is in only one portion of the color range (shadows, midtones, or highlights), levels may not do enough to make the correction. Curves are a more sophisticated means of fine-tuning color—either to make it exacting or simply more dynamic in a specific range. This is a correction you will make after, and in addition to, a levels correction.

> Those newer to "color correction" are probably sometimes misled by the term, which suggests there is a "correct" color to shoot for. Color correction remains more an art than a science, and corrections may reflect color that is more interesting, bolder, and more dynamic, rather than just "correct."

The problem is knowing exactly what to do with your curves. It is difficult to just look at an image and envision how a curve should look to make the desired correction. While it may be easy to determine what looks *wrong*, correcting it can remain a puzzle. Just fiddling with curves and hoping for a result will usually be a frustrating exercise—and if you do hit on a correction, it'll be an accident.

Say you are looking at an image and the color of the subject's skin just looks wrong. Skin color is something we are all familiar with, so most people can tell when it just doesn't look right. If the skin tone looks wrong, the image will look wrong. In fact, if you can correct for the skin tone, it is likely that everything else in your image will fall into place.

However, a problem arises when you try to correct for skin tone: The difference in skin tones is vast. Skin tone has many colors and shades, so no value can be an accurate reference—unless you measure it from the original subject, and there isn't much chance you'll be doing that. Certainly there are approximations, but you can just as well make approximations if you can trust your eyes (and monitor).

Paradoxically, the best reference are areas that should be grays. Grays can act as a reference because they are easy to measure: They should have even amounts of red, green, and blue. When you measure with the Eyedropper, the R, G, and B values displayed in the Info palette should all be the same—or very nearly so. Looking for areas that should be gray can give you a definitive value to adjust for.

In a perfect world, you could find areas of your image that should be grays of 75 percent (64, 64, 64), 50 percent (128, 128, 128), and 25 percent (192, 192, 192) black as reference in your images; you could then set accurate white and black points, and your images would balance nicely. It usually isn't too easy to find these references unless you place them right in your image. While you can do this using a reference card, it is not something that everyone will take the time to do. An example gray card can be as simple as printing shades of gray on a white sheet and getting that reference in the image.

A reasonable substitute for a gray card are grays that already exist in the image. If you look closely, you may find something that should be a flat shade of gray, such as a steel flagpole, chrome on a car, asphalt, ice skate blades, certain types of tree bark… Anything that should be flat gray, paradoxically, becomes very useful for color evaluation. While black and gray objects can vary in color to some degree, they will be easier to judge and correct for than something like skin (where there is no absolute reference). Making corrections for grays should become one of the more useful staples of your efforts in curve "corrections."

You'll try an example of this method next.

Correcting Color Using Gray Points

Once you determine your reference objects, curves can help you easily adjust image color. All you have to do is measure the tone and color of the gray object, and then adjust the curves to make those objects gray, while ignoring everything else in the image.

To determine the values for a gray object to use in correction, take the following steps:

1. Locate an object in your image that should be closest to gray.

2. Be sure the Info palette is visible and that one of the sample types is set to RGB Color (RGB).

3. Select the Eyedropper from the Tool palette. Be sure that the sample option is set to 3 or 5 pixels. The wider range is effective on images with greater resolution.

4. Put the tip of the Eyedropper over the reference area. Place a sampler by pressing the Shift key and clicking. This sampler will remain in place until you remove it. Values under the sample will appear in the Info palette (see Figure 1.21).

5. Note the RGB values in the Info palette. You may want to have another sample value showing the grayscale so that you know the approximate tone you are sampling from. Say you end up measuring these values:

Red	170
Green	150
Blue	160

6. Adjust the red, green, and blue channels with curves so that the color reflects an average of the RGB values. You will adjust the values in the example from the measured

Figure 1.21

Samplers stay in place in the image until you remove them by holding down Option/Alt and clicking the sampler. The image information read by the sampler(s) appears in the Info palette.

value (input) to the desired value (output). Just place points on the curve and then adjust by entering the appropriate Input and Output values. See Figure 1.22.

	Input	Output
Red	170	160
Green	150	160
Blue	160	160

When you have finished making the correction, the sample that was 170, 150, 160 will now be 160, 160, 160 (you can check this in the Info palette easily if you placed the sampler in step 4). Other values in the image will change based on the change in the curve.

With this level of control, your choice in selection of a gray reference is very important to the outcome. If you choose a gray that in reality is supposed to be slightly green and you don't allow for that, your corrections will end up somewhat warm. Again, visual inspection and the numbers have to work hand in hand to achieve the best result. The more reliable gray points you measure, the more accurate your curves correction will be. The next section looks at implementing this technique with gray values placed directly in the image just for that purpose.

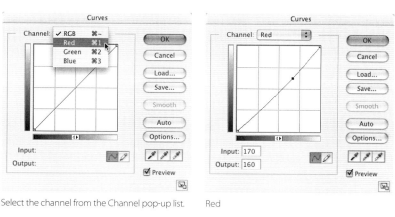

Select the channel from the Channel pop-up list.   Red

Green   Blue

Figure 1.22

Make adjustments by number, one adjustment for each channel in the Channel drop-downlist.

Tempering Curve Corrections

When using an object that you are not sure is gray (e.g., tree bark) as the reference, you may only want to make a percentage adjustment, rather than just assuming you want a completely flat gray. That is, you may want to give some credence to the existing values. This is similar in concept to not cropping off the entire tail in levels, since you will be looking to make only part of the correction as a compromise. Instead of making a drastic change, you make only part of it.

For example, if the difference in the colors is broad, or skewed to one of the channels, it may be preferable to average 50 or 75 percent of the difference. The more positive you are that the value you are measuring should be gray, the stronger the percentage you should apply; the less sure you are that it should absolutely be gray, the less percentage you should apply.

To change by a percentage, you would take the difference between the measured and average value, multiply by the percentage you choose, and add it to the measured value: Target value = measured value + {[(average value) - (measured value)] x percentage}. Using the numbers from the last example, your calculation for the red channel will look like this:

Target value = 170 + ([160 - 170] x .75)

Target value = 170 − 7.5

Target value = 163

The following list shows how the table would look if making only 75 percent of the change:

	Input	Output
Red	170	163
Green	150	158
Blue	160	160

Figure 1.23

If using several sample grays, place them on the curve for each channel in one step. This curve shows a red correction for 64, 128, and 191 levels changed to 51, 137, and 184.

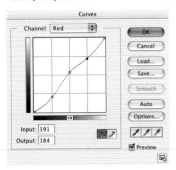

Compound Curves Correction

Simply correcting for one gray won't really give you a much better correction than using levels. What you'll really want to do to benefit from curves is correct for several grays. The more levels of gray you correct for, the more accurate your correction. Try to space out the tones of the grays you measure. For example, sample grays at the quartertones: 25, 50 and 75 percent gray. If you measure several grays, make the corrections all at once by placing as many points on each curve as you have sample spots (see Figure 1.23). This will ensure that you are changing the measured spots relative to one another; if you change the values sequentially on separate curves, the changes will work against one another rather than together. The more evenly you divide the gray levels used for the correction, the better.

Figure 1.24 shows an image that was photographed with a homemade 25 percent, 50 percent, 75 percent gray card. To correct the image, you'd open it, correct the levels (which sets the white and black points), and then make corrections using the values for the gray card as your target Output (result) values.

Let's run through the correction for the image.

1. Open lillycard.psd from the CD.

2. Place a sampler in each of the three gray card areas in the image to measure the grays. You should see these measurements, or something very similar to this:

	25%	50%	75%
Red	170	119	75
Green	196	153	85
Blue	213	148	52

3. Open a Curves adjustment layer by choosing Curves from the New Adjustment Layer menu: Layer → New Adjustment Layer → Curves. You can also choose Curves from the Create New Fill or Adjustment Layer menu at the bottom of the Layers palette .

4. Select the red channel by choosing it from the Channel pop-up list.

5. Add a point to the curve by holding ⌘/Ctrl and clicking on the darkest gray card swatch (75 percent). You can click directly over the samplers you placed.

6. Change the Output value to 63 in the Curves dialog box.

7. Add another point to the curve by holding ⌘/Ctrl and clicking the medium gray card swatch (50 percent).

8. Change the Output value to 128 in the Curves dialog box.

9. Add the last point to the red curve by again holding the ⌘/Ctrl key and clicking the light gray card swatch (25 percent).

10. Change the Output value to 191 in the Curves dialog box.

11. Repeat steps 6 through 11 for the green and blue layer components. See Figure 1.25.

12. Click OK to accept the changes.

Figure 1.24

The gray card (to the right) can help balance color at three levels of gray.

Figure 1.25

Each of the curves should look almost exactly like the curves pictured here for red, green, and blue when you make the corrections.

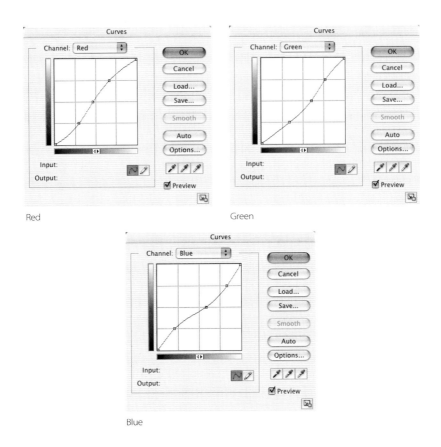

Red

Green

Blue

When you are done correcting the color, you can use the measurements to correct tone as well. Because you know that the card is 25, 50, and 75 percent gray (191, 128, and 63 levels), the measurements you checked will correspond to those values.

Now that the image is "correct," you may want to make other adjustments that are not quite so correct. In other words, this is where the artistic part comes in and takes over. The image may be technically correct in that it should be a reasonable match with reality, having realistic tone and color. While it may appear realistic, there can still be other problems, and you may want to make improvements accordingly. Additional adjustments could involve adjusting the curves further, or adding other adjustments (Color Balance, Hue/Saturation, etc.).

Sticking with curves for the moment, let's reopen the adjustment layer you have created (double-click the icon in the layer) and make our adjustments there. To adjust individual points, just click on them, and move the points while looking at the preview (either freehand or using the arrow keys). Note the initial Input and Output values (so you can return to those settings if desired); you may want to just duplicate the curve layer and play with duplicate, so you don't have to write down or remember the original values. If using a duplicate, shut off the original.

While it is possible that you can stumble into a correction for the color that looks better, it is more likely that you will get the result you want by observing and making targeted changes. For example, if you have a red that you think needs to be redder, you can set a sampler on it and increase the red, reduce the green and blue to darken (to *purify*), or add green and blue to lighten (to *desaturate*). Having a goal in your curve corrections rather than going at it at random will have you spending less time fiddling to get results. There are better tools to fiddle with (like Color Balance, as we'll see in a moment).

At the point where you have made the curve adjustment according to gray targets, the image is balanced. It is more likely that you will get pleasing results with curves when experimenting by applying them to image tone or color separately rather than to the RGB. Applying a curve to image color can help you work with image saturation (adjust the RGB curve) or in making specific increases/reductions in one of the component colors overall. Applying a curve to image luminosity can help you adjust tonality and contrast. The next chapter looks at many possibilities for isolating color and tone. You may actually get better color by making additional corrections and/or selectively replacing colors and tones, making corrections not so strictly tied to measurements, and in some cases by altering color completely. Making targeted and selective tone and color changes can help. Selective changes are covered in more depth in Chapter 3.

You can make other corrections using curves to adjust the image color and dynamic, but corrections without using targeted measures are less precision corrections than artistic decisions. Because they will also be based on the image preview, you will have to trust your perception (and your monitor) to go this route.

CORRECTING SPECIFIC COLORS

Color correcting doesn't just work for grays. You can correct for known color values as well. In instances where you know any specific color in the image, you can use curves to make your correction but just target the color. Say, for example, you take a picture of a business and know that the logo color on the building is an official color. You can target the change in color according to that measurement. Just take a measurement of the color in the image (after a levels correction), and use the RGB value for the target color as the output values. If you don't have a gray card and want to use paint swatches (gray or otherwise) from a local paint store, as long as you know the color values, you can make the adjustment for that color. Other adjustments may be necessary to other levels of the image (just as when you use multiple gray sources) to adjust the image over the entire range from highlight to shadow.

The Art of Color Balance

While levels and curves corrections are excellent tools for normalizing color, you might note one problem with making corrections by the numbers: This approach may make for pretty accurate correction, but it may not always produce the most pleasing color. If you don't know where to start your correction, the techniques we've looked at so far are definitely a fine start and will get you moving in the right direction. A final tweak of color balance may do quite a lot to enhance your image's color.

The idea of the Color Balance function (see Figure 1.26) is to allow you to shift the balance between opposing colors. Cyan balances against red, green against magenta, and blue against yellow, with separate adjustments for highlights, midtones, and shadows. While you could make similar changes with curves, the Color Balance dialog box is a friendlier and easier way to make these changes. The result is usually a fine-tuning to help bring out the interesting and inherent character of an image.

Rather than trying to calculate a result, you'll find it easier to work with color balance interactively. The goal is really to achieve more vibrant color:

1. Continue working with the lillycard.psd you have open (corrected in the previous section).

2. Open Color Balance by pressing ⌘/Ctrl+B.

3. Start with the Midtones (under the Tone Balance panel), and slide the Cyan/Red slider between −50 and +50, watching the effect on the image. Narrow down the range that looks best by swinging the slider in smaller ranges until the best position is achieved based on the screen preview.

4. Repeat step 3 for the Magenta/Green slider.

5. Repeat step 3 for the Yellow/Blue slider.

6. Repeat steps 3 through 5 for Highlights.

7. Repeat steps 3 through 5 for Shadows.

8. Repeat steps 3 through 7.

While the steps here might seem an oversimplification, this is really all you have to do. Your result can be a dramatic change in the image, even with small movements of the sliders, and changes will influence color, saturation, and dynamics.

The color result of a correction on the lillycard.psd appears in the color section, showing the original image, the image corrected for grays, and then the image color balanced with curve saturation and tone enhancements. The original looks bluish due to the overcast sky; the image corrected for gray shows a flat response and realistic color; and the enhanced version shows how the scene would look with warmer, yellowish lighting (note the cast on the card).

These general corrections are something you will probably do to any image. Yet, there are still a number of ways to further break down image color and get very specific about the changes you will make—and why you will make them. Making the best color changes after general corrections will be a matter of knowing how to properly purpose images by adjusting color and tone. Control over this aspect begins with understanding separation (breaking color and tone out of an image into separate components), which we will look at in Chapter 2.

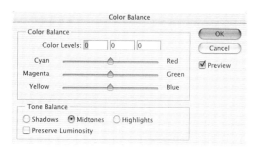

Figure 1.26

The Color Balance dialog box provides an easy, intuitive interface for adjusting color cast and balance.

Chapter 2

Color Separations

Photoshop provides many tools that seem to produce some magic behind the scenes. Channels, one of the most prominent of these tools, allow you to work directly with components of a color model, such as RGB or CMYK. But, as we saw in the previous chapter, channels can actually be simulated using some simple light theory. Understanding what the channels represent can help you make more intelligent color and correction decisions, and can very much change the way you work with images.

Not only does learning about separation help you understand what is going on in an image, it also frees you up to use different tools and techniques—because you can apply them to get a more targeted result. Good use of separation can give you the opportunity to make selective changes to image areas based on color or tone, and opens the door to advanced manipulations, selections, and calculations using targeted masking.

Turning color to grayscale

Adding color to tone

Separating CMYK color

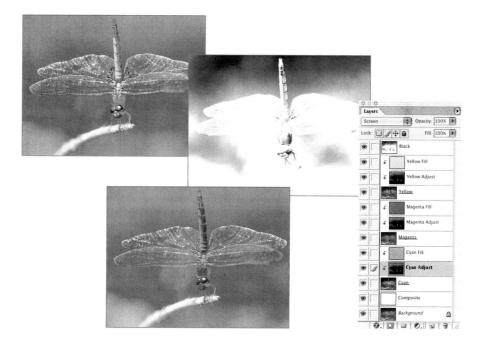

Turning Color to Grayscale

When I was learning to work with digital images, one of my first experiences was preparing images to be printed in black-and-white photography books. Problems often arose when photographers submitted their images as color scans. Converting RGB color scans to black-and-white was pretty easy—I could just choose Grayscale mode and was done with it. This approach resulted in a quick conversion so the images looked like black-and-white images, but it didn't always produce the most predictable—and not nearly the best—result. Just doing the conversion wasn't enough for a photography book; the goal was for the reader to see the best possible grayscale representation. Because it was extremely important how things looked when all was done and printed, I started looking for other solutions.

Grayscale images are quite a different animal from color. Because there is only tone—no color to worry about—it is natural to think that working with tone should be easier than working with color. There are fewer possibilities because images only have 256 shades of gray as opposed to 16 million–plus colors in an 8-bit image. However, the simplicity of the tone makes getting a good conversion important; with fewer ways for the difference in an image to be displayed, every tiny variation becomes critical.

You might think that converting an image to grayscale would be simple, since it is a simplification of the image. Besides that, Photoshop gives you several ways to make the conversion quickly, such as choosing Grayscale mode or selecting Image → Adjustments → Desaturate. However, there are hundreds of ways to convert images from color to grayscale. And just as there are various types of film with different-flavored results, users can control the flavor of their grayscale conversion. Clever use of information in an RGB image can even mimic other processes, such as infrared film.

Converting to grayscale is not only important for printing black-and-white images. Once images have color removed, you can create duotones and hand-colored images, or use the image information for repair by defining tone-based selections, for creating masks, and for adjusting and repairing channels. You may find different techniques and conversions to suit different situations. More important, you may find that dealing with tone is, in reality, easier to handle for getting good color results.

Desaturating to Grayscale

The easiest way to convert a color image to grayscale is to *desaturate* the image. Desaturating neutralizes pixel color by equalizing the red, green, and blue components to a single value. When the red, green, and blue values are the same measured value for a pixel, the pixel displays as gray. The calculation takes the highest and lowest measures and averages them, ignoring the middle value. Averaging may not be a good representation of actual tone because it doesn't do much to account for color. For example, RGB values of 255, 255, 0 and 255, 0, 0 both have a desaturation result of 127, 127, 127.

The obvious way to desaturate is to use the Desaturate function. Just choose Image → Adjustments → Desaturate. You can also open the Hue/Saturation dialog box and slide the Saturation slider all the way to the left. If you try creating a new image and filling different areas with pure RGB color (255, 0, 0 for red, 0, 255, 0 for green and 0, 0, 255 for blue), then convert to black-and-white by desaturating, the color becomes indistinguishable as tone, because all convert to a medium gray (127,127,127). Other methods of converting may salvage some of that difference.

Extracting the Brightness

Another means of changing an image to grayscale from RGB is to extract the image tone. You can do this in several ways with somewhat different results. Essentially you want to display the image brightness, based on grayscale as measured by luminosity in Lab mode or Brightness/Lightness in HSB (Hue, Saturation and Brightness) or HSL (Hue, Saturation and Luminance). Two easier methods are to extract directly from RGB or extract the luminosity after converting to Lab mode.

Use the Pumpkin.psd image from the CD to make the following conversions (see Figure 2.1 and the color section).

Extracting Grayscale from RGB Using Channel Properties

You can extract the tone right from an RGB image without the averaging that desaturation imposes. One feature of channels is that they can be loaded as selections based on their content: Just hold down the ⌘/Ctrl key and click on the channel you want to load. Brighter areas of the channel will be selected while darker areas will not. Loading a channel as a selection can be used to create a tone extraction as in the following steps:

1. Open Pumpkin.psd and create a new layer at the top of the layer stack. Name it `Brightness From Channels`.

2. Fill with white, and shut off the visibility for the layer.

3. Hold down the ⌘/Ctrl key and click on the RGB composite channel in the Channels palette. This will load the channel as a selection based on its brightness.

4. Activate the Brightness From Channels layer created in steps 1 and 2.

5. Fill with black. The image will appear as a negative.

6. Deselect and invert the layer (Image → Adjustments → Invert).

This result is the image brightness based on RGB tone—a result of loading the channel as a selection.

Figure 2.1

This pumpkin has some pretty vivid coloring (see the color section), which will translate in different ways to grayscale.

Extracting Brightness from RGB Using Layer Properties

Another way to accomplish about the same thing is to extract the brightness using layer properties:

1. Using the same image, shut off the view for the Brightness From Channels layer and create a new layer at the top of the layer stack; then fill with white and shut off the layer view by clicking the Adobe eye icon.

2. Create another new layer, then press ⌘+Option+Shift+E/Ctrl+Alt+Shift+E to merge visible to the top layer.

3. Change the layer mode to Luminosity.

4. Turn on the view for the layer created in step 1 (click the Adobe eye, but don't activate the layer).

5. Merge the two layers created in steps 1 and 2.

6. Name the layer `Brightness From Layers.`

If you compare the Brightness From Channels and Brightness From Layers layers, you may see a slight difference. To compare visually, toggle the view of the Brightness From Layers layer. To make a digital comparison, you can set the layer to Difference mode. Difference Mode will reveal any difference as lighter areas against black. These may be hard to see with the naked eye, but you can note the difference by viewing a histogram.

Converting to Grayscale from Lab Color

The Lab color model breaks down color using channels that represent brightness and color balance. The Lightness channel represents the tone, while the a and b channels represent the color balance between redgreen and blueyellow, respectively. The result is somewhat different than when you extract tone from RGB because of the difference in the color modes themselves. RGB works only with mixing color; there is no pure tone representation. Lab's Lightness channel directly represents image tone.

This extraction can also be done in several ways. All you are looking to do is convert to Lab mode and copy out the Lightness channel to an RGB image.

EXTRACTING THE LUMINOSITY FROM A LAB IMAGE BY DUPLICATING LAYERS

First, let's see the steps involved in extracting the luminosity from a Lab image by duplicating layers:

1. Using the Pumpkin.psd image, shut off the view for the Brightness From Channels and Brightness From Layers layers.

2. Click the Background in the Layers palette to activate it and copy it to a new image. (Use Duplicate Layer from the Layers palette pop-up menu and select New as the target.)

3. Change the mode of the new image to Lab. To do this, select Image → Mode → Lab Color.

4. Click on the Lightness layer in the channels.

5 Change to Grayscale mode and discard other channels when offered the option by clicking OK in the dialog box that appears. Since the appearance is already grayscale, you should see no change in the image.

6. Choose Duplicate Layer from the Layers palette and select Pumpkin.psd as the target. The grayscale background of the converted image will appear in the Pumpkin.psd document as Background Copy.

7. Change the name of the Background Copy layer to Luminosity.

EXTRACTING THE LUMINOSITY FROM A LAB IMAGE WITH APPLY IMAGE

A second way to move the extracted luminosity from a Lab image is to the use Apply Image command. The advantage of this approach is fewer steps, numerous options for application and masking.

1. Be sure all other layers you added are off and add a new layer to the top of the layer stack in Pumpkin.psd. Call it `Applied Image`.

2. Duplicate the background from Pumpkin.psd to a new image.

3. Change the duplicate image to Lab mode.

4. Activate the original image, Pumpkin.psd.

5. Choose Image → Apply Image and use the following settings (see Figure 2.2):

    - Source: The name of the duplicated image (from step 2)

    - Layer: Merged

    - Channel: Lightness (the choices here reflect the Lab channels in the source document)

    - Blending: Normal (several modes will accomplish the same thing)

    - Opacity: 100% (to achieve a complete fill)

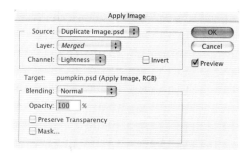

Figure 2.2

Apply Image is a powerful tool that can be used for quick calculations between open images. These settings will complete the duplication between images for you in the current example.

The dialog box will display your target as Pumpkin.psd. Click OK to apply.

Once you complete step 4, the Luminosity channel from the duplicate will be copied to the top of the layer stack in the original image. You can achieve nearly the same result by changing the image to Lab Color and then Grayscale mode and back to RGB. The result is not exactly the same as direct Lab conversions, because the conversion process includes some extra steps. The differences can be traced back to your color-management settings.

Just to prove a point, try this:

1. Shut off the visibility of all the layers except the Background, then create a new layer at the top of the layer stack in Pumpkin.psd. Name it **Desaturate**.

2. Press ⌘+Option+Shift+E/Ctrl+Alt+Shift+E to merge visible to the layer created in step 1.

3. Desaturate using the Desaturate feature (Image → Adjustments→ Desaturate), or press ⌘/Ctrl+Shift+U).

4. Compare the grayscale results by Option/Alt clicking on the visibility icon for the Luminosity, Brightness From Layers, Brightness From Channels and Desaturate layers. This will turn on the view for the view for the layer you click and shut off the others.

In step 4, the differences between each layer should be apparent on your screen. You should see a difference in each of these results (see Figure 2.3), but which is the best may not be clear. This will happen no matter what image you use. For some images one conversion will look best, and for another a different conversion will work well. These simple examples represent only the start of the subtle differences you'll note in conversions. You

Figure 2.3

The colorful pumpkin (see the color section) can easily break out into different grayscale representations depending on how it is converted.

Brightness From Layers

Brightness From Channels

Luminosity

Desaturate

Green (see the next section on RGB

can achieve a very different result by working with tone from separations into RGB and CMYK, and by combining results from different channels and separations. The point is that there is no best process or best conversion approach to getting black-and-white from color. You have to know many methods, and you have to try to visualize results to get them. Sometimes the easy route pays off, and sometimes you need to go a long way to make a great color image look decent in black-and-white.

RGB Separation to Grayscale

When creating the RGB image from the Prokudin-Gorskii plates in Chapter 1, you saw that scenes can be simplified to grayscale representations of red, green, and blue as tone. Chapter 1 showed you how to put together color from what's already separated. Taking apart the color is just about as easy! Not only can you use this separation for color correction, but separating layers can also help you create custom black-and-white images.

Separating RGB from a Color Image

Separating the image you put back together in Chapter 1 is an interesting challenge. Depending on your level of expertise and understanding, you may or may not absorb what is going on here right away. You may have to do it a few times before you grasp the details. Being able to separate RGB will help you understand how images go back together again (and how they are sampled by scanners and cameras). It all breaks down to a simple filtering of three colors.

However, users of any level can do this by following the steps outlined here. Once you become familiar with this process, it will help you understand both layers and RGB color. There is an action on the CD that will complete the RGB separation steps for you. You will find the action useful in automating the process, and it can also help by walking you through if you have difficulty with the steps. The action can be used to separate any RGB image into RGB layers.

1. Open the kushbeggi.psd image you saved in Chapter 1 (or kb-L.psd on the CD).

This technique will work with any image. The first few setup steps (creating the background and templates) help you move through the procedure easily.

2. Duplicate the background, name the layer **Source**, and then shut off the view for the Source layer.

3. Change the Background layer to black (to use as your projection screen). To do this, press D to reset to the default colors on the toolbar, and press X to exchange the colors, making black the background color. Then, activate the background by clicking it in the Layers palette, hold down ⌘/Ctrl, and press Delete/Backspace.

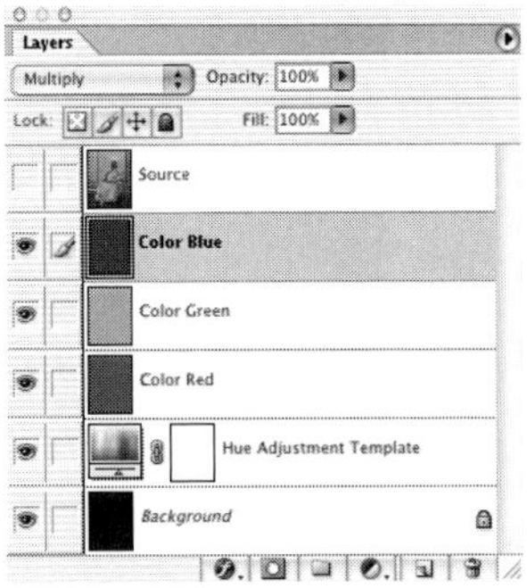

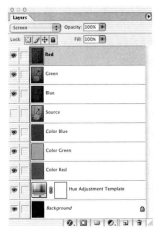

Figure 2.4

You'll use these layered components to make some repeated moves and separate out the color components in the next few steps.

Figure 2.5

After you complete step 7, the layers should look like this.

4. Create a color adjustment template layer. You will use this layer as a template that you can duplicate so that you don't have to keep re-creating the adjustment. To make the template, create a Hue/Saturation layer and set it to Hue 120, Saturation 0, and Lightness 0. Change the name of the layer to `Hue Adjustment Template`. This will not affect the black background but will help you rotate the color around the color wheel at 120° increments.

5. Create the Color Filter layer templates. Again, you will use these as templates that you can duplicate so that you don't have to re-create color-filled layers:

   • Create a blank layer named `Color Red` and fill it with pure red (255, 0, 0). Change the Mode of the Color Red layer to Multiply.

   • Duplicate the Color Red layer, and rename it `Color Green`.

   • Duplicate the Hue Adjustment Template layer and move it above the Color Green layer. This will change the effect of the layer from red to green.

   • Merge the Hue Adjustment Template layer with the Color Green layer by pressing ⌘/Ctrl+E.

   • Duplicate the Color Green layer, and name it `Color Blue`.

   • Duplicate the Hue Adjustment Template layer, and drag it above the Color Blue layer. This will change the effect of the layer to blue.

   • Merge the adjustment layer. At this point, your layers should look like they do in Figure 2.4.

6. Duplicate the Source layer, name it `Red`, and be sure it is at the top of the layer stack as viewed from the Layers palette. Then, duplicate the Color Red layer, move it above the Red layer in the Layers palette, and merge the Color Red Copy into the Red layer. Set the Mode to screen. This will make the layer serve as the red light component.

7. Repeat step 6 using the Color Green and Color Blue layers. Each time, start by duplicating the Source layer. To duplicate, drag the layer to the Create A New Layer button at the bottom of the Layers palette. Name the Source Copy layers `Green` and `Blue` in turn. Be sure to pair the Green layer with the Color Green layer and the Blue layer with the Color Blue layer, putting the Color layer above. When you are done, you'll have a simple separation showing the layers in red, green, and blue colors (see Figure 2.5). View them separately by toggling the layer views. Shut off the view for the Blue and Green layers before continuing.

8. Convert each of the color layers to grayscale representations:

   - Start with the Red layer. Duplicate this layer (leave the name Red Copy since it will be temporary).

   - Duplicate the original Hue Adjustment Template layer and drag it above the Red Copy layer. This will turn the Red Copy layer green (note the similarity to step 5). Commit the change by merging the Hue Adjustment Template layer with the Red Copy layer.

   - Duplicate the Red Copy layer (now actually green in color from the 120° color rotation).

   - Duplicate the original Hue Adjustment Template layer and drag it above the new duplicate (you may need to resize the Layers palette to do this). This will turn the Red Copy 2 layer blue.

   - Merge the adjustment layer with the Red Copy 2 layer to commit the change.

   - Link the Red, Red Copy, and Red Copy 2 layers (click the Link box as shown in Figure 2.6), click the Red layer to activate it, and choose Merge Linked from the Layers menu (or press ⌘/Ctrl+E). This will merge the layers into a single Red layer as grayscale.

> Adding even amounts of red, green, and blue will give you gray. In step 8, you have created three-color representations of the same tone, and the result of multiplying them together is gray.

Red Before merge

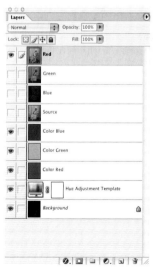
Red After merge

Figure 2.6

Link the layers prior to merging.

9. Repeat step 8, using the Green and Blue layers. Each time, shut off the view for the color component you have merged and turn on the view for the color component you are working on; then make the duplicate, apply the Hue Adjustment Template layer, make the second duplicate, apply the adjustment, and merge. When you have finished, the result will look like Figure 2.7.

Figure 2.7

At the top of the stack are Red, Green, and Blue layers that are accurate RGB color component separations.

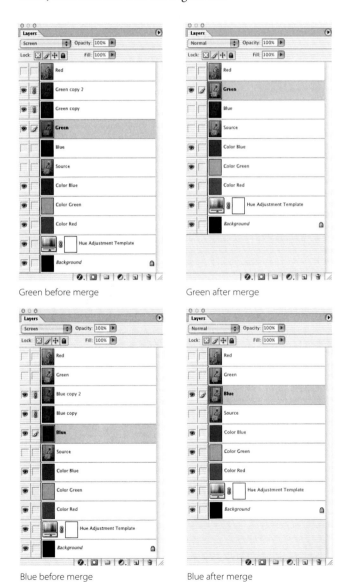

Adding Color to the RGB Separation

At this point in the example, you have filtered out the color channels. To complete the process and add back the color, you can clean up the template layers you won't need anymore, and then use the Color Red, Color Green, and Color Blue layers to re-color the image, as we did in Chapter 1. Follow these steps:

1. Throw out the Source and Hue Adjustment Template layers by dragging them to the Trash icon at the bottom of the Layers palette.

2. Change the mode of the Red, Green, and Blue layers to Screen. When you are done, leave the Red layer active.

3. Move the Color Red layer above the Red layer; then group them by pressing ⌘/Ctrl+G.

4. Move the Color Green layer above the Green layer; then group them.

5. Move the Color Blue layer above the Blue layer; then group them. The layers should look like they do in Figure 2.8.

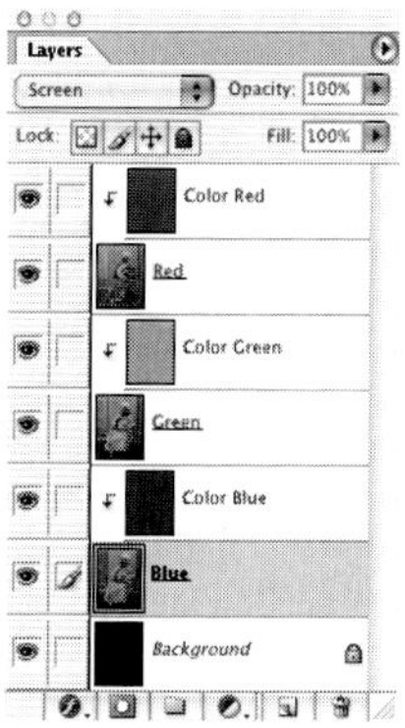

Figure 2.8

The image will be re-created in full color, in essence, projected as light onto the black background screen.

Can you accomplish this in other ways? Sure. You can copy the channels into layers and apply fill color to accomplish the same result. But what's pretty interesting is that the result is exactly the same. This process should show light theory applied to make your separation into RGB. The Split RGB action provided with the Hidden Power Tools on the CD executes the steps just described.

That may seem like a lot of work, so what does it get you? Flexibility. Now you can use channels and control them using layer properties in a way that is more intuitive than working with them in separate palettes. This approach offers many opportunities for color and tone correction and conversion based on additive light theory.

Earlier we were looking at some simple conversions of the pumpkin into grayscale. Open the Pumpkin.psd image again and run the Split RGB action. If you look at the separations as grayscale (to do this, shut off all the layer views except the channel you want to view), the green channel will be most like the tone as you might expect it to look in a black-and-white image. Red tends to look more like infrared and the blue like ultraviolet. Green, being closer to the center of the range of visible light, often looks most like you expect tone, but matching this up to a luminosity or brightness extraction will often reveal some pretty steep differences.

This look at extracting the RGB tone is all well and good, but it tells only part of the story. Another advantage of the separation to gray components is that you can also mix the channels using layer properties to achieve still other results. How you choose the combinations depends on the image. Having the channels as separate layers allows you to enhance and customize the conversions. Your choice may be based on theory or experimentation.

For example, going back to the kushbeggi.psd image you just finished separating, shut off the color fill layers, and change the settings for the Blue, Green, and Red layers as follows:

- Blue layer: Opacity: 100%; Mode: Normal
- Green layer: Opacity: 30%; Mode: Normal (this blends in 30 percent of the Green layer)
- Red layer: Opacity: 30%; Mode: Normal (this will blend back 30 percent of the Red layer)

This is yet another representation of the black-and-white conversion. Now try this: Activate the Green layer, set the opacity to 0%, click in the Opacity field on the Layers palette, hold down the Shift key, press the Up arrow on the keyboard. Press the Up arrow again. This will increase the opacity of the Green layer in increments of 10 percent. Keep doing this while watching what is happening on screen—and take snapshots when the opacity of the Green layer is at 30, 60, and 90 percent. Then click the snapshots in turn to view the differences. Each should have its own interest and appeal—though each is a very different result based on the tone of the image. See Figure 2.9.

If you see how easily different tone separations can be combined, the possibilities move exponentially from here. For example, you can mimic infrared effects by manipulating channels and how they go together:

1. Open the sheep.psd image from the CD.

2. Duplicate the background and name the new layer **Color Shift**.

3. Create a Hue/Saturation adjustment layer, and load Infrared.ahu from the Extras folder (or enter the Hue/Saturation values shown in Figure 2.10).

4. Group the Hue/Saturation adjustment layer and the Color Shift layers. Set the layer mode of the Hue/Saturation adjustment layer to Color, then merge the Hue/Saturation layer with the Color Shift layer. This targets the change to the color only.

You can do more or less to affect the outcome depending on your preference and the image. Increasing the Lighten and Saturation sliders will intensify the shift and brighten the infrared effect.

30% Green   60% Green   90% Green

30% Green   60% Green   90% Green

Figure 2.9

These two series show examples of mixing channel tone in layers to get different gray-scale results.

5. Change the Advanced Blending Channel of the Color Shift layer to R (shut off the G and B Channels checkboxes in the Layer Styles dialog box) to keep the change targeted to the color. Change the Mode to Color and then use Gaussian Blur to soften the color a little (say 5 pixel radius).

6. Flatten the image and play the Split RGB No Stops action.

7. Shut off the view for the Red layer and the Green layer, and throw out the Color layers (Color Red, Color Blue, and Color Green) by dragging them to the trash.

8. Hold down the ⌘/Ctrl key and click the blue channel in the Channels palette (any of the channels will actually do). This loads the light portion of the blue channel as a selection.

Figure 2.10

Loading the Hue/Saturation setting makes an adjustment to shift cyans, greens and yellows toward red. Look at the preview bar at the bottom of the palette to see the effect. It should show yellow, green, and cyan (upper bar) shifting toward red (lower bar).

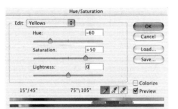

Select Yellows from the drop list

Select Greens from the drop list

Select Cyans from the drop list

9. Duplicate the background, name it **Blue Mask**, and move it above the Red layer. This will be used in the next steps to create a mask to darken blues in the image.

10. Invert the selection created in step 8 (press ⌘/Ctrl+Shift+I). This makes a selection of the dark portion of the original blue channel.

11. Delete the selected area (press Backspace/Delete), and change the layer mode to Multiply. This leaves the more intensely blue areas of the shifted color by removing the dark areas of the blue channel.

12. Duplicate the Red layer, change the mode to Normal, name it **Black Blues**, and drag it above the Blue Mask layer.

13. Group the Black Blues and Blue Mask layers. This uses the red content masked by the blue to darken bluer areas of the image; this targets the darkening to areas which are not red or bright but have strong blue components.

14. Duplicate the Red layer, name it **Infrared Glow**, and drag it to the top of the layer stack.

15. Hold the ⌘/Ctrl key and click the red channel in the Channels palette (again, any of the channels will do).

16. Invert the selection and delete. This will leave just the highlights.

17. Deselect (press ⌘/Ctrl+D), then blur using Gaussian Blur (3–10 pixels). Set the mode to Screen.

18. Turn on the view for the Red layer.

Luminosity conversion

Mock Infrared conversion

Figure 2.11

A more traditional conversion using Luminosity is shown here in comparison to a more radical mock infrared conversion.

The result of these steps mimics a type of infrared black-and-white. Since infrared film (properly filtered) is sensitive to red and infrared light, the idea of the conversion is to play up the red response of the capture, while choking the blue image area (steps 4–8), and adding a characteristic infrared glow in bright spots (steps 9–12). Steps 2–5 shift the gamut of yellows, greens, and cyan toward the red spectrum in an attempt to mimic infrared's tendency to make foliage glow. As you can see in Figure 2.11, the effect is noticeably different from a conversion based on Luminosity.

There are other means of improving the result (such as adding film grain), ways to accomplish similar results, and ways to mimic other specific film types according to their response (different black-and-white or infrared films). While this mock infrared will never be exactly like real infrared (infrared light is not stored separately on color film or in RGB images, after all), this should give you an idea of how far you might take conversions. I have included an Infrared action with the Hidden Power Tools so you can experiment with, and re-create, this series of steps.

This type of mixing of channels is what happens (to a lesser degree) when you use the Channel Mixer function. The Channel Mixer can help you achieve similar results, but using the tool will not allow you the same flexibility you achieve working with the results as layers, where you are afforded the luxury of modes, opacities, and selective custom (rather than channel-based) masking.

When scanning color images to turn them to black-and-white, you may be tempted to scan to grayscale. This offers only one possible grayscale result. Pouring through these options—both simple and complex—it should becomes obvious that there may often be good reason to consider scanning images that you plan to use in grayscale as RGB first. This will allow you some additional freedom to experiment to get the best black-and-white result.

As we've seen, extracting image tone from color can be complex, and can be much more of an art than science. Considering that tone is the basis of digital color representation, the complexity of your digital images increases exponentially when you're working with color. To achieve a result, you need to have control over two, three, or more color components in your image to represent the color, and you need to be able to balance the color and tone. Let's now look at how the complexity builds by adding color to tone.

Adding Color to Tone

One thing that is simple when you hear it, but not so obvious, is that color depends on tone—not just as a means of encoding the RGB color, but to represent color intensity, depth, and brightness. You can't have a dark color without dark tone, and you can't have light color without light tone; tone and color go hand-in-hand.

We've taken a look at pulling tone out of color and also at how to add RGB separations back together to make a color image (in the first chapter). There are a number of ways to add color to tone, including making duotones, creating gradient mapping, and painting in custom color (or essentially what amounts to hand-coloring). Let's look at these options next.

Applying Duotone to Color Black-and-White Images

A duotone is an image using at least two tones rather than just black (as in a simple grayscale image). When creating your own duotones, you replace the single tone of your grayscale image with two or more tones. The tones often work together to create a subtle, colored effect in an image, such as sepia toning. Originally, duotoning was a process used to introduce color and richness to black-and-white prints in the darkroom using a chemical process. In digital imaging and color process printing, duotones are used to achieve a toned effect (creating the colorized equivalent of a duotone color), to create a richer feel for black-and-white images, or to add a little color and increase the dynamic range of a printed image.

Figure 2.12

Setting the Hue to about 10% will give a decent sepia when you use the Colorize option with any black-and-white image.

Photoshop lets you create a duotone digitally in a number of ways. For example, you can rather quickly emulate a sepia tone by opening the Hue/Saturation dialog box, clicking the Colorize option, and shifting the slider to achieve a duotone effect (see Figure 2.12). When you print to an inkjet, the result will often be satisfactory.

This may give you the effect of duotone color in RGB, but it may not be the best solution for achieving the ultimate duotone effects in print. Certainly duotones can be pleasing to the eye, but the result would probably require all of the CMYK colors to print. This means that it wouldn't technically be a two-toned (*duo*tone) print.

In many cases, duotone images are used in spot-color jobs where there is a desire to limit color due to budget constraints but some color interest is needed. To create effective duotones for this purpose, you have to be able to control the separation for two inks (e.g., black and a spot color). If not, you will have to pay a technician to do the separation for you, or worse, pay for four-color work (CMYK printing) on what could be a two-color job—and then possibly not get the color you thought you applied (some spot colors will not separate to CMYK equivalents for printing). Using more than one ink to print your halftone images takes advantage of multiple screening angles, which can do a better job of presenting ink and color. Other advantages to using duotone over black ink alone include both lessening the appearance of halftone dots and increasing ink coverage. Creating a true duotone effect can also help with correcting and emphasizing subtle tonal detail.

> Even using two black inks can improve an image printed as a halftone because the two sets of dots will be screened differently, for better array of printer dots in application of inks.

Solving the problem and understanding the application requires a little knowledge of duotoning as well as knowing how to work with separations and spot color. We'll take a look at the whole process, from breaking down and applying spot-color inks in preview to getting actual duotone print effects on your inkjet and on press—with and without using Photoshop's Duotone function.

Background on Duotones

A key difference between duotone color and four-color printing (CMYK) is that four-color printing attempts to imitate color that exists in the image. Duotoning is pretty much the opposite: It is a means of adding color based on existing image tone. The image tone (either as grayscale, or however the color is converted to black-and-white) is used once for each ink/color. The color components are adjusted to influence which colors display more prominently to achieve specific shading and color effects.

The components are considered "ink" because the idea is to set up a representation of inks that will be applied in print in separate ink passes. The mix of the inks is controlled using tone adjustments (most often curves) to specify how the individual inks are emphasized in specific tone ranges. This adjustment will most often be different for each ink/component.

> The application of inks in duotoning is not based on reproducing original image color as CMYK printing would. It's possible to use multiple inks with this method for spot color and additional press options, like varnish (which adds gloss). Using color in sets of three (tritone) or four (quadtone) will often be referred to generically as "duotone" despite the existence of these more accurate terms.

Selecting and mixing color using the tone adjustments controls how the colors interplay and affects the duotone result. The changes applied to the tone of each component manipulate how selected inks are applied. When the image goes to print, the adjustments create the interplay of color in the printed result. The component colors, or channels, become synonymous with the inks they represent on a press.

Manipulation of the image tone is usually controlled using curves—though it can be accomplished in other ways as well. Setting the adjustment (curves) without some sort of technique or method might prove quite fruitless and frustrating in that the results could be difficult to predict.

Likewise, picking color you like rather than color that will be effective can be troublesome in producing the desired result. Your plan for creating a successful duotone image should be:

1. Select inks that are compatible and that can accomplish your goal in duotoning.

2. Set up the image and apply curves to make the most of the inks you have chosen in the image you have.

There is a little art to experimenting with color selection and application, but some pretty straightforward science is involved as well. A 25 percent gray ink at 100 percent strength still shows at 25 percent gray when printed; it just covers 100 percent of the paper (see Figure 2.13). It can never get darker than 25 percent gray unless mixed with another color. With this in mind, any color affects an image mostly in tonal areas that are lighter than the 100 percent strength of the color. That is, a 25 percent gray ink will be able to more effectively influence tonality in 1–25 percent grays—though it will affect darker colors that it mixes with, it will be less effective in manipulating the image between 25 and 100 percent gray. A dark color can represent lighter tones, but the opposite can never happen. A good rule of thumb is to use at least one color that is dark or black for your duotone so that you can maintain the dynamic range in the image.

Figure 2.13

Magnification shows black ink (100 percent black ink) at 25 percent gray (25 percent coverage) and gray ink (25 percent black) at 25 percent gray (100 percent coverage) in halftone printing.

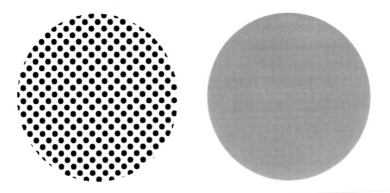

Figure 2.14

Unrealistic expecta-tions can yield bad results in your duo-tones. You want blended tones to be able to flow evenly from dark to light (A). Bad choices can limit tonal range (B) or lead to applying color inappropri-ately (C).

When choosing colors for your image, work with colors that are harmonious and sensible. In other words, select colors that can blend easily to produce a smooth white-to-black gradient (see Figure 2.14). For example, you might choose a black, red, and light yellow, or a black, blue, and sky blue to keep tones in the same family to make a successful tritone. The emphasis of the colors should be in their most effective range. Harmony between colors will make it easier to set up effective blends, and it will allow you to work successfully with various levels of image tone. If you choose difficult color combinations or have unrealistic expectations, you will have twice as much trouble getting the blends to be effective—or you may simply make it impossible.

Simply put, the lighter colors you use emphasize the contrast and tone in the brighter or highlight/midtone range of the image, and the darker colors emphasize the shadow details. You will most often want to use colors with varied tone, rather than all dark or all medium-toned inks. Splitting the effective range of the colors you pick can improve your image by giving you a choice of colors that have varying specialties. If you select a light and dark color for a duotone, the light color can be run with a greater density in the lighter image areas and the dark in the shadows. This will help you to most effectively work with (rather than against) image tone. The mixture of inks can give the image more of the feel of continuous tone and create a more photographic appearance.

Curves serve as translators for how ink density is to be applied. The curves are applied to the original tone of the image to target application strength. Throughout the tonal range, the inks blend to form shades and tones, which can be finessed to the advantage of the image. A good rule of thumb is that if you want to apply a 25 percent gray ink, curves should show high intensity at 25 percent on the curve graphing for that ink (shown in Figure 2.15).

Figure 2.15

This is an example of how a curve might look when using a light (25 percent gray) ink using both standard curves and the curves from the Duotone dialog box. Depending on the color, desired effect, and image, the curve can be even steeper than pictured here.

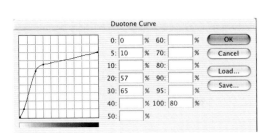

Duotone dialog curve

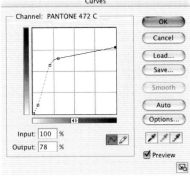

Standard curve

Deciding how to set the curves is part art and part science. Darker inks are often steeply graded in the shadow tones, whereas lighter inks are more steeply graded in lighter tones. This often easily and naturally makes a desirable result with lots of contrast. Other inks require different handling. If you use two shades of black ink, for example, you probably want to de-emphasize the total density of the inks or you will darken the image; however, in decreasing density, setting both curves the same way may not take advantage of potential dynamics in the image. Figure 2.16 shows curve settings used in a scenario with two dark inks.

When applying the same duotone colors to different images, you can't always apply those colors with the same curves. The result depends on the image and its tonality. What works fine for normal and low-key (naturally dark) images may not work as well for high-key (naturally light) images, which would probably suffer from the attention to shadow detail. Curve presets might get you in the ballpark (you can save your curves using Save in the Curves dialog box), but you have to adjust the curves for optimal performance as carefully as if you were making image corrections.

You can use more than one technique to build a separation-ready duotone in Photoshop. *Separation ready* means that you will be able to use the duotone with process color printing. These techniques include creating a manual separation and using the Photoshop Duotone function. To fully understand the process, we'll do the manual version first, and then we'll use Photoshop's function. Being familiar with both techniques will give you more control over the result, as well as a better understanding of using spot color.

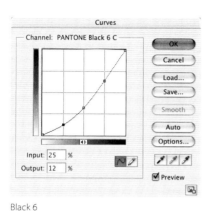
Black 6

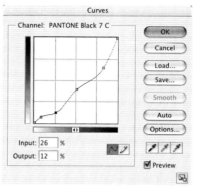
Black 7

Figure 2.16

In applying two black inks in a duotone, this example shows curves that emphasize contrast in the shadows (Black 6) and contrast in a smaller portion of the range (Black 7), almost like you would use a curve for tone correction.

Manual Duotones

Creating duotones manually is something you will want to do to achieve ultimate control over the duotone result and better understand the application of colors. Working in RGB allows you to create color ink components (also called "plates" or "color plates") using more intuitive light processes while defining spot color without compromising it as a spot channel or CMYK equivalent.

To create duotones manually, you will use existing image tone along with some tricks that we've seen hints of in both using curves and in making RGB separations. If your original image is an RGB image, you should convert to grayscale (see the previous sections on converting to grayscale for these options). Curves are used to adjust the tone for the separate inks, and RGB preview techniques are used to look at the result of combining inks. When the preview looks the way you want, you can create separations that can be used to print duotones at home or to your printing service as grayscale image plates. Here are the steps involved in the manual process:

1. Open an image that is Grayscale mode, or turn a color image to grayscale by the methods described earlier in this chapter. Be sure the image tone is corrected—you won't want to do this afterward—and be sure the image is flattened. See the sample image used in Figure 2.17.

2. Change the mode of the image to RGB. RGB mode will allow you to preview colors.

Figure 2.17

Figure 2.17

This western scene (wagontrain.tif on the CD) can garner some additional authenticity by using a sepia tone.

3. Decide on the colors to use for the duotone effect. In this example, to create something of a sepia tone, let's use black and an RGB value close to Pantone 472 (RGB: 255, 155, 125).

4. Add a new layer, fill with white, and call the layer **Composite**. This layer will be used as a background to display the duotone result.

5. Duplicate the background to create a new layer, and drag it to the top of the layer stack.

6. Rename the new layer **Duotone 1**. You may want to identify the layer by the color/tone you expect to apply (e.g., Black 6), by generic names like "Duotone 1," by RGB values, or by Pantone color names.

7. Change the mode of the layer to Multiply. Multiply mode will ensure that the layer content acts like ink on paper, darkening the composite layer.

8. Add a new Solid Color layer (Layer → New Fill Layer → Solid Color), group it with the Duotone 1 layer, and choose the darker color selected in step 3. Change the mode of the layer to Screen, and name the layer **Color 1**. Screen mode will convert the tone to a representation of the selected color.

9. Activate the Duotone 1 layer.

Since you have started with a grayscale image, the layer color will technically be black without the fill layer. I added this here just to keep consistent with how you generally want to work with spot colors for this procedure and to show how to handle other blacks (e.g., a Pantone black).

Figure 2.18

This curve for the darker Duotone 1 ink was used to increase contrast in the grassy midtones.

10. Add a Curve adjustment layer by choosing Layer → New Adjustment Layer → Curves. Enable the option Use Previous Layer To Create Clipping Mask in the New Layer dialog box so that the adjustment affects only the Duotone 1 layer. In the example, use the curve shown in Figure 2.18.

11. Repeat steps 5 through 10 to add the second duotone color. Name the layers you create **Duotone 2** and **Color 2**. Figure 2.19 shows the curve used for the fill color and how the layer stack should look.

Figure 2.19

The curve for the lighter Duotone 2 color concentrates on influencing the highlights and midtones.

When stacking colors, run them from darkest at the bottom to lightest at the top. This will improve your organization and application.

The result of the steps can be seen in the color section.

For the layer order, the curves should be directly above the duotone layer they are adjusting, between the tone and the color. If you put the curve above the color, your curves will influence the color as well as the tone. Grouping the curves ensures that the curve influences only the duotone color where it is applied. If you want more spot colors, repeat steps 5 through 10.

You can use a gradient bar as part of the process to judge the quality of the gradient you are creating when combining the colors. To do this, add a blank layer above one of the duotone layers (Duotone 1), make a selection where you want the bar to appear, and fill the selection with a gradient from white to black (left to right, or right to left). Duplicate the layer containing the gradient and move it to just above the other tone layer (Duotone 2). Duplicating the layer ensures the gradients are identical. The gradient should appear relatively smooth and even after placement, unless you are using the duotone for some type of image correction or special effect.

I have provided a sample gradient bar action with the Hidden Power Tools on the CD. You can set up a duotone in layers using the Duotone Layer Setup action, and then add a gradient bar without a lot of fuss by clicking Duotone Preview. Removing Duotone Preview will delete the gradient bar layers.

You can use this to check how smooth your mixing is or to help while developing curves for application. This action will work for any duotone set up as described using Duotone 1 and Duotone 2 as the naming convention. When you are done with the preview, just delete the bar layers.

With the result on screen, you have several options for generating prints. You will handle this differently depending on what you want to accomplish. In the simplest scenario, you just flatten the image and print, but this result will not be much different than applying duotone via the Colorize option in Hue/Saturation. In more advanced scenarios, you will want to separate the duotone layers and use them to control the printed result. You can do this using techniques discussed in the "Printing Duotones" section later in this chapter.

Duotones via Spot Color Channels

A second way to achieve manual duotoning is to create the effect using spot color channels. This creates an image with the spot color built in, and essentially it will be press ready as a separation. In the following techniques you will use both the manual layer method just described in the previous section and Photoshop's duotone interface to create duotone results.

1. Open the wagontrain.psd from the CD.

2. Change the mode from RGB to Grayscale. You can also use other means for conversion, but since the image is already grayscale, the difference in the conversion shouldn't matter.

3. Duplicate the Gray channel.

4. Double-click the Gray Copy channel to open the Channel Options dialog box. Change the options to Spot Color, 0% Solidity, and pick your spot color from the Color Picker. The dialog box should look like the one shown in Figure 2.20. We'll use Pantone 472 for the spot color in this case to get something of a sepia tone; the name of the channel automatically changes to the pantone selected.

5. Repeat steps 3 and 4, creating a second color channel with the same settings: Spot Color and 0% Solidity. We'll use black for the second color; you can use a Pantone black, or set the Color Picker to 0, 0, 0 in RGB and Photoshop will change the channel name to Black.

6. Click on the background layer to be sure it is active, press D to set the default colors (white in the background), select all (press ⌘/Ctrl+A), and then press the Delete key. This will clear the original image and the gray channel.

7. Make the Pantone 472 and Black channels visible by clicking in the visibility box on the Channels palette to turn on the Adobe eye for each. This will show a preview of the duotone.

8. Make curve adjustments as desired to each of the channels. To make the adjustment, click once on a channel to activate it, then select Image → Adjustments → Curves, or press ⌘/Ctrl+M. The dialog box will appear.

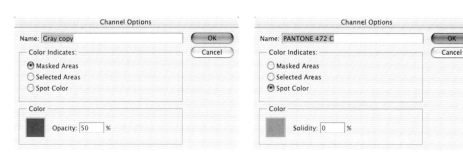

Figure 2.20

The Channel Options dialog box allows you to change the behavior of individual channels in the Channels palette. Changing the Color Indicates option from Masked Areas to Spot Color tells Photoshop to handle the channel like a color.

While this technique offers immediate feedback in the previews and a finished format, there is a drawback to not being able to adjust the curves more fluidly; changes you make with the curves are more or less a once-shot-deal in that they affect the channels directly. The previous layer technique allows you to return to curves as often as you'd like before committing any changes.

It is possible to combine these techniques somewhat so that you use the adjustability of the layer technique and the final format advantage of the channel technique. If you start with the layer technique to create the curves, you can later apply those curves settings to the duotone channels. Try this:

1. Run through the steps for creating a manual duotone. Use the Duotone Layer Setup action in the The Hidden Power Tools to speed you through this step.

2. Save the curve settings by double-clicking the curve adjustment layers in turn to open the Curves dialog box, and then click the Save button to save the settings to a file. Save the file in a place you will find easy to get to, using a name that makes sense. For example, you might want to save to a Curves folder that you create in the Presets folder in the Photoshop program file directory. If you name the files Pantone 472 and Black and date them, you can locate the right curves. These curve files will have an .acv extension appended to them during saves.

3. Click the original History state (Open) or initial snapshot in the History palette. This will return the image to the original state.

4. Set up the duotone channels using the Duotone Channels Setup action in the Hidden Power Tools. This will do the basic setup described in steps 1 through 7 in the previous procedure.

5. Instead of making curve adjustments by following the instructions in step 8, load the curve settings saved in step 2. To load these settings, click on a channel once to activate it, choose Curves (press ⌘/Ctrl+M), click the Load button in the Curves dialog box, and select the curve you saved for the active channel.

These steps allow you to make custom adjustments to the curves before you make the spot channels. In other words, you can play freely with the curves to get the settings right and using the on-screen previews, and then save the settings to apply them to the spot channels.

There will be several problems here as well. The first is that the color in RGB layers may be slightly different than the PMS color. This can be due to color settings or conversions. However, you are more likely to get a satisfactory result from combining the methods than you can trying to get it perfect in one shot.

Using Photoshop's Duotone Interface

You can change a grayscale image directly into a duotone format using Photoshop's Duotone interface. This dialog box, shown in Figure 2.21, opens when you convert a grayscale image to Duotone mode.

To create a basic conversion using the Duotone interface:

1. Choose Image → Mode → Duotone. This command will be available only from Grayscale mode or Duotone mode. The dialog box opens with either the current (when the image is already duotone) or previously used settings.

2. Choose a setting from the Type drop-down list. This can be Monotone (one color), Duotone (two colors), Tritone (three colors), or Quadtone (four colors). Choose the setting based on the number of colors you expect to apply. After you make the selection, the views will activate for the number of colors you selected.

3. Click the color swatch for each of the colors in turn and choose the color from the Color Picker. For this example, choose the same colors as in the previous example: Pantone 472 and Black.

4. Click the Curve boxes in turn and set the curves as appropriate for the color application. To do this with the same settings as the previous examples, load Duotone_black.acv for the Black ink and Duotone_P472.acv for the Pantone 472 ink from the Hidden Power Tools.

5. Accept the changes by clicking OK.

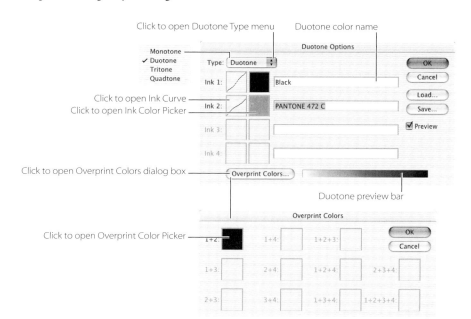

Figure 2.21

Photoshop's Duotone dialog box allows you to assign color and curve application based on the original tone, but does it all in a one-layer image.

If you don't like the idea of fiddling with layers as in the manual method, this can prove less troublesome, but it also can offer fewer options and opportunities for making changes and controlling the result because of the inherent limitations of the mode and the lack of channels. Therefore, it may actually prove harder to use for advanced applications. For example, if you want to adjust spot color density with a brush or add spot color type, these files can prove difficult to manipulate.

Files created using the Duotone interface may appear different (on screen and in print) than those created using the manual technique—even when exactly the same settings are used for colors and curves. The difference depends on the color-management settings you are using—specifically the dot gain settings, which tell Photoshop how much a printed dot can be expected to expand on press. The result may be better or worse depending on the process.

The Curves dialog box you use when working with duotones is somewhat different than the Curve dialog box used in image adjustment. This is because the behavior is more akin to using Transfer Functions, affecting the ink, rather than technically changing the stored values for the pixels in the image. You are somewhat more limited in the number of curve points that can be placed; there are 13 positions. Curves you load that were saved from adjustment curves will be transcribed.

The Overprint Colors dialog box is a means of adjusting the preview to fit the inks you are using. If, for example, you are using a metallic ink that has 100 percent solidity and will overprint even black ink, you can adjust the overprint mix of black and the metallic ink to look more like the metallic. Of course, this has its own problems since the metallic will not represent well on an RGB screen. Do not make changes to the Overprint settings unless you have tested the output and know the result. Any changes in the overprint settings do not affect the printed outcome—changes here affect image preview only.

Printing Duotones

When trying to print your duotone, one of several things will happen, depending on the equipment you are using to print and the expertise/experience of the prepress people you are dealing with. Your duotone and spot color channel files might be acceptable as is for PostScript processing, but not for printing to a home ink-jet printer. You would usually just save the file as an EPS (perhaps a DCS, or Desktop Color Separation, for the spot color channel type), insert that file into your layout, and print. Files created with separations as layers will need to be converted by moving the layers to spot channels, or possibly by creating separate plates—the latter option may be less desirable.

However, there are times when you will want to convert the Duotone mode file to spot color channels to separate EPS or TIFF, so you can use the channels from that file as you would with a manually created duotone. Just flattening the file and sending it to your home ink-jet is not what you want to do after you've gone to the trouble of keeping the information separated. It is most likely that the file will be converted and re-separated on-the-fly (with your home printer, and a number of other digital processes), and the result may be anything from simply unexpected to a real disaster.

What you actually have by the time you are done with either of the manual procedures as described is a bona fide duotone separation: two tones of ink, not necessarily the equivalent of the RGB or CMYK process. This is different from a Duotone mode file, which applies what are essentially transfer functions to the reference tone for the image. If you flatten the manual duotone images and change to CMYK or RGB, the color for the manual-layered duotone and Photoshop duotone will be converted to that mode rather than handled as a true duotone. If you attempt to print the manual file to a home printer with spot color channels, you may get a conversion (to RGB and back to CMYK!) or nothing at all (because the additional color channels may not be recognized). Treating the image as a true duotone will help you get the best duotone results. This generally means using the inks/channels separately and applying them in the intended colors on a press that can handle custom color.

> Transfer functions are curves stored with your image and applied during processing for print, resembling a printer profile more than an adjustment curve.

When printing any of these duotones, you can best handle the duotone color information by splitting it out into different channels, or representations of ink intensity. The separated channels can then be recombined into a CMYK, RGB, or grayscale image as spot colors or existing tones (e.g., K in CMYK), or can be colored and used with a home ink-jet printer in a multiple-pass technique that imitates press processing. While the Duotone mode file and the spot channel duotone are really press ready, the layered duotone will require adjustment in order to be used as a true duotone. On the other hand, trying to print spot color won't be good for all situations, such as home printing on an ink-jet. We'll look at both options more closely in the following sections. First let's make sure you can separate the ink tones from the image.

Table 2.1 attempts to clarify just what you can use your duotones for. If a file is "Press Ready," it means that you can send it to process with spot color as is; if it is "Home Printer Ready," it means that the file can be sent to your home printer as is but that you should expect a CMYK result rather than spot color one.

<table>
<tr><td>

Table 2.1

Uses for Duotones

</td><td>

DUOTONE TYPE	PRESS READY	HOME PRINTER READY
Manual layers	No. You have to separate out the duotone channels from layers to create a press-ready file.	No. While it will print, you will get a conversion from your hard-earned separation. You will probably have to flatten the layers and print from RGB or convert to CMYK before placing the image in layout programs. You must separate the channels to use the multiple-pass printing method (described in the section "Multipass Printing" later in this chapter) to get true duotone results.
Manual spot channels	Yes.	No. You may be able to print it, but you will get a conversion unless you separate out the channels and treat them like manual-layered duotone results. To get any color at all, you may have to merge the channels (change to RGB or CMYK mode and choose Merge Spot Channels from the Channels palette pop-up menu) because the additional channels may not be recognized. No ink will print if the channels are not recognized.
Photoshop Duotone	Possibly. Layout programs and drivers may recognize the Photoshop Duotone as a viable separation. Test-print or ask your service to be sure. You can also separate out the channels to create a pre-ready file.	No. Layout programs and drivers may recognize the Photoshop Duotone as a viable color file, but the result will, again, be a conversion to CMYK or RGB. You will need to separate the channels to take advantage of the multiple-pass printing method used with manual-layered duotone files.

</td></tr>
</table>

Creating the Duotone Channels

Depending on whether you used the layer method or Photoshop Duotone to create the duotone information, you will have to extract the channel information differently. Having to separate out the channels doesn't apply to the channel method since the channels are already created, but you may still want to separate the channels to make prints at home. The goal here is to isolate the channels in their own images so that you can combine them however you'd like. Creating a separate image for each channel gives you many options for combining the information and allows you to combine multiple channels—perhaps separated using different methods. This may also create options for adjusting tone and can help with management of non-duotone spot colors that you might use in files.

If you created the duotone using the layer method, extracting the channels is fairly straightforward. You can do this by merging the curve adjustments with the duotone layers, and then duplicating each duotone layer to a new image (using the Duplicate Layer command and targeting a New image). The new image will be in the same mode as the original file; you can change it to grayscale, if necessary. You'll have one image for each channel you extract. You may want to attach names to the layers as they are duplicated to the new image so that you know which is which.

In order to extract channels from a duotone created with the Duotone tool, the best and easiest result is typically obtained by changing to Multichannel mode. Doing this will apply the curves and create a single channel for each ink during the conversion. After the Multichannel file is created, use the Split Channels command on the Channels palette pop-up menu to create separate channels. When the channels separate, Photoshop will name the new image "[*file name*]. [*channel name*]," which should help you keep track of what the images represent.

Creating separate images for channels from duotones made using the channel method is the easiest of the bunch: just choose Split Channels from the Channels palette pop-up. This step isn't necessary for printing this type of file with spot colors on press. However, there may be other instances in which you will want to revert to manual control of the channels—such as when you are repurposing the file to print to a home ink-jet.

With the channels separated into individual files, you can combine them in different ways to print as spot color or to make separated prints at home with the multipass method.

Duotone Prints as Spot Color

Part of the trick of successfully using duotone color is incorporating it correctly into image files. Duotone information can be compiled into a single file to print as spot color, or as part of existing color spaces. For example, if you had a duotone created from black and cyan, you could combine the duotone channels into a CMYK image as the Cyan and Black channels. If the colors don't correspond to a process color, you can incorporate them as spot color.

With the duotone channel files open, you can quickly incorporate them into a single image file. The following steps assume you are still working with the wagontrain.psd example and that you have converted the channels to separate files.

1. Open a new image in Grayscale mode and make it the same size as the originals. Do this quickly by selecting All and copying one of the originals and then opening a new document; Photoshop will size the image to those dimensions for you.

2. Choose Merge Channels from the Channels palette pop-up menu.

3. When the Merge Channels dialog box opens, choose Multichannel and set the number of channels to 3: one for the grayscale channel, and one each for the duotone colors.

4. Assign the image you created in step 1 to the grayscale channel and the duotones to the other spot color slots (see Figure 2.22). Click OK.

Figure 2.22

Because the new image is blank, assigning it to the grayscale channel will not affect the duotone result.

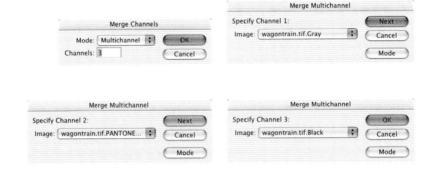

5. Open the Channels palette and double-click the Alpha 2 thumbnail. This will open the Channel Options dialog box.

6. Change the Color Indicates selector to Spot Color, change the Opacity setting to 0%, and specify a color that matches the color selected for the duotone channel. You assign the color by clicking the swatch to open the Color Picker.

7. Repeat step 6 for the Alpha 3 channel.

8. Click on Alpha 1 in the Channels palette and change the image mode to Grayscale. As a result, Photoshop names and incorporates the spot color channels correctly in the new file (see Figure 2.23).

Figure 2.23

Converting to Grayscale from Multichannel allows you to save the file and spot channels in a broadly supported file type.

If saved in a format that allows and recognizes additional color channels (TIFF or EPS), the file will carry the information to a layout program that can recognize spot color, and will print separated spot color plates when sent to print in a PostScript workflow.

Multipass Printing

On a press, ink gets put on paper one press color at a time. You can mimic this process printing at home by sending a sheet of paper through your printer multiple times. Use this method to create single copies of your duotone images, both to test the duotone settings on your home printer and to create prints for display that use true duotoning methods.

While in some cases it may be redundant to do this (there is no need to print CMYK in separate passes on a CMYK printer most of the time), this approach may be the best way to get the results you planned using your ink-jet when printing duotones. It will let you imitate press separation and process printing by laying down color one "ink" at a time, though you will actually be processing four inks in each pass to imitate specific tones. By applying colors in this way, you can imitate the result of spot color printing at home (so long as the colors you choose are in the CMYK range). This will probably work best with an ink-jet or liquid ink printer rather than a laser or pigment printer. Inks will mix better than toners.

When working with the multipass technique, keep the tones for each color in separate images, color them using the appropriate fill color, and send the result to the printer one at a time *on the same sheet*! Print light colors first, and follow with darker. Allow some drying time in between colors. In this way, you will build your print similar to the way it would be created on a printing press. As long as your printer has reasonably accurate paper gripping, you'll get a pretty refined result. Because each pass can create color using CMYK ink mixtures, you can imitate many Pantone colors.

> Be sure that your manufacturer does not warn against running printed sheets through the printer a second time. Some printers and processes may cause trouble and possible damage if used incorrectly.

Blacks will often be richer and darker when you're printing with multiple passes. You'll notice a greater tonal range because the blacks will be darker—even though you are dealing with the same number of levels of grays in the image. This works somewhat like putting on a second coat of paint. You may need to allow a few seconds of drying time between passes, and using a good quality photo-print paper is recommended.

USING DUOTONE FOR TONAL CORRECTIONS

Duotone curves can be used to make subtle changes and corrections in difficult black-and-white images. Although the images will not retain the richness of duotoning or the effect of multiple inks when printed in black and white, using duotone may help you visualize the change you want to make by adding more variables to the tone. Creating duotone effects to correct grayscale images can help strengthen subtle detail that already exists in the image.

For example, if you have an image with subtle highlight detail (such as a wedding picture where the dress detail can become somewhat washed out or faded due to harsh flash lighting), you can create a duotone to change the image emphasis in different tones. Open the image in black and white, and then create a duotone. In the case of the wedding dress, you might pick a black and a light-gray ink for your duotone colors. Use the light gray to emphasize the highlight area of the image; this will allow you to make fine adjustments.

With the duotone information separated into channels within the file, you have more flexibility to manipulate the file and get the desired results. For example, if you wanted to add type to your image in pure spot color, or in a specific mixture of colors included in the file, you can do that by manipulating the channels. This is just about impossible to pull off in a Duotone mode file.

To add type that is a specific mix of colors that won't be a natural mix of the duotone curves (say 100 percent of the light color and 25 percent of the dark), you need to adjust the tone in the channels separately. You can do this by creating a type layer and using that layer as a selection source for manipulating the channels:

1. Using the file from the previous example, choose the Type tool and click on the image to create a type layer.

2. Type in the text you want (to follow the example, type *Wagontrain West*), and then position the type and size it to fit. The color of the type doesn't matter at all, but you might want to select a color that comes close to how you imagine the result (to help with your preview).

3. Hold down the ⌘/Ctrl key and click the type layer in the Layers palette to load the type as a selection.

4. Choose the channel/color you want to adjust and fill the selection with the percentage of that color that you want the type to have in grayscale. For this example, choose the Pantone 472 channel and fill with 100 percent black.

5. Choose the other channel/color and fill it. For our example, choose Black and fill with 25 percent black.

The channels that result from these steps are shown in Figure 2.24. While it may be best to handle the type in a separate file (using vectors) to get the sharpest result, this example should help you see how manual duotones allow more potential in manipulating files and results. These changes can also be made in an earlier stage in the layered channel file by directly adjusting the Duotone 1 and Duotone 2 layers using the selection.

Figure 2.24

With the type at 100 percent Pantone 472 (A) and 25 percent Black (B), the channels will look as they do here when adjusted.

a

b

Separating CMYK Color

RGB differs from CMYK in that RGB is a *reflective* light scheme and CMYK an *absorptive* one. When you add color (light) in RGB, the result gets brighter. When you add more CMYK color (pigment/ink), the result gets darker in what is just about exactly the opposite process. In fact, CMY and RGB have an interesting relationship as opposites, as we saw briefly in the first chapter.

Photoshop provides automated separation to CMYK. To make the separation all you have to do is choose CMYK from the Mode menu, and Photoshop will separate your image according to your specified color preferences (This can be one of the predefined standards from the CMYK Working Spaces in the Color Settings, or a custom definition). The CMYK command can be a godsend, but it almost completely disconnects you from the separation process. Once you can do a CMYK separation manually (few people who use Photoshop can), the reasoning behind the process will help you make good CMYK handling choices, and it will allow you to customize your separation results. Custom CMYK separation in Photoshop is not that easy because the program wrests control from you to simplify the process. In most cases this is handy, but it can certainly hamper your understanding of the color process.

CMYK separation can be a complicated topic, and this topic alone could fill an entire book. Let's now look at the process of manually separating CMYK right from RGB and examine some additional theory. Initially this discussion will just be a learning tool so that you can see the possibilities and complexity of CMYK separation options.

We'll walk through the separation process in three sections: the basic CMY separation, the handling of black separation, and the application of black to the image.

Step 1: Making the Basic CMY Separation

In theory, a CMY separation (with no K) is the inverse of RGB. In the RGB color scheme, cyan is a combination of pure blue and pure green, magenta a combination of pure red and pure blue, and yellow a combination of pure red and pure green. You can see color combination in action by opening the RGB.psd file on the CD. With this file open, move the colors around to see how they combine.

Blue is also really the inverse of yellow, green the inverse of magenta, and red the inverse of cyan. Note that they are in directly opposite positions in RGB.psd, CMYK.psd, and in ColorWheel.psd (all on the CD).

You can separate an image into CMY either by using the primary cyan, magenta and yellow colors as a filter or by using the RGB colors that make up those components. Screening an RGB image for blue and green will reveal cyan, screening for red and blue will reveal magenta, and screening for red and green reveals yellow. You can achieve the same effect by creating the RGB channels in layers and inverting each of the channel colors in turn. Completing the separation will give you a very basic CMY separation that works on screen—and in a perfect world. Because pigments (and the surfaces they are used on) are not 100 percent efficient in absorbing light, black is added to CMY to make CMYK. The added black increases the efficiency and dynamic range of the result—similar to the idea of using more than one ink in a duotone to extend dynamic range.

The four steps involved in creating the basic CMY separation are preparing the image, separating the color, converting separations to tone, and applying color for preview. We'll use the dragonfly.psd from the CD shown in Figure 2.25.

Preparation

Set up the separation by duplicating the image background once for each of the CMY inks. Once the initial layers are created, you will be ready to start extracting color separations:

1. Duplicate the background layer of the flattened dragonfly.psd image.

2. Change the mode of the duplicate layer to Multiply.

3. Change the name of the layer to `Cyan`.

4. Duplicate the Cyan layer, and change the copied layer name to `Magenta`.

5. Duplicate the Magenta layer, and change the copied layer name to `Yellow`.

6. Activate the background layer.

7. Create a new layer.

8. Fill with white and name it `Composite`.

Figure 2.25

See the color section for more detail of this dragonfly.

You can complete these same steps by running the CMYK Setup action from the Hidden Power Tools. The image will look awful at this point, but that doesn't matter. Figure 2.26 shows how the Layers palette should look.

Separation

This next set of steps continues from the previous. Screening each ink layer by the color components (C, M, and Y) isolates information for the ink while simultaneously creating a preview for the color. This state of the separation is temporary. To make this a really useful separation, you'll have to convert the separated information to grayscale:

1. Activate the Yellow layer.

2. Create a new layer choosing Use Previous Layer To Create Clipping Mask and call it `Yellow Fill`.

3. Fill the layer with pure blue (0, 0, 255 in RGB), and change the mode of the layer to Screen.

4. Invert the layer (Image → Adjustments → Invert, or press ⌘/Ctrl+I).

5. Activate the Magenta layer.

6. Create a new layer by choosing Use Previous Layer To Create Clipping Mask and call it `Magenta Fill`.

7. Fill the layer with pure green (0, 255, 0 in RGB). Change the mode of the layer to Screen.

8. Invert the Magenta Fill layer.

9. Activate the Cyan layer.

10. Create a new layer by choosing Use Previous Layer To Create Clipping Mask and call it `Cyan Fill`.

11. Fill the layer with pure red (255, 0, 0 in RGB).

12. Change the mode of the layer to Screen.

13. Invert the layer.

You can run through these steps manually or by running the CMYK Color action in the Hidden Power Tools.

If you complete these steps without a hitch, you'll be looking at the same image you started with and the layers will look like Figure 2.27. If you shut off any two of the three color plate layers (e.g., Cyan and Yellow), you'll see the separation named in the remaining layer (Magenta).

To make a viable separation, you have to convert the color layers to include grayscale representations of a color as tone.

Figure 2.26

With this setup, you are all ready to separate the CMY colors.

Figure 2.27

The basic RGB-CMY separation setup

Converting Color to Tone

Continuing on, the following steps adjust each layer to display tone only. You have to merge the filter with the channel to isolate the color and then neutralize layer color to isolate the tone.

1. Activate the Cyan Fill layer.

2. Press ⌘/Ctrl+E to merge the fill with the Cyan layer.

3. Make a Hue/Saturation adjustment by choosing Image → Adjustments → Hue/Saturation. Choose Cyans from the Edit drop-down list, and move the Saturation and Lightness sliders all the way to the left (see Figure 2.28). This removes the color from the Cyan layer to make the Cyan tone.

4. Activate the Magenta Fill layer.

5. Press ⌘/Ctrl+E to merge the fill with the Magenta layer.

6. Make a Hue/Saturation adjustment by choosing Image → Adjustments → Hue/Saturation. Choose Magentas from the Edit drop-down list, and move the Lightness sliders all the way to the left. This shifts the color from the Magenta layer to grayscale to make the Magenta tone.

7. Activate the Yellow Fill layer.

8. Press ⌘/Ctrl+E to merge the fill with the Yellow layer.

9. Make a Hue/Saturation adjustment by choosing Image → Adjustments → Hue/Saturation. Choose Yellows from the Edit drop-down list, and move the Saturation and Lightness sliders all the way to the left. This removes the color from the Yellow layer to make the Yellow tone.

These steps commit the changes to the layers so that the layers are grayscale tone. They also remove the color, which means no preview is available. In the next set of steps, you will add the color back by reintroducing color screens to the plates. Running the CMYK Tone Seps action from the CD will complete the steps to neutralize the tone and add back the preview color (completing the steps from the next section).

Figure 2.28

The Hue/Saturation settings for changing the cyan separation to a grayscale cyan plate

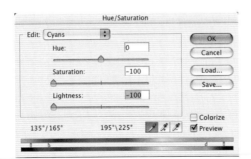

Reapplying Color for Previews

Follow the steps in the section "Separation" to add the preview color back (to do this independently, play the CMYK Color action in the Hidden Power Tools). The Layers palette should now look like Figure 2.29. See the color section for a preview of the CMY separation results.

Step 2: Handling the Black Separation

CMYK separation from RGB requires separation into CMY, and then generation of elements and masks to generate black (K). The way you handle implementation of black can vary depending on your preferences. We'll look at one style that should help you understand the idea behind the process.

Now that you have the base plates, the black separation can be based on color saturation (or lack of) and luminosity (the darker portion of the image). These steps continue from completion of the basic separation in the previous section.

To complete black separation, you'll have to know how to create saturation and luminosity masks. Both of these sources come from a luminosity and color separation, which mimics some of the properties of Lab mode in maintaining color information separate from tone.

This exercise should give you a hint as to the complexity of adjusting CMY for printed output, but it also offers you the opportunity to see inside the process and concepts behind how black is generated and how it is targeted to optimize print results.

Figure 2.29

A complete CMY color separation should look like this with all the layers.

Making the Saturation Mask

Creating a saturation mask allows you to target gray areas of the image and replace the purer grays with black rather than a CMY mix, which can shift hues depending on their mixture. Follow these steps:

1. Duplicate your background image to another document by choosing Duplicate Layer from the Layers palette pop-up menu. Choose New as a Document Destination in the Duplicate Layer dialog box. This opens the background in a new image.

2. Duplicate the background two times. Change both the name and mode of one of the duplicates to `Luminosity`, and change the other duplicate's name and mode to `Color`.

3. Activate the background layer, create a new layer called `Composite`, and fill with 50 percent gray (RGB 128, 128, 128). At this point, the layers should look like they do in Figure 2.30.

4. Shut off the view for the Luminosity layer and move it to the top of the layer stack (if it is not there already).

5. Duplicate the Composite layer.

Figure 2.30

This setup is the basic luminosity and color separation. You can use this in different ways to adjust the black result.

6. Merge the Color layer with the Composite Copy. You can do this by activating the Color layer and pressing ⌘/Ctrl+E. This commits existing color.

7. Set the layer mode to DifferenceThe image now appears brighter in areas where there was more saturated color. Merge that layer with the Composite layer to commit the result.

8. Open Hue/Saturation. Set Saturation to –100%. This will neutralize the color.

9. Open the Levels dialog box by pressing ⌘/Ctrl+L. Set the sliders to adjust tonality by moving the white slider to 128. This adjustment can vary depending on the image and on what you want to accomplish and how you want to affect the separation. Setting the slider to 128 will exclude light and fully saturated colors from containing additional black. Making a stronger change will eliminate a greater portion of saturated color and confine black generation to less saturated areas. Making a lesser change will include saturated color in black generation. Name the layer **Saturation**.

At this point you will have a saturation mask. It should look something like Figure 2.31. It represents a mapping of color in the image from most saturated (lightest) to least (darkest).

Figure 2.31

The saturation mask shows lighter in areas where the color is most pure (has the least gray).

Making the Luminosity Mask

A luminosity mask helps you target image tone based on light and dark. You use it to isolate the dark areas of the image where adding black will matter most. To create the mask:

1. Add a layer above the Saturation layer. Name the layer **Black** and fill with gray (50 percent gray or RGB 128, 128, 128).

2. Activate the Luminosity layer.

3. Open the Levels dialog box by pressing ⌘/Ctrl+L. Make the adjustment by moving the white slider to 128. This changes the mask so that only 50 percent grays or above will appear as gray (0–50 percent gray input will appear as white). This adjustment is optional. A smaller change allows black to substitute in lighter gray areas of the image; a greater change confines black substitution to only the darkest parts of the image. The Levels dialog box should look like Figure 2.32.

4. Merge the Luminosity layer with the Black layer. The layer should be named Black after the merge.

5. Move the Saturation layer above the Black layer and change the mode of the Saturation layer to Screen. This will brighten (dodge) areas of the image that are saturated.

6. Merge the Saturation layer with the Black layer. The result is your Black (K) plate; it should still be named Black.

Several interesting things happen here. The black is generated to substitute in areas where the image is darker than 50 percent gray. In the lighter area, saturated color is spared the effect of black mixing in. Overall, this allows black to work where it is most effective: pure gray and dark colors.

While you have generated the black from existing image information, you have done nothing to apply it. You still have to introduce the black back to your original and make adjustments. You can complete the black separation following these same steps using the CMYK Black action after completing the CMY separation and preview. (This same action completes the steps outlined in the section "Copying the Black Separation to the Original.")

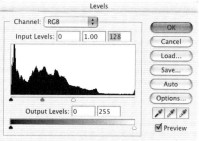

Figure 2.32

The dark portion represents the darkest half of the image (50–100 percent black).

Step 3: Applying the Black Separation

Having the black separated completes only part of the process. You could just overlay the black on the other colors, but more than one thing could go wrong. One of these problems is over-saturating the inks. Black is really added to replace some of the other color; the black needs to be used to target and remove some of the color to balance the result.

First, you need to copy the black layer back to the original image you were working on. Next you will want to remove some of the CMY ink in areas where the black will take over the responsibility (similar to duotone work, applying black where it is most efficient and reducing the effect of other ink). This serves the additional purpose of reducing the amount of ink used in black areas—which in turn can shorten ink drying time and lower the possibility of streaking or other over-inking effects.

Copying the Black Separation to the Original

This is the easy part. All you have to do here is copy the Black layer back to the CMY layered image you were working on:

1. Copy the Black layer that was the result of completing steps 1 through 6 in "Making the Luminosity Mask" back to the original CMY image using the Duplicate command from the Layer palette pop-up menu.

2. Close the image used to generate the Black layer.

3. Move the Black layer to the top of the layer stack. Set the layer mode to Multiply.

Removing Color Under Black

To reduce ink use and to get better results on press and in your prints, decrease the amount of ink printed in the darkest areas of the image in accordance with the amount of ink you are adding. This can keep the ink from over-saturating, streaking, and drying poorly. Ideally, it might seem that you would want only a maximum of 300 percent ink: The darkest areas of the image would have 100 percent each of cyan, magenta, and yellow if no black were introduced. You have to remove CMY inks to make room for the black to maintain the 300 percent maximum.

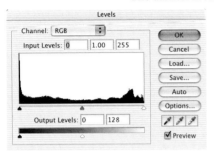

We take a simple route here, but you may want to fiddle with this result to achieve different ends.

To use the black ink information in removing the color below it, use the black layer information as a mask. Inverting the black will help you use it to lighten the CMY inks. A simple adjustment lets you control exactly how much total ink you will have.

Figure 2.33

Adjusting the Levels determines how much of the color below the black you will be taking out of other color plates— and that constrains the total ink.

1. Duplicate the Black layer and invert it by choosing ⌘/Ctrl+I.

2. Open the Levels dialog box (⌘/Ctrl+L) and change the white output slider to somewhere between the 128 and 191 levels. The 128 setting is used by default in the action supplied. For the example, the Levels dialog will look like Figure 2.33.

> Using 128 will remove 50 percent of the color under the black ink, and 64 will remove 25 percent of the color. At 64 (25 percent removal), your maximum ink outlay in black areas will be 325 percent (C75 + M75 + Y75 + K100), which is a little higher than what is usually suggested for press work. At 128 (50 percent removal), your ink outlay changes to a maximum of 250 percent (C50 + M50 + Y50 + K100). You are just making a flat change here because adjustment can get really intricate. For example, you may choose to use curves to set the removal and adjust removal at separate levels for each ink. Standard CMYK separations for black typically use a few more percentage points of cyan.

3. Move the Black Copy layer to just above the Yellow layer and name it `Yellow Adjust`. This should place it between the Yellow layer and the Yellow Fill layer.

4. Change the mode to Screen. This reduces the gray values in the Yellow layer by the intensity/density of the black ink.

5. Repeat steps 1 and 2, and move the new copy above the Magenta layer. Change the mode to Screen and name the layer `Magenta Adjust`.

6. Repeat steps 1 and 2, and move the new copy above the Cyan layer. Change the mode to Screen and name the layer `Cyan Adjust`. Your layers should look like Figure 2.34.

Figure 2.34

With the Black Copy layers in place, you've essentially completed the look of the separation.

That's it. What you have now is a complete separation that shows the cyan, magenta, yellow, and black with color removed under the black to reduce the density of inks so there won't be over-inking on press. The results appear here in Figure 2.35 as gray components, and you'll find the printed result in the color section.

Black

Yellow

Magenta

Cyan

You may see the potential here for manually adjusting the performance of your images. That can be valuable in some rare instances. What we have really taken a look at is something similar to what goes on behind the scenes during creation of your CMYK separations in Photoshop. This particular calculation is perhaps not complete in that there are many other variations you can make. For example, cyan ink is usually reduced less than yellow and magenta when removing color under black. The color is also often reduced using curves rather than levels as we did here. Any separation requires a little testing to achieve the best output.

With the separation layers in place, you can make adjustments to the image in CMYK, just as you would adjust an RGB image or layered duotone. That is, if you feel there is a little too much or too little of any color, you can reduce the amount by insinuating a curve or levels layer just above the plate color layer and making adjustments. You can preview the changes directly in the image as you make them.

Actions are included in the Hidden Power Tools so you can experiment with this process of separation. There are actions for each segment and one that plays the whole CMYK series. Encompassed in this process are most of the behind-the-scenes functions that go on in Photoshop when you convert to CMYK. You can adjust this procedure to your liking, and automate the result by duplicating the CMYK action and adjusting it to fit your needs. It will also help in looking at custom settings for generating automated CMYK separations, which we will look at more in a little bit.

Using the CMYK Separation

Once you have the separation, you'll want to be able to test it out. You can do this in one of several ways, including splitting out the layers as separate images that you can merge with the Merge Channels command—which is probably the easiest testing method.

1. Merge the Adjustment layers with their associated color layers to accept the changes. This will leave you with the plates and their color preview layers.

2. Change the mode of the image to Grayscale. Don't merge the layers when offered the opportunity.

3. Duplicate each of the ink layers to a new image in this order: Cyan, Magenta, Yellow, and Black. Name each image according to the layer you are duplicating. You should have a total of five images when you are done, including the original and four others named Cyan, Magenta, Yellow, and Black.

4. Flatten each of the four new images (Cyan, Magenta, Yellow, and Black).

5. Choose Merge Channels from the Channels pop-up menu.

6. Select CMYK from the Mode drop-down list and click OK.

7. Adjust the selections in the Specify Channels list so that Cyan is Cyan, and so forth. Click OK.

Photoshop reassembles the image as a CMYK image. You can use it as is or make additional adjustments. Once you have determined your process and the way you like to separate images, it may require fewer post-conversion adjustments. The file can be saved as any other CMYK file.

Keep in mind that there will be a difference between this RGB-to-CMYK separation and Photoshop's. Photoshop uses an even more sophisticated procedure to go from RGB to Lab to CMYK. This allows the program to take advantage of Lab during the conversion process to help match and remap RGB to CMYK colors. If you stick with the action as is without making finer adjustments, your results will be mediocre.

On the other hand, you may benefit from the theory we've used for other corrections. First, make a levels correction as you would for RGB on the CMY channels. Then make a curve adjustment for one of the midtone colors to balance the gray. Increase the contrast on the CMYK curve—perhaps using a luminosity layer (see the following section). Apply Color Balance; if you do it right, you'll note that the color won't be far from the original.

Once you arrive at settings that work for you in adjustments, you can reuse them over and over again for the same output device for a variety of images. For example, if you note that your prints are all a little magenta heavy, you can add a curve to the Magenta layer as part of your process to reduce the magenta influence. At the same time, you can adjust the correction to maximize the potential of the image. In this way, you can make custom corrections to your CMYK content that you simply can't control otherwise in Photoshop.

> To print any of the plates on a home ink-jet for proofing, follow the same instructions as you did for printing duotones. When printing to your printer, you can apply the color screens to the plates and print them separately. When separating the plates, throw out the screening layers and save the plate layers as separate files.

We've completed our look at the separation process, and you've seen the potential for customizing that process. For CMYK conversion, color has to be remapped from RGB to CMY, and black has to be introduced through calculations. You need to optimize these calculations for the output, taking into account how heavy you want the black generation to be, what exactly you want the black to replace, how the device and paper handle color (so you know how to adjust for dot gain), and perhaps even differences in the colors of your ink. These considerations are handled by Photoshop in automated CMYK conversions, based on choices you make in the Color Settings dialog box. With that in mind, let's have a look at your conversion options.

Automating Customized CMYK Generation

Photoshop offers some advanced tools for adjusting your CMYK output that are probably hidden (intentionally) in the interface within the bowels of the Color Settings dialog box. The purpose of these settings is to allow you to set up your CMYK separations so that you can customize them for output without having to generate them manually every time. Photoshop allows you to create and save custom setups that you can recall when using a particular device or paper, with the aim of optimizing your output.

In the Color Settings dialog box (⌘/Ctrl+Shift+K), click on the CMYK Working Space drop-down list and scroll up to the top to select Custom CMYK. This will open the Custom CMYK dialog box shown in Figure 2.36.

Figure 2.36

Custom CMYK is just the beginning of potential custom adjustments you can make to CMYK output.

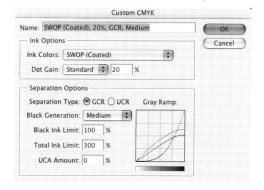

In this dialog box, you enter a name for a custom setup and choose ink and separation options. You can then save the setup you create and reuse it at a later time. First, let's look at the Ink Options settings.

> Before making changes to *any* settings in these custom areas, know what you are doing and be sure you are making the changes for a specific reason. This may mean making a change based on the suggestion of your printing service or because of sophisticated measurement using such devices as a reflection densitometer, colorimeter, or spectrophotometer.

Ink Options

The basic Ink Options dialog box allows you to define color and absorption behaviors by selecting from a set of color standards from a drop-down list and by specifying the dot gain. You can customize ink colors by choosing Custom from the Ink Colors drop-down list (see Figure 2.37), and you can customize the dot gain by entering percentage right in the field or by choosing Curves from the Dot Gain drop-down list (see Figure 2.38).

Colors in the Ink Colors dialog box can be entered as Yxy coordinates or L*a*b* measure right on the screen. You can open color pickers for each of the nine swatches and enter such values as RGB, HSB, or Lab; or you may choose to sample colors via the Eyedropper (as you might do from a scan). Users can then measure and enter accurate depictions of device response. If you can determine accurate measures, Photoshop can look at these values and make better, targeted conversions.

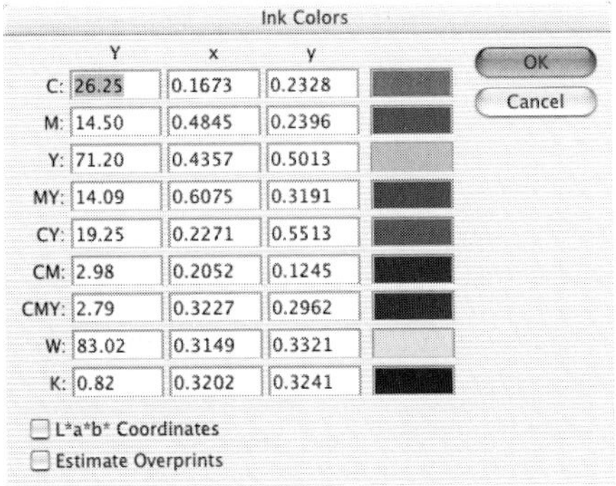

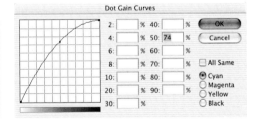

Figure 2.37

The Ink Colors dialog box allows users to enter colors measured from printed pieces to accurately reflect device reproduction.

Figure 2.38

Dot Gain curves let the user enter a dot gain response of a particular device.

Separation Options

The Separation Options dialog box offers means of controlling generation of black separation. The Separation Type setting can be GCR (Gray Component Replacement) or UCR (Under Color Removal). UCR replaces CMY color with black only in gray areas; GCR replaces grays and some darker areas of color components. As you'll recall, the manual separation involves removing color under grays and darker saturated areas, so that process is more like GCR.

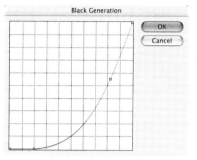

Figure 2.39

Customizing black generation curves affects black output.

Black generation lets you determine how closely generation of blacks will match image luminosity. None means no black generation; Light, Medium, and Heavy are mix variations generating less or more total black ink; Maximum generates all tone as black; Custom allows you to adjust a custom generation curve (see Figure 2.39). In the manual separation, you have the opportunity to control black generation by adjusting curves and levels to target tonal range and impact.

Assigning a Black Limit means that you tell Photoshop the maximum percentage of black ink that can be used for any color or tone. Often this will be 100 percent (which tells Photoshop to use the entire dynamic range), but lower percentages allow for richer blacks and ink mixes. Total Ink Limit works in conjunction with Black Limit to calculate a result. Percentages can be as high as 400 percent (100 percent of all four inks), but using less ink has advantages such as reduced drying time and less saturation. The manual example uses a 300 percent ink limit. UCA Amount (Under Color Addition) allows you to increase the amount of color inks used in darker areas of the image. This may enhance rich blacks and help retain subtle shadow details.

Any changes in the settings in the Separation Options dialog box affect changes in the Gray Ramp graph. This graph shows how the inks will generate blacks based on the current settings by displaying changes in the CMYK output graphs.

If you have the equipment and are interested in indulging these settings by printing and measuring your results, or if you get recommended settings from your printing service, color and separation adjustments can help maximize the effectiveness of your output and give you intricate control of separations and results. Best of all, the separations will be automated, removing the need for manual efforts—though there may be instances where you will want to combine manually separated components into a CMYK image, such as to achieve totally customized or enhanced black generations based on properties that standard settings don't provide.

Lab Color

In the section "Converting to Grayscale from Lab Color," we looked at taking the tone from an image by separating it from the color. Part of the idea behind this was based on the Lab color model, which treats color separately from tone. Separating tone from color can come in handy when manipulations require that you treat one or the other, rather than both. In CMYK or RGB models, color and tone are essentially inextricable: If you change one of the components, the tone and color of the image are altered. With tone separate from color in Lab, you can make adjustments to the image tone without having the by-product of affecting color change at the same time.

So, say your image is a bit flat (lacks contrast) but you think the color is good. Splitting the image tone (luminosity) from the color allows you to make a curve adjustment to the tone to increase the contrast with no real effect on the color. Lab is also great for making targeted color change (e.g., changing the color of a dress) because it is easier to work on the color in isolation from the tone.

The conversion to Lab is as simple as choosing Lab mode. Because Lab is able to reproduce more colors than either RGB or CMYK, it can represent all the colors the others can. However, after you make manipulations in Lab, returning an image back to RGB or CMYK will be less friendly to the image information: Some data may be compromised in either case during the conversion. Converting to Lab and back to CMYK will also cause the image to be re-separated, so any changes you have made in customizing separations may be lost. Therefore, it is best to use Lab in correction stages—before targeting your image for CMYK output.

Figure 2.40

You have created five new layers in steps 2 through 6. Before you continue, they need to be in the order shown here.

Working separately on color and tone offers distinct advantages when you're working in layered separation in RGB, Lab, or CMYK. The idea is to create separate layers to carry the image luminosity (or lightness) and another to carry image color (the A and B channel information). Making changes to the Luminosity layer affects only the tone, and changes to the Color layer affect only color as long as those changes are grouped to their target layers.

Let's take a look at the basics by separating luminosity and color in layers:

1. Open JuliaButterfly.psd.

2. Duplicate the Background and name the layer `Color`. Change the mode to Color.

3. Duplicate the Color layer and name the layer `Luminosity`. Change the mode to Luminosity.

4. Activate the Background and create a new blank layer. Name the layer `Composite` and fill it with gray (50 percent).

5. Duplicate the Composite layer two times. Change the layer copy names to `Commit 1` and `Commit 2`.

6. Move Commit 1 above the Color layer. The Layers palette should look like Figure 2.40.

7. Activate the top layer (press Option/Alt+Shift+]), link Commit 1, and then press ⌘/Ctrl+E to merge the Luminosity layer with Commit 1. If the Luminosity layer is not the active layer and the layers are not linked, the name can change to Commit 1, rather than retaining the name Luminosity.

8. Change the layer mode of the Luminosity layer to Luminosity. This changes to Normal automatically during the merge.

9. Activate the Color layer (press Option/Alt+[), link to Commit 2, and then merge by pressing ⌘/Ctrl+E. Change the mode of the layer to Color. The result will look the same as the original, but the color will be separated into Luminosity and Color components as in Figure 2.41.

Figure 2.41

While not exactly like Lab, which separates two color layers, this setup will give you much of the advantage of Lab color mode without switching to Lab.

The color dynamic of the Color layer is virtually the same as if you had switched to Lab, except that you won't adjust the A and B layers separately. In this case, it can actually be an advantage. If, for example, you have an image with a lot of color noise, you can clear up the problem by just blurring the Color layer—depending on the image, you may be able to blur the Color layer by an almost obscene amount. You can combine the blur effect with specific areas of color noise as applicable. In any case, you can blur and not affect the tone because it is in a separate layer and is self-contained. In other words, the shape of the image will be held by the tone. You will see more of the advantage of this separation when we discuss masking in Chapter 3.

Of course, you can always switch to Lab mode and make corrections to the Lightness channel and blur the A and B color channels to reduce noise. Yet another option is to move to Lab mode and use the Color and Luminosity tool to split luminosity and color within the Lab mode image. This approach may let you handle the desired corrections more easily.

RGBL Hybrid Separation

A hybrid type of separation can be created using luminosity to control tone along with creating an RGB separation for control of color. The result is that you get the simplicity and intuitive arena for color correction and a dynamic control of tone isolated from one another.

All you really have to do is separate RGB in layers and add a luminosity layer to the top of the stack. When you are done, you will have successfully separated color from tone *and* separated the tone into a light-based representation of colors. This is something that would be very difficult to do using channels alone.

1. Follow the steps to separate RGB channels as layers from the section "Separating RGB from a Color Image" Or play the Split RGB No Stops action.

2. Create a new, blank layer at the top of the layer stack. Name the layer `Luminosity`, and set the mode to Luminosity.

3. Press ⌘+Option+Shift+E/Ctrl+Alt+Shift+E to merge the visible image into the Luminosity layer.

4. Create a new layer and fill with 50 percent gray (HSB: 0, 0, 50).

5. Move the Luminosity layer above the layer created in step 4, group them, and merge.

6. Set the merged layer mode to Luminosity.

This gives you an image that freezes the current image Luminosity. It allows you to make drastic and controlled changes to the color without affecting the shape of the image. In other words, you can take advantage of and correct the RGB channels by making corrections below the Luminosity layer using curves, for example.

By this point, we have sliced and diced images in innumerable different ways, and this last section shows that you can mix and match color schemes to some extent to take advantage of different theories and separations without necessarily converting the image to a different mode. Being able to extract targets for tone, color, saturation, and different channels gives you greater power over your images in affecting your targeted change. Practice taking your images apart and putting them back together. The better you understand these procedures, the better you can grasp and integrate the chapters to come.

Part II

Altering Image Objects

One thing you can trust is the content of your image. If you see a ball, a smiling face, or a piece of garbage in an image, none of it will be going away soon unless you remove it. If you zoom in to 200 percent or more, you will see all the information in the image, pixel by pixel.

When looking at the image, you'll want to consider the content and make notes—mentally, on a piece of paper, right on a printed copy of the image—so that you know what you may want to change later to improve the image composition, to remove damage, to reduce image noise, to eliminate debris, and so forth.

In making these changes, you generally begin with basic corrections first, such as the overall color, and then move on to the specifics, either by isolating the area in layers or by using masking or selection tools. Often you will use techniques that rely on separation and tone. In this chapter, we take a broad look at manipulating image content.

Chapter 3

Image Change and Repair

It was surprising to see the general reaction to the Healing Brush in Photoshop 7: People who should have known better were suggesting that Healing was the biggest innovation since layers. All that happens when you apply the tool is that image information is copied from one area of the image to another. The application is a clever trick—but not magic. In reality, it is just another technique for image repair. Similar results can be achieved without it.

If you know what you are doing when you go to work on an image, you control your results and don't rely on magic—or anything that seems to be magic. Some tools can speed up a process or simplify steps, which is good. You gain control of images when you can visualize the result, not when the magic "do it for you" tool jumps in and wrests control from your hands. If you choose the latter, you are trusting that tool to use calculations to make an artistic judgment that it is probably not qualified to make.

Repairing and adjusting images almost always entails duplicating image areas—either from the current or other images. You might mask the areas or apply modes, transformations, and other adjustments, but the basis for the changes is substitution—substitution over magic. This chapter looks at the substitution process, beginning with a simple review of the basics to an in-depth look at the most complex adjustments. We'll examine the following topics:

Changing and repairing your images

Using the Clone tool

Understanding masking and selective change

Using filters

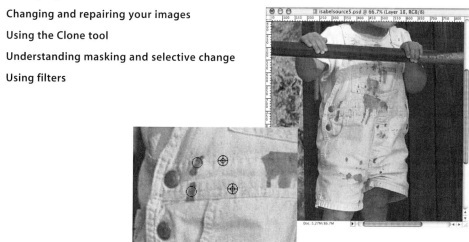

Cloning

The simplest, most straightforward means of making repairs is to duplicate image areas by using Copy and Paste. You just look at the image, define what should be fixed, find a replacement, and assimilate the replacement.

Figure 3.1 shows a kid at the top of a slide. She's had an altercation with an ice cream cone, and the once-white clothes aren't white anymore. To work with this example, open the playground.psd file on the CD.

The laundry list for correcting this image could be pretty long. There is the dripped ice cream problem, the rust on the bar, the shortened pant leg, the sock frill flipped up, glare from the slide causing two-tone on one leg—and this is after some other problems had already been corrected. Of course, the image could stay as is: It is obviously just a casual summer fun shot. In fact, there should rarely be a time when the corrections you might want to make to an image are this extensive; if so, it would probably be better to reshoot (or be sure to get in all the shots you want before handing out the ice cream). But this particular image offers us some interesting challenges of shadow, tone, and pattern.

Figure 3.1

We'll be working with this image to show you the cloning process and look at improving image flaws.

All of the trouble here can be easily fixed by using cloning and duplicating areas from the existing clothes that remain unblemished to cover the stains. That is all you have to do: duplicate clean areas to cover the dirty ones. You create the basic copy by selecting an area of the image using any selection tool, pressing ⌘/Ctrl+C to Copy, and then pressing ⌘/Ctrl+V to Paste. Pasting automatically makes a new layer, and you can move the clone into place. Copy and Paste is the simplest form of duplication and has a wide range of uses. The Clone and the Patch/Healing tools can also help with variations on basic cloning.

There are better (and worse) ways to make the corrections, depending on where the damage is, how much there is, and what type it is. You have to be aware of patterns, color, and tone, and work with image information to make the best corrections. At times, you have to rely on more than just a straight application of any one tool. The process may involve masking, blending, changing modes, erasing, and other tool options in order to finish the job.

Using the Clone Stamp Tool

The Clone tool lets you do simple copying and pasting from one point to another in the shape of the currently selected brush (using brush dynamics). Let's start with a simple cloning and look at options for other variations. The simplest means of making a clone is the Clone Stamp tool.

1. Open the playground.psd file on the CD.

2. Choose the Clone Stamp tool and make sure the settings are as follows:

   - Use All Layers: Enabled.

   - Aligned enabled

   - Opacity: 100%

   - Mode: Normal

   - Brush is semi-soft (80–90% hardness). A softer brush will help your clones blend into the surroundings.

3. Create a new layer and move it to the top of the layer stack (if it isn't already there; Photoshop creates the layer above the currently active layer, wherever it is).

4. Sample a replacement area. This should be an area that is clear of other damage or detail (e.g., clothing seams or pockets, as in this example). To make the sample, hold down Option/Alt and click the spot in the image that you want to use as the sample area.

5. Apply the sample by releasing Option/Alt, moving the cursor over the area where the clone will be applied, and then clicking in that area.

Steps 4 and 5 will apply the clone to cover the target area by copying the sampled area and painting it into the application area (see Figure 3.2). Save this image at this point to continue our example in the next section.

Figure 3.2

Using the Clone Stamp tool is just a fancy (and convenient) way of applying copy/paste.

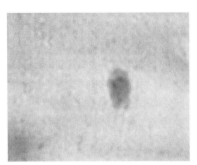

Original image area

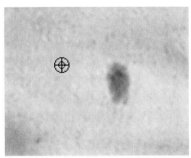

Target showing sample area

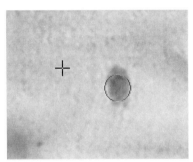

Sample crosshair and destination brush shape during application

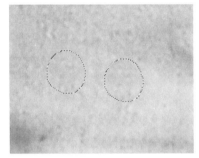

Area duplicated from origin to destination

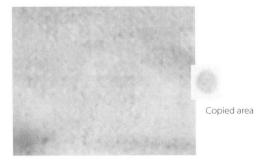

Copied area

Completed result

Optimally, the size of the brush should be just slightly larger than the area you are cloning to, but not so large that it extends beyond the area you're targeting for the clone. You will often want to use a slightly soft brush so that the changes blend into the background. Too soft a brush can lead to corrections that look blurred. For best results, be sure the color and tone are similar in the clone-from and clone-to area, and that the area you are cloning from is already clear of defects. Checking the tone may require using the Eyedropper and Info palette; failing to use a clean sample area will replicate defects to the new area. It is a good idea to zoom in close and clean up with a small brush first, picking up little bits of damage before moving on to larger patches. This will help clear sample areas for larger cloning.

It is helpful to have several presets at the ready for the Clone tool to make switching back and forth between brushes easy. You create the presets by setting up the tool options and choosing New Tool Preset from the Tool Preset Picker pop-up menu (the Tool Preset Picker for the Clone Stamp is on the options bar when the Clone Stamp tool is selected). Naming the preset with the hardness, opacity, and tool name should help you quickly locate tools in the future. These presets will prove handy:

- The largest brush diameter you will need at 90 percent hardness and 100 percent opacity
- The smallest brush diameter you will need at 90 percent hardness and 100 percent opacity
- A brush diameter midway between these smallest and largest brushes at 90 percent hardness and 100 percent opacity
- The largest brush diameter you will need at 90 percent hardness and 50 percent opacity
- The smallest brush diameter you will need at 90 percent hardness and 50 percent opacity
- A brush diameter midway between the smallest and largest brushes at 90 percent hardness and 50 percent opacity

It is also a good idea to consider the setup of your workspace and customize it for working with specific tools, then save the setup. For the Clone Stamp, you may want to show the Brush, History, Tool Presets, and Info palettes prominently, so you can quickly change brushes to custom sizes, undo many steps at once for a comparison, and check tone and/or color in original and destination areas. Having a workspace set to your normal setup and one for brush use can be handy when you're switching modes of work; that way, you don't have to deal with palette clutter.

You could get away with fewer presets by making brush-size adjustments using the bracket keys. Pressing the [key will shrink the brush size, and] will increase it. The brush size changes in increments, depending on the current size, as shown in Table 3.1.

For the most part, the areas you should target with the Clone Stamp are the smaller spots. It isn't the best tool for cloning a subject's head from one image to another, for example. For larger areas, you will want to use patching, as long as there is a reasonable replacement area.

Table 3.1

Brush Size Increments

BRUSH SIZE BETWEEN...	INCREMENT
1 and 10	1 pixel
10 and 100	10 pixels
100 and 200	25 pixels
200 and 300	50 pixels
300 and 2500	100 pixels

The softer brushes can be used for smoothing out correction areas where you don't have a suitable match or where slight blending is called for. Above all, keep your coverage to a minimum. Start working on the image from the CD, zoomed in 200–300 percent, cloning to a new layer (just create a layer at the top of the stack). Pick up the smaller spots and damage over the clothing. Your results should end up similar to Figure 3.3, which shows the before and after of our cloning work, with a separate shot of just the clones.

Movements with the Clone Stamp tool are usually spotty, click-and-move actions, rather than blowing away large areas of the image. You'll want to resample often, changing angles and position of the sample to appropriate areas (you'll do this far more often than changing the brush). At times you'll switch modes to Color or Luminosity to help move only the color or lightness component of the sample area rather than both. For example, you may want to sample the tone from one area and the color from another to get a good match.

For this image, we have accomplished the bulk of the minor cleanup with the Clone Stamp tool, which is not unusual. The repair on the pocket area is fairly heavily clone-stamped, which may be a bit more unusual. The change reflects the result of many tiny clones to help prepare for later, larger patches.

Figure 3.3

The area of the pocket on the viewer's right is more cloning than you usually want to do. Your cloning should generally be limited to spotty cleanup, as exemplified in other areas of the image.

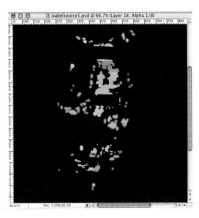

There are some specific spots left behind knowing that we could more easily repair these areas by patching (manually) or by using the Healing brush (or Patch tool). In this case, the right of the smaller pocket on the overalls (from the viewer's perspective) will be re-created using a duplicate of the left, and the larger cleared area at the left of the waistline will become a patch for the center (where the ice cream stained that difficult area heavily). We'll look at healing those few leftover spots first.

Healing

The Healing brush can be used for spot cleaning in addition to the Clone Stamp, and can often make quick work of lines, wrinkles, dust specks, and other damage in relatively isolated image areas. Correcting damage in areas where you expect to do a lot of cleanup can lead to some unexpected results: The tool can actually cause more trouble because of the way it works.

Healing is a clever application, really, in that it does a comparison of the source and the target and combines the image information, saving you the complicated steps of blending, sampling, and blurring. In essence, Healing adds the texture of the sample to an averaged area of the target (an area around the target), and then blends on the edges to create a seamless patch. It can make some great corrections to, say, wrinkles on a forehead. However, using the tool indiscriminately is not recommended, because of its blurring and blending behaviors.

Here are some guidelines for using the Healing brush:

- Use only if you can cover the entire area of damage with the source in one step.
- Don't use it (without a selection that contains the application area) if you will apply or sample near the edge of areas that contrast significantly in tone or color with that sample or target.
- Be sure the source is the texture you want to replace in the target; ignore the color.

If you don't cover the entire area of damage—with a little overlap—that uncovered damage area will be used in samples to calculate the result and will blend (actually blur) back in as part of the correction. Because the result samples pixels around the target, getting too close to an area that contrasts in tone with the area you are sampling from or correcting will make for a bad result. Texture should be the main consideration; You want the texture from the source to replace the texture in the target. Think of the texture as the noise rather than the overall tone of the sample area.

What ends up getting placed is not so much the sample as the texture of the sample, which is lightened or darkened based on an average of the tone in the area surrounding the target. For example, you can stamp from a large tattoo (be careful to avoid its edges) to cover a mole on an area of skin where there is no tattoo; only the texture of the skin has to be a good replacement.

When using the Healing brush, cleaning up a stray eyelash fallen on a cheek is different (easier and more straightforward) than cleaning stray hairs right at a dark hairline (or the edge of that tattoo). Getting too close to the hairline tends to shade the "healed" area unnaturally.

To work with the Healing brush:

1. Be sure the version of the playground.psd file you were working on in the previous section is open.

2. Create a new layer and call it **Healing.**

3. Choose the Healing brush (press J, or scroll the tool while pressing Shift+J). The brush you use should be hard (100 percent) and large enough to easily cover at least the thinnest diameter of the damage. Tool Presets might include several brushes of various size (though you can change size with the bracket shortcuts we mentioned earlier). The Source will usually be Sampled, unless you create a pattern to use (Chapter 5 shows you how to create seamless patterns that might be used for this). For this example, use:

   - Mode: Normal
   - Source: Sampled
   - Enable Aligned
   - Enable Use All Layers

4. Identify an area to fix, and look for a replacement area that seems to mimic the texture of the targeted replacement area (see Figure 3.4). This area should have a similar texture (and perhaps contour) to the target.

5. Sample the replacement area as you would when using the Clone Stamp tool (press Option/Alt and click).

6. Apply the Healing brush to the target area by moving the cursor over it and pressing the mouse button. Cover the entire area to be replaced in one step as shown in Figure 3.5. When the area is covered, release the mouse button.

7. Toggle the view for the Healing layer to see before and after results.

Figure 3.4

The spots here obviously need fixing, and a decent replacement (circled) seems to be not far above in the image.

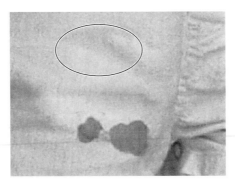

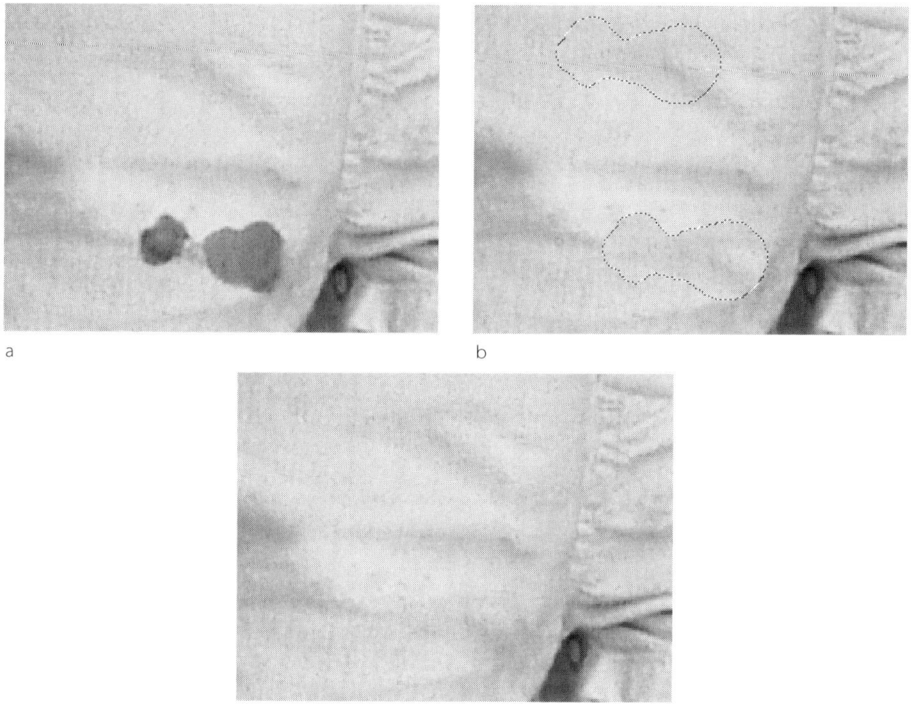

a

b

c

Figure 3.5

The area to be fixed (a) is covered entirely with the sampled area; when the mouse is released, the area will seem to transform from looking like a straight clone (b) to something more fitting to the target area (c). The delay is due to the tool calculating the result.

From here, the function of the Healing brush is similar to the Clone Stamp tool. One final warning: Don't become overdependent on the Healing brush. Although it can make some pretty neat changes, it is not always superior to using the Clone Stamp tool or manual patching. Let's take a look at using the Patch tool on the same spots and how this correction differs.

Using the Patch Tool

Using the Patch tool is much like using the Healing brush, at least as far as the results and applications where it is most useful. In fact, the correction from the previous section can be made in a nearly identical way. The chief differences in using the Patch tool are:

- It provides a handy preview of what will be applied to the target area as you drag to search for a sample.

- You use a selection tool rather than a brush to define the target area.

- You cannot patch to a blank layer, so changes can't be layered.

- You can't patch using all layers content is applied to and from the currently active layer only.

Because you can preview the change, the Patch tool can be a better means of tackling larger patch jobs—such as cleaning up the spots from the previous example. For this example, turn off the Healing layer in the image and let's tackle those same spots using the Patch tool:

1. Make a new blank layer at the top of the layer stack and call it **Patch**.

    As stated, you can't patch to a new layer. The idea of these steps is to keep the correction separate. It will also offer a way to make a patch adjustment so the patch can stand alone on its own layer.

2. Press ⌘+Option+Shift+E/Ctrl+Alt+Shift+E to copy the visible area of the image to the current layer. If you don't merge the content to this layer, you will get an error when moving the patch.

3. Choose the Patch tool. Set Patch to Source to use the selection made in step 4 as the target for the patch. If you chose Destination instead, you would use the area you selected to patch the area that you move it to.

4. Make a selection around the damaged area by click-dragging the Patch tool around the area. This selection will look like the selection in Figure 3.6. You will most likely want to use a hard selection (no aliasing or feathering).

5. Click in the selection area (created in step 4) and drag around the image; keep an eye on the preview in the target area. It is a good idea to have a source in mind before you start to move the selection.

6. Position the source for the patch so that you match any contour of the target area as best you can. When the preview looks like a good match, release the mouse button.

Figure 3.6

Select the entire area of damage

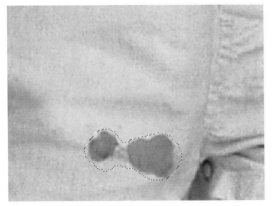

At this point, Photoshop applies a behind-the-scenes calculation similar to the one it uses when you apply the Healing brush. You can turn the view for the Patch layer on and off to compare the change before and after.

After completing these steps, you will still have the original selection. You can use this selection to isolate the patch on the current layer. If you are using a hard selection (not one you feathered), you can just invert the selection (⌘/Ctrl+Shift+I) and press the Delete key. If the selection is feathered (e.g., created with a selection tool that allows feathering), you should adjust it before inverting and deleting the selection to encompass the entire area affected by the change. To do this, follow these steps:

1. Change to Quick Mask mode (press Q).

2. Open the Threshold dialog box and slide the slider all the way to the left. This will change the Quick Mask so that all of the area affected by the change will be transparent.

3. Switch back to Standard mode (press Q again).

4. Invert the selection.

5. Press Delete to remove the selected area.

This is not exactly the same effect you'd get with the Patch tool, but it is the entire area that is potentially affected by the change. You can trim the area further and more accurately with the following steps:

1. Duplicate the Patch layer, set the mode to Difference, name it `Patch Difference`, and move it below the Patch layer.

2. Shut off the view for the Patch and Patch Difference layers.

3. Create a new layer, and drag it below the Patch and Patch Difference layers in the stack. Name the new layer `Original`.

4. Merge the visible content to the Original layer (⌘+Option+Shift+E/Ctrl+Alt+Shift+E).

5. Activate the Patch Difference layer and merge down.

6. Hold down ⌘/Ctrl and click the RGB channel in the Channels palette.

7. Switch to Quick Mask (press Q).

8. Open Threshold and adjust the Threshold setting by sliding the slider all the way left.

9. Switch back to Standard mode (press Q again) and Invert the selection.

10. Activate the Patch layer and press Delete.

11. Delete the Original layer.

These steps separate out pixels that actually changed from the original—no matter how much they changed. It is still not the same as isolating the correction by applying the Healing brush to a second layer. If you want an isolated correction of a larger area, it may be best to first do some checking around using the Patch tool, note the approximate coordinates, and apply the actual correction to a new layer using the Healing brush instead of the

Patch tool (which will not apply changes to a blank layer). You can get pretty exacting using the Info palette to determine the source and target areas. The following steps will keep the correction isolated:

1. Choose the Patch tool and set to Source.

2. Make a selection around the damaged area by click-dragging the Patch tool around the area.

3. Click in the selection area, check the Info palette for the XY coordinates, and drag around the image (watching the preview of the patch in the target area).

4. Position the source for the patch so that you match any contour of the target area as best you can. When the preview looks like a good match, check the coordinates and release the mouse button.

5. Step back in the image history to before step 2.

6. Create a new layer and name it Healing Patch.

7. Select the Healing brush.

8. Sample at the coordinates determined in step 4.

9. Apply at the coordinates determined in step 3. Cover the entire area of damage.

You can use a preexisting selection made with any selection tool to apply your patch. That is, if you would find it easier to create the selection with the Magnetic Lasso, or define it with calculation or create it using Quick Mask mode, you can do that, and then switch to the Patch tool to use that selection to apply your patch. This could prove handy in a situation where you have a large area (such as a sky) where a scan reveals a lot of dust. You can use the tone of the image to help select the dust, and then apply a patch to heal the damage. We'll look more at selection later in this chapter.

At this point, you should try to use the Patch tool to correct the isolated ice cream spots near the snaps to the viewer's left. This correction should prove to be just about impossible to do in one step because the stitching is unique at that spot in the image. You'll find that the pattern created by the stitching is better covered in two steps. Because this is the case, undo the patch and try the Healing brush. Using samples from different angles (concentrating on matching the pattern and direction of the stitch), this process won't necessarily work better than two moves with the Patch tool, but it will be faster since sampling is quicker than making selections. Figure 3.7 shows some potential substitutions.

Leave the stains over the pocket and in the center of the belt line for manual patching, the topic of the next section.

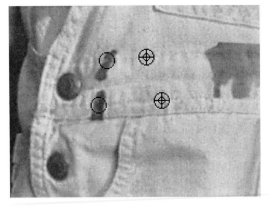

Figure 3.7

Use the stitch line to orient your sample and application points.

Manual Patching

The last two larger areas of damage in the sample image could potentially be cleaned up using the previously discussed tools, but not without an extraordinary amount of fuss and bother. A better way to fix these larger areas is to use manual patching. With the manual approach you can redefine the shape of the patch being applied (which you can't do with the Patch tool). We can use additional tools between what is essentially sampling (selecting the source for the correction) and application (targeting and committing) to shape replacement areas to better fit where they have to go. Let's continue with the image used in the previous section:

1. Create a new layer at the top of the stack and merge the visible content to that layer.

2. Choose the Lasso tool either from the toolbar or by pressing L (press Shift+L if you need to cycle through the Lasso tools).

3. Change the lasso options to Feather 0.

4. Make a rough selection of the area around the stain by click-dragging the lasso around the stain. See Figure 3.8.

5. Move the selection to an area of the image that you want to use to patch the shirt (see Figure 3.9). The selection should, optimally, fit over an area that is already free of damage—because you've already cleaned it up using one of the techniques covered earlier. Fitting the selection over the area can include changing the orientation of the selection (Select → Transform Selection) or snipping off areas that you don't want to copy (hold down the Option/Alt key to subtract from the selection).

6. Press ⌘/Ctrl+C to copy the image area.

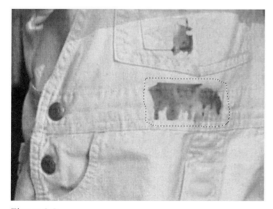

Figure 3.8

This selection will serve as a template for choosing an area to substitute for the stain, similar to what you did to choose a source with the Patch tool.

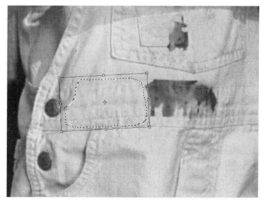

Figure 3.9

The selection is adjusted, in this case to leave behind the shadows in the upper left and follow the stitch pattern of the original area.

7. Press ⌘/Ctrl+V to paste the image area into a new layer. Name the layer **Patch**.

8. Choose Transform (Edit>Transform>Free Transform), then Move (click on the area and drag), Rotate (click outside a corner of the area and drag) and Distort (hold down Command/CTRL and drag a handle) the replacement into position. See Figure 3.10.

This simple procedure will make a template for the repair (the selection in step 4), create the replacement piece (steps 5 through 7), and allow you to move and adjust it (step 8).

A byproduct of the reshaping is a slight feathering, which will help your patch blend in with the surroundings. If the blending is not enough (or if there is little need to distort the patch), you can adjust using the Eraser tool at the edges of the patch area. Erasing content with a soft brush causes it to blend with the underlying content. However, as you run the risk of losing pixels that you may later want to restore, it may be better to use layer masking, which lets you duplicate image areas and then adjust without erasing and permanently losing those pixels you may want to keep. Follow these steps:

1. Hold down the ⌘/Ctrl key and click the Patch layer in the Layers palette. This loads the transparent portion of the layer as a selection.

2. Choose Layer → Add Layer Mask → Reveal Selection to create a layer mask based on the transparency of the Patch layer. At this point, nothing in the image will have changed, though the Layers palette will display the layer mask. Leave the mask active (note the slight highlighting frame on the thumbnail for the mask).

3. Choose Gaussian Blur and move the slider so that just a hint of the area that you had repaired appears in the image; then reduce the blur slightly so that the damage is covered. If the repair is very tight to the damage, you may want to consider stepping back in the image history and reshaping the correction to give yourself a little more play for the blending adjustment. While you can make this adjustment after applying the mask, you will introduce more blurring and interpolation.

Figure 3.10

Depending on how well the areas for the source and target match, you may not have a lot of work to do. In this case, the stitching needs to match on each end of the replacement area.

Blurring the mask will affect the blending at the edge of the mask area. Applying the blur may be enough to blend the correction in with the background, but you can enhance the correction to the mask in a variety of ways. For example, painting the mask with black using the Brush tool will achieve the same results as using the Eraser. Using a brush with white will do the opposite and restore areas you have masked. By switching between black and white, you can customize the shape of the mask to best blend the patch with the background, with more flexibility than if you'd just erased the area.

Other adjustments can be helpful for refining the mask as well. For example, you can use the Curves dialog box (Image → Adjustments → Curves) to change the blend of the blurred mask from step 3. After opening the Curves dialog box, leave the default points in place and add points. For the mask you have created, adjusting the curve to make the mask result darker increases the amount of the information used from the original; making the mask result lighter removes original information by allowing more of the sample to show. The curve must be applied to the layer mask and not the layer content, so a curve adjustment layer will not work here.

In order to finish the cleanup for the jumper, let's now take care of the pocket and the spot on the label. We made earlier corrections with the Clone Stamp tool to clean up the left side of the pocket (from the viewer's perspective). To combine those corrections into a new layer, use the ⌘+Option+Shift+E/Ctrl+Alt+Shift+E shortcut. Make a rough selection around the pocket area that you want to duplicate, then copy and paste it so it appears in a new layer. After pasting, you can flip and transform the object to replace the other side of the pocket (see Figure 3.11).

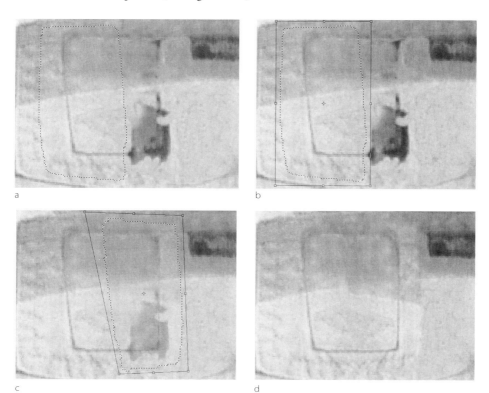

a

b

c

d

Figure 3.11

After making a selection (a) and copy/pasting the image area (b), you can set the opacity of the layer to 50 percent to temporarily see through the patch for placement and use the Transform function to flip the copy and then distort it into place (c). When you switch back the transparency to 100 percent, the result (d) requires some touchup but will get you most of the way there.

With the pocket in place, a smart touch-up is to use the Clone Stamp tool in Color mode to recolor some of the portion of the upper pocket that is stained. Fixing the label requires creating a patch from another portion of the label. Using a similar manual patching approach, you can straighten the pant leg and fix the up-turned frill on the sock.

It is sometimes best to see if problems are isolated in channels or other portions of an image that you can separate out and work on individually. In essence, using tools such as Clone Stamp in Luminosity or Color mode will affect only a portion of the image information, which lets you target the change. At times you may want to target a change to a color channel, or make changes as part of a layered separation (using techniques from the previous chapters). While you can make changes in the channels using cloning methods, it may be best to make those types of changes in layered separations because it will be easier to target and control using separate clone-to layers. Changes to the channels themselves have to be made directly (or by using Advanced Blending Channels checkboxes). It is also possible to isolate areas for change using selection and masking. Let's take a more in-depth look at Masking and Selection next.

Masking and Selective Change

Another means of isolating image areas is to use selection and/or masking. These terms are somewhat interchangeable. The purpose of both is to mark areas subject to change. With cloning, the shape of the brush acts as a selection, both for sampling and targeting the application of new pixels. Patching is somewhat like masking in that to use it effectively, you should define the shape of the target area by making a selection of it first. The method is nearly identical to cloning if you consider the predefined selection as just a custom-shaped, disposable brush that will be used for one quick application.

When using masking and selection, you define the shape of the target area to isolate areas outside that target from change. Masking can take many forms:

- A selection created with selection tools that appears only on screen
- A layer mask that appears attached to a layer in the Layers palette (and can be viewed as a channel)
- A clipping mask that works based on the transparency of the bottom layer in a layer group
- Conditional blending using Blend If functionality, which lets you mask areas of an image from view, based on a comparison of layers

For the purpose of brevity, we'll assume you're familiar with the basic selection tools (Marquee, Lasso, Magic Wand, Quick Mask, etc.). Essentially, you create a selection using one of the freehand tools and simply use the selection to corral some image information into an isolated area. There are perhaps some less obvious and more powerful means of selection based on tool combinations and calculations. In these cases, you can use tools to isolate areas according to color or tone, which will help you make accurate selections along complicated edge areas.

There are several ways to make reasonably clean selections of even complex image areas given a little thought and ingenuity. Often, helpful image information can be dredged up from channels and other separations and that, in turn, can be emphasized or adjusted to turn out the mask you need. Everything won't always be perfect the first go around, but observing image content and leveraging it to your advantage can save you hours of complicated manual work.

Here is where understanding separations can really shine and the experimenting you did in the first two chapters begins to pay off. If you think of color and tone in zones or ranges, you can do some pretty amazing things to create selections and masks using just a few tools. Let's look at several options for targeting change with masking, including masking based on tone and color, calculating masks, and using Blend If options.

Tone-Based Masking

The basics of tone-based masking can be summed up by separations. If you can separate some component of an image out into a tone, you can use that tone for masking, targeting that area or isolating it from change.

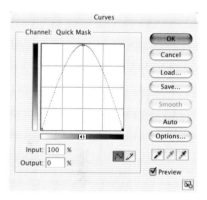

Figure 3.12

This curve will emphasize the midtones. Note that the Curve dialog is in percentage mode.

Basic tone masking can be accomplished using highlight or shadow masks to confine changes to the lighter or darker ranges of an image. To do this, you load the RGB channel as a selection by holding the ⌘/Ctrl key and clicking the RGB channel.

But say you want to mask midtones and affect highlights and shadows with changes? In that case, try this:

1. Load the RGB channel as a selection.

2. Change to Quick Mask mode (press Q).

3. Open the Curves dialog box and change the points as shown in Figure 3.12.

4. Change back to Standard mode by pressing Q again. This will shut off Quick Mask mode.

5. Duplicate the background, and then invert it. Change to Overlay mode.

6. Use the Layer → Add Layer Mask → Reveal Selection command to apply the selection as a layer mask.

If you look at the result by saving the selection and viewing the resulting channel (shut off the RGB channel), you will see that the highlights and shadows are both white. Black areas of the mask show what will be protected from change (in this case, the midtones, slightly biased toward the shadows), and light areas show what will be changed. In this next series of steps, you will darken the highlight and lighten the shadows while protecting the midtones from change by applying what is essentially the negative of your image. In a high-contrast image, this can help bring out highlight and shadow detail.

To get a more accurate selection of the midtones, work with the image luminosity and make the curve adjustment to that rather than the Quick Mask.

1. Separate luminosity from a flattened image using the Add Luminosity action provided with the Hidden Power Tools.

2. Duplicate the Luminosity layer, and name it `L-duplicate`.

3. Apply the curve shown in Figure 3.11 to the L-duplicate layer. If using an adjustment layer, group it with the L-duplicate layer.

4. Load the RGB channel as a selection.

5. Trash the L-duplicate layer. This should leave you with the Luminosity layer active.

6. Invert the Luminosity layer and change to Overlay mode.

7. Apply the selection as a layer mask using Reveal Selection.

The result of these steps will be slightly different than what you accomplished with Quick Mask because the mask more accurately reflects pure midtones (the Quick Mask version will skew toward the shadows).

Ensuring accuracy in a vague area of midtones is less important than ensuring accuracy when you're targeting specific tonal ranges that you measure. By altering a copy of the Luminosity layer to target a range, you can accurately target change to specific areas according to tone. For example, say you are interested in targeting a change to a specific area of an image. Using the Eyedropper, you can measure the tone range by sampling what appears to be the light and dark areas. Say the range you measure is 44 percent and 77 percent. You can make a mask based on those measurements to help keep changes confined to that area of tone. After measuring, follow the steps we just outlined and apply the curve shown in Figure 3.13 in step 3.

Figure 3.13

This curve turns the L-duplicate layer white in the 44 to 77 percent range, and masks other content.

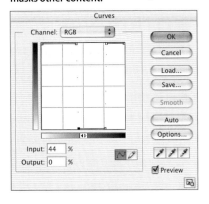

This technique can be useful for many purposes, in targeting or excluding image areas from change. For example, say you had a scan where the sky was dusty, leaving black specks in the image. If the sky ran from, say, 12 to 34 percent, you could set your range to 35 to 100 percent, effectively creating a mask for the sky and allowing you to quickly eliminate the dust only (without changing the masked area of sky). You duplicate the sky, run a destructive filter (like Dust & Scratches), and then apply your mask to limit the areas of change to only the damaged areas.

Using the image luminosity to create tone-based masks is only one option. If you recall how you separated colors into tone in previous chapters, you will find many more options for targeting change. Each tone separation comes with its own map to help you build masks that target, say, the Cyan in the midtones. We'll look more at targeting based on color in a moment. First, let's take a look at the Blend If options.

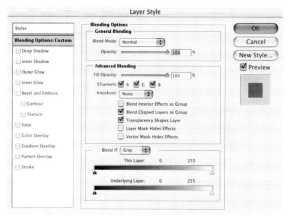

Original slider positions

Targeting with Blend If

Like the trilobite image you'll work with later in this chapter, Blend If is a Photoshop fossil. It was introduced with layers in Photoshop 3 and has barely changed at all since. This tool is somewhat hidden in the interface and is probably the least utilized, most misunderstood function in Photoshop. At the same time, it is unique in its means of quickly targeting image areas by color or tone and creating layer transparency, and it can make quick work of some changes that could prove massively difficult and time consuming using other methods.

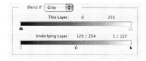

Positions to exclude midtones

Enhanced midtone exclusion

The tool is not entirely intuitive, which is part of what makes it tricky to use. However, with the right technique it can be used for everything from coloring black-and-white images, to blending layer content, to being used as a substitute for, or along with, masking.

In the tone-based targeting example earlier, you had to create additional layers and masking, which can prove cumbersome, depending on what you are trying to do and the level of accuracy you want. With Blend If, the change is simplified to a single adjustment. All you have to do is know your range, convert the measurements, and adjust the Blend If sliders for the layer.

To mask the midtones with the Blend If sliders as you did using curves and luminosity, first create a new layer, double-click to open the Layer Styles dialog box, and change the Underlying Layer sliders to look like Figure 3.14.

The change in either of the adjustments (b or c) tells Photoshop to blend any content of this layer 100 percent with anything in the layer below that is white or black (0 or 255 levels grayscale) and blend 0 percent with anything that is a midtone (128 level grayscale). Blending between slider points is linear; the effect for b will be 50 percent at 64 and 191 levels with this setup. The result here will be different again than when you used the curve and luminosity method because the blend is linear. C excludes the whole range of midtones (from 64 to 191 levels of gray) from change, targeting the change to between 0–64

Figure 3.14

The original position of the sliders (a) is black left and white right, including everything to the left of white and right of black. You can split the sliders (hold down the Option/Alt key and click on one of the slider halves) to blend changes linearly between halves of that slider. When black/white right/left positions invert (as in b and c), right of black, left of white still holds true, excluding the area between markers.

and 191–255 levels. Anything you add to this layer (for example, stamp visible and then invert and change to Overlay mode, as we've been doing) will affect only the areas of the image outside the excluded range. If the content of the layer below changes, the blending will react accordingly.

Applying absolute ranges is easier still. In the example where the range was 44 to 77 percent, you would set the slider range to 59 (black) and 133 (white).

Applying Blend If options is probably most confusing when you're using the This Layer slider set because any changes to the layer affect how the layer is applied. Because this may make changes difficult to predict, you will usually not use the This Layer sliders if you plan to make changes to the current layer after setting the Blend If sliders. If you do make changes, you will essentially be working blind because you can't see all of the content of the layer accurately. In the same way, you would probably not want to make changes to the layer below when using Underlying Layer settings.

Because Blend If creates transparency in the current image layer, you can convert that transparency to a clipping mask. You create the mask using This Layer sliders to target a range of tones to either keep or throw out tones (based on slider positions):

1. Duplicate the layer you want to make into a mask and name it `Blend Mask`.

2. Determine the range of tone you want to use in the layer as a mask using measurement or conceptual ranges (e.g., midtones).

3. Create a new, blank layer below the Blend Mask layer (create above and drag under).

4. Activate the Blend Mask layer and set the This Layer range.

5. Merge down, and change the name of the layer to `Transparency Mask`. This commits the apparent transparency to the Transparency Mask layer based on the Blend Mask layer and the This Layer slider settings.

CHANGING MEASURES BETWEEN TONE LEVELS AND PERCENT

The numbers are converted from the measurement in percent:

$255-(44\times2.55)=133$

$255-(77\times2.55)=59$

To convert % to levels, you have to multiply by 2.55 and subtract from 255:

$255-(\%\times2.55)=levels$

$\%=255-(levels/2.55)$

So, if you have a tonal range in mind that you would like to isolate to work on, you can just set it according to the value in levels. Splitting the slider by several levels (say 5 to 10 percent or 12 to 25 levels) will help the changes you make blend into the surrounding areas of tone.

You can now group layers with the Transparency Mask layer (using the Transparency mask layer as the base of the clipping group) to make changes in the targeted area. This commits the Blend Mask and allows you to make changes to the area without having to worry about the transparency changing; adding clipping layers above the Blend Mask layer before committing the transparency shifts the result according to changes in tone that are affected by the clipping stack. Steps 3 through 5 lock the transparency based on the Blend If range according to the original tone.

To set up a highlight mask based on transparency in the current layer, split the black slider to 0 and 255. To create a shadow mask, split the white slider to 0 and 255. To contain changes so they are 100 percent across only the lightest parts of the image (0 to 50 percent gray), split the black slider to 0 and 128. As you can see, Blend If can be very effective in targeting tone. If color is isolated as tone (as you can do with RGB, CMYK, or other separation), application areas can be based on specific ranges within a color component. Blend If can also make a change based on specific color ranges by using color range sliders along with tone, as we'll see in the following section.

Figure 3.15

This trilobite has many ribs that protrude, making a manual selection cumbersome. Techniques for selection and isolation lurk in using color separation.

Creating a Color-Based Mask

The trilobite in Figure 3.15 (see the color section and trilobite.psd on the CD for color) would prove to be a very tedious selection to make manually. The general shape, along with the lumps and bumps, could take hours to trace in contour with one of the manual tools. The mixture of light and shadow make any kind of selection based on tone difficult or even impossible.

Using a combination of tools, however, it is possible to isolate an area based on color, and then convert that to a selection or mask. If you want to take this image and change the color behind it, you may not have to go so far as to select the beast from its background to make the change. If you use Hue/Saturation, you can quickly target a color range change by following these steps:

1. Open the trilobite.psd file on the CD.

2. Duplicate the background layer and name it **Source.**

3. Open Hue/Saturation (⌘/Ctrl+U).

4. Choose Blues from the Edit drop-down list (if you were looking to change a green or magenta, you should select that range instead).

Figure 3.16

5. Change the Hue/Saturation slider to –100 (see Figure 3.16).

Figure 3.16

This desaturates the areas that Photoshop considers part of the blue range.

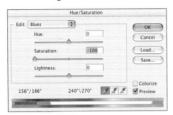

6. Click Add To Sample in the Hue/Saturation dialog box. Click in areas of the image using the sampler 🖋 where there is still color that's not included in your target range (anything blue for this example; see Figure 3.17). All areas of blue should be desaturated (gray).

At this point, you could just shift the Saturation slider back to 0 and make a hue adjustment (see this same image with a green background in the color section). But you can also use this targeting to make a selection. Continuing from Step 6:

7. Click OK to accept the change of the blue to gray.

8. Activate the Background layer by clicking it in the Layers palette, and then create a new layer (⌘+Option+Shift+N/ Ctrl+Alt+Shift+N) and fill with 50 percent gray (Shift+F5). Name the new layer `Commit 2`. Duplicate Commit 2 and name it `Commit 1`. See Figure 3.18 for the setup.

9. Change the mode of the Source layer to Color and merge down. This isolates the color for the Source layer.

10. Change the mode of the Commit 1 layer to Difference, and merge down. This reveals the difference between the color of Commit 1 and gray.

Figure 3.17

Clicking in the two areas shown here should desaturate all the blue. If areas of other color desaturate, choose Subtract From Sample and click on the areas to re-saturate them.

11. At this point, you can possibly jump ahead to step 14, but let's enhance the difference to make that step easier. Duplicate the Commit 2 layer and change the mode to Linear Dodge. Linear Dodge lightens areas of the layer below based on the current layer by doubling the RGB values. You'll note that the image gets significantly brighter.

12. Press ⌘+Option+Shift+N/Ctrl+Alt+Shift+N, then press ⌘+Option+Shift+E/ Ctrl+Alt+Shift+E. This creates a new layer and then copies the visible image to the layer that you created.

13. Press Option+Shift+W/Alt+Shift+W to change the layer mode to Linear Dodge, and then merge down (⌘/Ctrl+E). Repeat steps 11 through 13 to enhance the difference even more.

14. Change the name of the current layer to `Mask Source`. The layers should look like they do in Figure 3.19.

To make a mask from the information in that layer, you can do one of the following:

- You can use the Magic Wand to make a selection of the black and delete it to use the remaining opaque pixels as a clipping mask.

- You can use that same selection and invert it to clear the colored areas to white so that you can convert this to an alpha channel or layer mask.

- You can use the Threshold setting to define the black/white balance from the information so that you can convert this to an alpha channel or layer mask.

- You can make the content invisible using Blend If and use that as a source for a somewhat different clipping layer.

The last of these options may be the most interesting since the result is flexible, you can edit it easily, and you don't have to fiddle with making the result into a layer mask or alpha channel. Although you can get a similar result by using Threshold, extra steps are involved. The Blend If result can also easily be converted to an alpha channel or layer mask.

We'll use the last option and continue with the step by step:

15. Double-click the Mask Source layer to open the Layer Styles dialog box.

16. Under Blend If, click the black slider for This Layer and slide it to the right while watching the image. Slide right only 1 or 2 levels. The black should disappear from sight in the image. Close the Layer Styles dialog box by clicking OK.

17. Clean up the mask. You can do this with the Paint Brush using black to remove/create transparent areas, and paint with white (or anything lighter than black) to make areas opaque.

> You can continue to adjust the mask using a variety of techniques that will affect the tone in the layer and cause change in the blending. For example, using Gaussian Blur, the Threshold setting, and curves can help with adjustments. Blurring will smooth edges and expand the selection, and curves and/or Threshold can reestablish the edge position.

18. Activate the Background layer. Create a new, blank layer.

19. Merge the Mask Source layer down into the blank layer to commit the transparency. Name the resulting layer `Clipping Mask`.

20. This result can be used as a clipping layer. Duplicate the background, name the duplicate `Original Trilobite`, move it above the Mask Source, and then group those layers. Your image will be restored to the original look, but you can now alter the background without affecting the trilobite. See the layer stack in Figure 3.20.

Figure 3.18

The layers should be Source, Commit 1, Commit 2, and Background.

Figure 3.19

After these steps, only the background and Mask Source will be left in the layer stack.

Figure 3.20

The Clipping Mask layer can be adjusted, but after committing the transparency, you will have to add or reduce opacity, as you would using the Paint Brush tool or Eraser, respectively.

To test this out, add a Hue/Saturation change to the background by activating the background and pressing ⌘/Ctrl+U. Move the Hue slider to make the change.

Here's what's happening here: Blend If redefines the visual relationship between layers in the image. When you move the black This Layer slider to the right, the black areas of the layer are eliminated from view (though not yet deleted). You are telling Photoshop to exclude information in this layer from view if it isn't black. If the range has been selected properly (all the blue was desaturated), the only color areas left in the image will be in the trilobite (the color you see in step 9), because desaturated areas will be changed to black in step 10.

The solid area of the Clipping Mask layer can, of course, be converted to a layer mask or alpha channel. To convert to a layer mask, activate the layer you want to apply the mask to, and load the Clipping Mask layer as a selection by holding down ⌘/Ctrl and clicking the layer. With the selection active, choose Layer → Add Layer Mask → Reveal Selection. If you apply the layer mask to a copy of the background, this isolates the trilobite. To store as an alpha channel, just choose Save Selection after loading the Clipping Mask layer as a selection.

Blend If, Selection, Cloning, Masking and Patching are all means of targeting image areas. They can be used together or separately to your advantage, and for their advantage in working together with other tools. Once you have areas properly isolated and targeted, you are free to make changes without affecting other parts of the image. This can give you greater control over image content by object, shape, color, or tone.

In the next chapter we'll look at using filters to make changes to image content.

Chapter 4

Filters for Correction

With most of the filters on the Filter menu in Photoshop, applying them can be a session of trial and error where you try one, have a look, adjust, and try again. It's a creative process; to achieve the effect you want will almost always involve multiple filters. Photoshop's new Filter Gallery is useful in helping with this type of experimentation.

If you are using Photoshop for correction and repairing images (as opposed to creating digital art), creative application will usually not be what you want. Photoshop includes a handful of practical and predictable filters that are exceptions to the general rule. You will probably use these filters often, perhaps even on most images, and you might use them alone.

This chapter describes some of the filters used for repairing images—filters such as Unsharp Mask, Add Noise, and Gaussian Blur—and also looks at targeting your filter applications. This chapter covers these topics:

(Un)sharpening and enhancing contrast

Addressing image noise

Using the selective blur

(Un)Sharpening and Boosting Contrast

You may be confused by the name *Unsharp Mask*. It sounds like another term for blur, or even masking to keep the unsharp parts of an image from change. The purpose of Unsharp Mask is to make an image appear sharper. Unsharp Mask does this by enhancing contrast along object edges. Doing this accentuates edge lines, resulting in a sharper appearance. Unsharp Mask is probably the most useful and commonly used of the tools on the Sharpen filter menu. The name comes from the darkroom process where a blurred (unsharp) negative is sandwiched with an original to create a mask that can enhance edge contrast during exposure for prints. The unsharpened mask creates an accurate mask based on shapes and contrast that exist in the image. Photoshop's Unsharp Mask works using calculation. Other manual processes can get closer to mimicking the idea and application of the darkroom technique.

The idea of sharpening is not to make a fuzzy image sharp. Sharpening will never rescue a badly out-of-focus image and make it crisp. Just as in other corrections where the idea is to enhance what you have been able to achieve in capturing the image, the idea is to work from the best possible source.

Sharpening can be used for enhancing contrast between objects in an image. Used with a smaller range (radius and intensity), sharpening will work to accentuate smaller detail (and noise); used with a greater range, the effect will work more generally to enhance contrast and separation between objects and colors. You can use sharpening to enhance the look of an image or improve the resulting image in print by helping to *alias* (distinguish and separate) edge areas. Enhancing edges can help when you're printing halftones depending on the conditions: Increased aliasing between colors and tones may keep inks from running together or appearing less distinct after halftone processing.

Applying the Unsharp Mask Filter

Figure 4.1 is an image of a goose that could be sharper, and is further marred with a bit of image and digital noise, characteristic of the 2.5-megapixel digital camera it was taken with. You can find a copy of the original image on the CD. The contrast is generally a little low (note the center-weighted histogram when you open the image), and there isn't a lot of variety in the color—though the color that is there has fairly good definition. Some sharpening could enhance the subject of the image, but so could some selective blurring, as we'll see. Let's see how this image can be enhanced using Unsharp Mask, a type of manual layer sharpening, and applying edge masks to help target and localize sharpening.

Figure 4.1
This lone goose is not camouflaged by any means, but could stand out more in this image with sharpness adjustments.

While we could just apply the Unsharp Mask filter after opening, this image could benefit from more targeted sharpening. First make sure the image is properly prepared for sharpening, which is usually done near the end of the correction process:

1. Open up Goose.psd from the CD.

2. Adjust the image as desired for tone and color using techniques from previous chapters (e.g., levels correction, color balance, and perhaps curves and cropping as well).

3. Take a snapshot of the image using the Snapshot feature in the History palette so that you can return to this point with the corrections intact, if desired; then flatten the image.

4. Do a luminosity and color separation of the image using the Color and Luminosity separation action provided in the Hidden Power Tools.

   At this point you should have a corrected image split into color and tone. We'll use the color and tone as a source for both the corrections and the masking that we will apply.

5. Duplicate the Luminosity layer. Name the layer `Unsharp Mask`.

6. Open the Unsharp Mask filter (Filters → Sharpen → Unsharp Mask). Look at the difference between the following settings as applied to this image:

   - Intensity: 80%

   - Radius: 2 pixels

   - Threshold: 0

   and

   - Intensity: 20%

   - Radius: 30 pixels

   - Threshold: 0

The setting with the higher intensity and lower radius will appear to enhance finer detail; the setting with the higher radius will have a broader effect on tone. Apply both of these adjustments to the image on the Unsharp Mask layer in separate applications of the Unsharp Mask filter. Figure 4.2 shows a comparison.

Figure 4.2

Using different settings with the Unsharp Mask filter enhances fine detail (a) and local contrast (b) separately.

Original

(a) High intensity, low radius

(b) Low intensity, high radius

Radius determines how far the filter is applied (the distance from the contrast edge); the Intensity setting affects how strong the effect is applied over the selected radius.

These steps show slightly more than the basic application of Unsharp Mask. You should see some enhancement to the apparent sharpness of the image and better separation between objects. You can take additional steps to adjust sharpening. The simplest of these adjustments is to reduce the opacity of the Unsharp Mask layer. You can also apply the Unsharp Mask from step 6 in different layers so that the sharpening is not compounded, which could lead to oversharpening in some areas of the image. Oversharpening becomes apparent in the image as halos, which are bright glows that usually form around areas that already have high contrast. This halo effect can be avoided by blending back some of the original tone (e.g., from a separate layer), using a lighter application of Unsharp Mask, or by using other sharpening methods, such as the manual sharpening technique described in the next section.

Applying Manual Unsharp Masking

What the Unsharp Mask filter is doing is quite a mystery; you can apply it but can't see the means that create the change. The process involves applying a calculation to determine the result. The darkroom procedure of using an unsharpened duplicate is less of a mystery, and can be mimicked in a "manual" application of masking with an unsharpened duplicate. These steps assume you still have Goose.psd open from the previous section.

1. Shut off the view for the Unsharp Mask layer and duplicate the Luminosity layer. Rename the duplicate `Manual Sharpen`.

2. Open Gaussian Blur and set the blur radius to 10 pixels. The image will get a bit blurry. Don't worry that you are preparing an unsharpened mask.

3. Invert the layer, change the opacity to 50%, and set the mode to Overlay. The result should look like the layer setup shown in Figure 4.3.

This is a simplified application of manual sharpening that essentially duplicates the idea of darkroom sharpening. The application takes the image luminosity separated previously and applies it to the image in Overlay mode. Overlay mode will increase contrast in the highlights and shadows, by moving tones toward 50 percent—just about the opposite of what Unsharp Mask does by pushing tones out to highlight and shadow. Because there is no color in the layer (only tone), the overlay will affect the image tone only. If you attempt the same thing with a duplicate of the background (i.e., with color), you should see a pronounced difference that will also cause undesirable color shifts (toward neutral).

Inverted, blurred background copy

Figure 4.3

The blurred negative of the original actually helps accentuate the edge areas like an edge mask.

Original background

Sharpened result

Before going on, turn on the visibility for the Unsharp Mask layer and change the Opacity setting to 50%. This will blend the two sharpening effects you have so far. The effect will probably be more pleasing than either of the others alone. This is because the processes work differently: The manual process tends to reduce contrast in the image overall (increasing detail in highlights and shadows), and using Unsharp Mask tends to increase contrast overall (by pushing more detail to pure white or black).

Applying Sharpening with Edge Masks

Either sharpening action can be masked to target edge areas only. Limiting the effective area can help by keeping sharpening focused on edges and away from the bulk of noise and grain elsewhere in the image—which you really don't want to enhance. Let's look at a few ways to target edges, formed by tone, color, or both.

1. Duplicate the Luminosity layer and move it to the top of the layer stack. Change the name to **Edge Mask Source**, and change the mode to Normal.

2. Use Gaussian Blur to blur out image noise. This blurring will keep noise from being recognized as edges. It will probably only require 2–4 pixels here, but you can use more depending on the image and what you want to target. The more you blur, the less fine detail that will be included in the sharpening.

3. Run the Find Edges filter (Filter → Stylize → Find Edges). This will darken distinct edges and turn nonedge areas of the image white.

4. Use Threshold to define which edges will be included in the mask. As you move the slider, black areas indicate edges that are included; the more black you include, the stronger the overall effect.

5. Blur the Threshold result using Gaussian Blur. This will help feather in the edge masking and smooth out the response in the edges so that the change blends in well.

6. ⌘/Ctrl-click the RGB channel in the Channels palette to load the Edge Mask Source as a selection.

7. Shut off the view for the Edge Mask Source.

8. Activate the layer you want to apply the edge mask to. You can do this for the Unsharp Mask layer, the Overlay Sharpening layer, or both (by repeating steps 8 and 9).

9. Choose Layer → Add Layer Mask → Hide Selection. This will make the white area of the Edge Mask Source layer into a mask for that layer.

Figure 4.4

Putting the Overlay Sharpening layer on top allows you to look through it because it is only 50 percent opaque and blends the effects of the two sharpening techniques.

This mask confines application of the sharpening to edge areas. In this way, it doesn't increase noise in the rest of the image. If you apply the mask to both the Unsharp Mask and Overlay Sharpening layers, your resulting layer stack should look like the one shown in Figure 4.4.

Color may be considered an "edge" as well, and could be used as a source for creating an edge mask based on color rather than tone. It is a little more difficult to bring out, in that more steps are involved in converting the color to meaningful edges.

10. Duplicate the Color layer and move it to the top of the layer stack.

11. Create a new layer, and fill with 50% gray. Change the name to `Color Edge Source`, and move the layer below the Color copy layer.

12. Activate the Color copy layer and merge down. This result should retain the Color Edge Source name. This step commits the color mode.

13. Use Auto Levels (⌘/Ctrl+Shift+L) to enhance the color in the layer.

14. Use Gaussian Blur to blur out color noise. This blurring keeps noise from being recognized as edges.

15. Run the Find Edges filter. This step darkens distinct edges and turns nonedge areas of the image white.

16. Use Threshold to define which edges you want to include in the mask. As you move the slider, areas darker than white are included; the less white, the stronger the overall effect will appcar.

17. Blur the Threshold result using Gaussian Blur. This helps feather in the edge masking and smooth out the result in the edges so that the change blends in well.

18. ⌘/Ctrl-click the RGB channel in the Channels palette to load the visible layers as a selection.

19. Shut off the view for the Color Edge Source.

20. Activate the layer you want to apply the edge mask to. You can do this for another copy of the Unsharp Mask layer, the Overlay Sharpening layer, or both. You may need to remove and replace the mask. To create a new layer from the existing masked layers:

    a. Duplicate the layer you want to apply the mask to.

    b. Discard the layer mask (Layer → Remove Layer Mask → Discard).

21. Choose Layer → Add Layer Mask → Hide Selection. This turns the white area of the Edge Mask Source into a mask for the layer.

22. Add an identifier to the layer (e.g., Unsharp Mask Color).

Because some edges in the image are color and others are tone based, you may want to apply both edge masks at the same time. For example, around the goose's head there is very little tone distinction, but the color change is clear. Enhancing that edge will probably prove helpful.

You can do this by using a copy of the background and running through steps 1 through 9 to create an edge mask. However, having control over tone and color separately may prove to be an advantage, and can help yield a more accurate masking by dealing with components separately (see Figure 4.5). You have the separated component edge masks in the previous steps (10–22), so all you need to do is combine them.

To combine the Color Edge Source and Edge Mask Source layers into a single result, drag both to the top of the layer stack, set the mode of the upper of the two layers to Multiply, and follow steps 18 through 22. For step 19, you will shut off the view for both the source layers instead of just the Color Edge Source. Using Multiply mode darkens the lower of the two layers using the tone of the upper layer, effectively combining the tone of the color and tone edge masks without merging them. Your result will look something like the separate generation edge mask from Figure 4.5. Any variation between your result and what is pictured is a result of the selections you made for the Threshold and blur settings.

Simultaneous edge mask

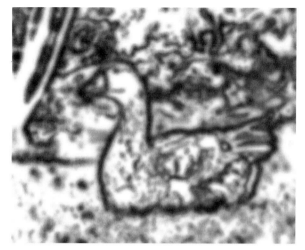

Separate generation edge mask

Figure 4.5

An edge mask created from color and tone at the same time comes out a little nondescript (a). The mask compiled from separate tone and color masks shows a clearer result (b) that looks more like the objects.

Selective Blur (Unsharpening)

Now that the goose in our image has been sharpened, it is somewhat more distinct, but a lot of image noise still exists in the way of background detail that detracts from the broader distinction of the bird. The image can benefit from some loss of detail—blurring select areas of the image to make those areas you want the viewer to focus on stand out. The idea is to enhance the blurring already in the image and mimic the effect of taking the image with a longer lens (or shorter depth of field) so that the subject is isolated from the surroundings (which waxes out of focus).

The primary thing you want to do is blur the background behind the goose. To do this, you need to isolate the goose from the background. The tricky part is maintaining the focus you have established without making the blur seem faked. You'll have to make a selection to isolate the effect, but the result calls for mixing and matching several techniques we've seen so far:

1. Flatten the image, or create a new layer at the top of the layer stack and copy the result to a new image.

2. Separate color from the image. Use the Add Color action included with the Hidden Power Tools.

3. Make an adjustment to the Color layer using Hue/Saturation. When you have the Hue/Saturation dialog box open, change Edit to Reds, and shift the Saturation slider to –100. Choose the Add To Sample tool 🖋 from the dialog box and drag it through

the goose's head, as shown in Figure 4.6. Switch to Cyan, choose the Add To Sample tool again, and drag through the goose's body. The goal is to remove all color from the goose (you'll use what's left to help make the selection).

4. Choose the Magic Wand, set the Tolerance to about 20, and be sure that Contiguous is checked and that Use All Layers and Anti-Aliased are not. Click inside the goose.

5. Change to Quick Mask mode (press Q), shut off the view for the Color layer, and clean up the selection to make a solid selection of the goose. Fill in areas with black to turn them red (which means they are excluded from selection) or with white to clear them (which means these areas are included in the selection). Feather the Quick Mask by a pixel or two to smooth the transition by blurring.

6. Change the mode from Quick Mode to Standard by pressing Q.

7. Create a duplicate of the background. Name the duplicate **Blurground**.

8. Cut and paste the goose into its own layer. Use the keystrokes ⌘/Ctrl+X, ⌘/Ctrl+ Shift+D, and ⌘/Ctrl+V. This cuts the goose, reloads the selection, and pastes the goose back in the same position as per the selection on a new layer. Name the new layer **Goose.**

Figure 4.6

Drag the Eyedropper through the goose's head and body. The result should desaturate the goose and leave the greenery.

With the goose isolated from the background, the two can be treated as separate elements. Blurring the background will not affect the goose.

9. Activate the Blurground layer and apply a Gaussian Blur of 10–15 pixels.

10. Duplicate the Blurground layer four times. The background should appear to be fairly blurry at this point. The duplication will help solidify the effect near the transparent area created by cutting out the goose.

11. Activate the Background, create a new layer, name it `Backblur Mask`, and fill with a gradient that runs from black to transparent. Run the gradient from somewhere near the creek to the base where the goose is sitting.

12. Link the Blurground copies and the Backblur Mask layers and group them. In this way, we'll use the Backblur Mask layer as a clipping mask for the Blurground copies. Change the Opacity setting of the Backblur Mask layer to 50%.

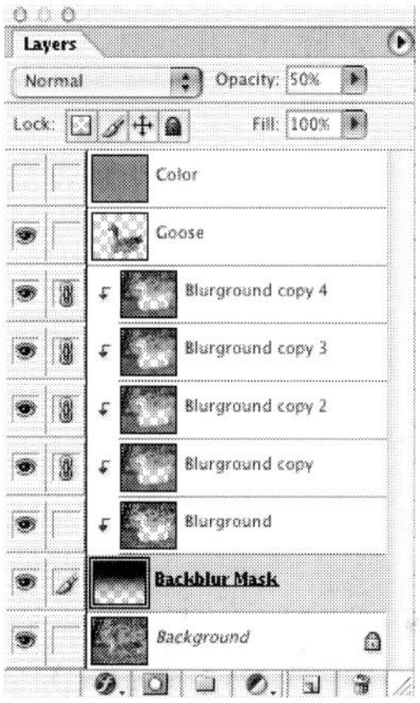

When you are done, this series of steps will have separated the goose from the background. Doing this allows you to blur the background to simulate depth of field. The goose, in its own layer, acts like a mask over the top so it is not affected by any of the blurring. The layer stack should look like that shown in Figure 4.7.

You can make additional adjustments to the Backblur Mask to make the depth-of-field effect more realistic. For example, the trees to the left should be somewhat more in focus than the extreme background (the other side of the creek), so you will want to make that apparent in the image. To do this, take the original background and make a selection of the tree—in a way similar to how you made the selection for the goose—and make the change for the tree in its own layer. You'll want to separate the distinct elements into different layers for the best result. If the tree is included in the initial blur, before extracting it the tree will cause darkening in the extreme background, which is not a realistic result. Essentially you want to repeat steps 2 through 8 to extract the tree using the Blurground layer instead of a newly duplicated background. This will actually allow you to increase blurring on the background (leave the Blurground Mask at 100% in step 12 and/or increase the Gaussian Blur in step 9 to 15–20 Radius).

If you step back and complete the tree extraction and blur of the tree (you can blur the tree directly in its layer, and you may want to duplicate the result as you did with the Blurground to adjust solidity), you'll see results comparable to those shown in Figure 4.8.

Figure 4.7

Look for the results of this series in the color section.

Before

After

Figure 4.8

The initial image (before) shows the goose in a noisy background that it has some difficulty remaining distinct from. After we adjust sharpness and blur, the goose appears more distinctly from the background (after), even in black and white.

Adjusting Image Noise

While the previous section discussed a means of removing image noise, that method merely obliterates detail that isn't crucial to the image. Other forms of noise appear in digital images, including JPEG artifacts, color noise, chromatic aberration, and the like. In a way, you might consider halftone dots as they appear in scans as another potential source of digital noise. This type of noise can be confounding in that it may appear throughout the image and competes with detail, and it can prove to be quite difficult to fix. Using some methods we have already looked at to isolate image areas (either to keep them from change or focus change in those areas) and combining these methods with other adjustments, we can tackle the various problems illustrated in Figure 4.9 without losing the desired detail.

Smoothing Out Color Noise

Color noise is really the easiest of these image noise problems to eliminate. You can isolate the color easily by separating the color and luminosity (use the Color and Luminosity action provided with the Hidden Power Tools).

Once the color is separated, you can blur it without affecting the appearance of the tone. A blur of just a few pixels (2–4) will usually wipe out offensive noise without causing any color halos (where mixing color edges makes for an offensive bleeding of one color into the next, compromising the look of the image). You could also use the Median setting

Figure 4.9

This image has fine detail in the sweater, skirt, and in the stencil on the chair, so we will need to retain fine detail in any corrections. However, JPEG artifacts and color noise require cleanup to enhance the image.

to quell the color noise. Median averages tone and color over an input Radius. Again, setting to just a few pixels should take care of true color noise. Follow these steps:

1. Open Girl_Sitting.psd from the CD.

2. Split the Luminosity and Color layers by clicking Color and Luminosity in the Hidden Power Tool actions.

3. Blur the Color layer using Gaussian Blur with a 3-pixel Radius setting.

While this move is all color oriented, you might expect that it would offer little difference when examined in print in black and white; this is the case if you are looking at tone conversion *only*. The color section shows a shot of a small section of this image before and after the color blur. However, the changes in the channels are dramatic, and this can be distinguished easily in black and white. Figure 4.10 shows the difference in the blue channel both before and after the color blur.

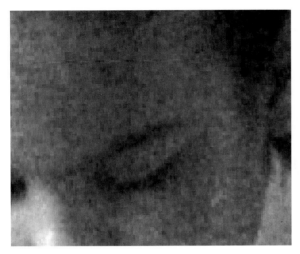 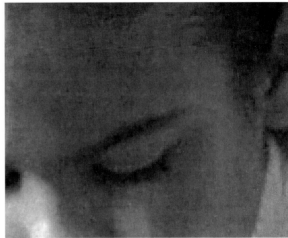

Before   After

Figure 4.10

The color blur does-
n't affect the tone in
the image but has a
dramatic impact on
noise in the color
channels. Here the
blue channel is
shown before and
after the color blur.
Note the distinct dif-
ference in the
smoothness of the
tone in the channel.

Of course, you can use edge masking to better target application of color blurring to nonedge areas. The Color To Edge Mask action will help with this targeting, or you can follow the steps in the previous section. You will find that you may not need to apply the mask at 100 percent to get the benefit you want from blurring the color; in fact, too strong an edge mask may leave behind some unnecessary noise. Lessening the effect of the mask once you have applied it is not as easy as reducing the opacity for the layer (in fact, if you try this, you'll get the opposite results; the overall effect of the blur is reduced). The solution is to adjust the mask itself. You can do this with any adjustment that allows you to fade the intensity of the black in the mask, weakening the masking and thereby letting more of the blur through. Figure 4.11 shows how you would do this using levels.

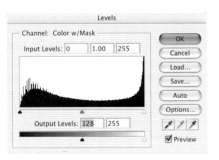

Figure 4.11

With the layer's
mask active, making
this adjustment will
reduce the masking
to 50 percent,

In some cases you might want to limit masking to just the edges or perhaps to a specific color. For example, chromatic aberration can occur when a camera's lens focuses different light waves at different depths. In some cases, this can produce a pronounced magenta glow at object edges. Where it would be ineffective to mask for tone or color edges, it may be a good idea to mask for the aberration color (which you might find easily in the color layer). With the trouble area targeted, you can blur or use a Hue/Saturation adjustment to reduce or eliminate the effect—or perhaps use a combination of these.

Note that in this image blurring a lot will compromise the color detail of the florets on the skirt. The color edge mask will help reduce or eliminate any troubles you would otherwise have in this "naturally noisy" image area.

Smoothing Out Tone

Troubles with image tone can be quite a bit more difficult to handle than trouble with color—tone is what tends to give an image its shape. Removing detail by blurring will generally not be appropriate or helpful without masking; while reducing the noise, it will obliterate important detail. With tone more so than color, you have to pick your battles and focus your changes on specific areas of trouble.

In the example image, it is clearly challenging to attempt to remove JPEG artifacts from the face while retaining the fine detail in the sweater and in the skirt print. However, clear lines of delineation exist in those areas, and enough differences are evident that you can make some remarkably easy work of minimizing the undesirable JPEG effect.

1. Open Girl_Sitting.psd from the CD and adjust the color noise, or continue from the previous exercise. Flatten the image.

2. Zoom in to the forehead area above the eye (to the viewer's right).

3. Choose the Marquee tool and make a rough selection of the area of the forehead that contains the JPEG damage.

4. Copy and paste this sample to its own layer. This area will be used as a sample to accurately target a range of color and tone to apply your changes.

5. Be sure the Info palette is visible and open the Threshold dialog box (Image → Adjustments → Threshold).

6. Change the position of the slider so that the sample turns all white, and then write down the value for the position. Now change the position of the slider so that the sample turns all black and write down the value for that position. After the positions are noted, close the dialog box without saving the changes. Figure 4.12 shows the positions we measured for our sample; your measurements may vary. We'll use these values to establish a range for targeting your changes.

7. Click on the red channel in the Channels palette and repeat step 6, noting the positions. These values will bracket the tone value range for the red color within the sample.

8. Click on the green channel in the Channels palette and repeat step 6, noting the positions. These values will bracket the tone value range for the green color within the sample.

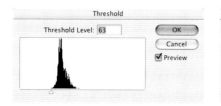

Figure 4.12

You can use the histogram to determine about where the sample will turn all white (left of the graph) and all black (right of the graph). The resulting numbers show your tone range for the sample.

9. Click on the blue channel in the Channels palette and repeat step 6, noting the positions. These values will bracket the tone value range for the blue color within the sample. Here are the values we came up with for the sample (again, your values may vary since your sample will probably be somewhat different and blur/color adjustment may affect the outcome).

Component	Low Range	High Range
Tone	62	121
Red	101	158
Green	49	107
Blue	29	95

10. Duplicate the image background and move it to the top of the layer stack. Change the layer mode to Luminosity, and name the layer `Smooth Skin`.

11. Apply a Gaussian Blur with just enough radius to blur the artifacts into their surroundings. You will probably use between 1 and 2 pixels for the radius.

12. Double-click the thumbnail for the Smooth Skin layer in the Layers palette. This opens the Layer Styles dialog box for the Smooth Skin layer.

13. Under Blend If, set the Gray sliders. Move the Underlying Layers black slider to your Low Range value, and the white slider to the High Range value.

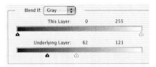

14. Change the Blend If selector to Red and set the sliders on the Underlying Layers slider to the low- and high-range settings measured in step 7.

15. Change the Blend If selector to Green and set the sliders on the Underlying Layers slider to the low- and high-range settings measured in step 8.

 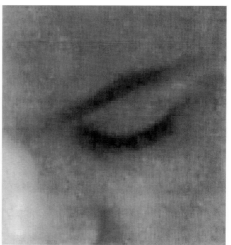

Before   After

Figure 4.13

This close-up of the skin area shows a marked improvement in the JPEG noise.

16. Change the Blend If selector to Blue and set the sliders on the Underlying Layers slider to the low- and high-range settings measured in step 9.

17. Accept the changes by clicking OK.

At this point, you will have made the Blend If adjustment, which tells Photoshop to blend the content of the current layer if all the criteria of the blend are met. If you look at the image and compare the before and after images by toggling the view for the Smooth Skin layer (Figure 4.13 shows both views), you will see significant smoothing in the skin. Now look down at the sweater and toggle the view. You will note that very little about the sweater changes since you have effectively limited the blending to a range outside the sweater color and tone.

In some areas, the smoothing may seem a bit too significant. In the next section, we take a look at how you can influence this by adding noise. But before doing that, you can affect the blending by other methods, including reducing the opacity of the layer or adding an edge mask. To add an edge mask:

1. Create a Luminosity layer by clicking the Add Luminosity action in the Hidden Power Tools.

2. Create the mask by clicking Luminosity to Edge Mask.

3. Apply the edge mask to the Smooth Skin layer.

This adjustment adds back some of the noise in detail areas along with the details. You can make spot corrections by painting with white to remove the masking in those areas of the mask. Paint with gray (50 percent) to mediate the effect of the mask.

If the edge of your blended areas seems too harsh, you can always split the Blend If sliders and use those to achieve a blend based on tone in the underlying layer. This may actually prove less valuable than blending with opacity in this case; the extremes will be the first pixels to blend back if you're moving the sliders to decrease the range. If you're moving the sliders to increase the range, the spread of the effect on the image will increase—though with lessened intensity. Depending on the accuracy of the sample area, increasing the range may not be desirable.

For the moment, leave the Smooth Skin layer aside and work through a correction for a patch of hair at the top of the subject's head, repeating steps 3 through 17 to create a second noise fix. Name the duplicate layer in step 10 `Remove Hair Noise`. To create the source layer for the sample, press ⌘+Option+Shift+N/Ctrl+Alt+Shift+N, and then press ⌘+Option+Shift+E/Ctrl+Alt+Shift+E. This stamps the visible area to a new layer. Call

the layer `Temp`, and delete it when you complete the steps. The changes you need will be targeted by the Blend If function set in the Remove Hair Noise layer, so the Temp layer isn't needed.

We'll continue working with this image in the next section. You should have several layers intact before moving on, and the Layers palette should look like the one shown in Figure 4.14.

Roughing Up Flatness by Adding Noise

Once you've finished applying Blend If to reduce noise in specific areas of the image, those same areas may look a little flat and unnatural when viewed with 100 percent opacity. Most tones and colors in images have some amount of noise, which comes from color variation and surface texture. Removing all the noise in areas can appear unnatural; in complexions, it can leave the subject looking plastic and false.

Although you may have to reduce noise to improve the image, you may need to add some noise back to make the result look natural. Reducing the opacity and other blending methods can help, but may not be the best approach. Randomly generating new noise can apply noise evenly and re-create texture without having to reintroduce the damage or noise you just replaced.

To add back noise, you'll continue from the previous section with the image as pictured in Figure 4.10.

1. Zoom in to the face so you can see the top of the head and forehead.

2. Click once on the thumbnail for Smooth Skin in the Layers palette.

3. Open the Add Noise dialog box (Filter → Noise → Add Noise) and enter **2%** for the amount. Use Uniform Distribution and deselect the Monochromatic option. You may want to experiment with other values.

> Hold the Shift key and press the Up/Down arrows on the keyboard to increase/decrease the percentage by .1.

4. Click once on the thumbnail for the Reduce Hair Noise layer and repeat step 3.

This application of the Add Noise filter makes a change directly to the layer, and you can then adjust the intensity by using opacity or by adjusting the edge mask. Noise can affect the change in tone only if you leave the mode set at Luminosity, or it can affect both color and tone if you change to Normal mode. Figure 4.15 shows the image close up before and after our adjustments.

There may still be other areas of the image that you want to target for change and smoothing, such as the top rail of the rocker. Create a new layer and new targeting for each of these areas. To finish up the correction for the image, you might want to use techniques we looked at earlier in the chapter for manual sharpening, which will reduce the contrast and increase detail in the highlights. Because we've managed to quell much of the important noise, the details will strengthen without making a nuisance of the noise that remains in the image. See the color section for before and after shots and the CD for Girl_Sitting_2.psd, which is a version of finished correction for the image.

Before   After

Figure 4.15

Noise introduces natural variation back into the image that was removed when we were reducing damage.

Painting with Filters

When you want to apply a filter, masking or Blend If may suit your needs on many occasions, but those options are not the only means you'd want to use for application. At times, a combination works best; other times you might wish you could just turn some brush into a filter so that you could make spot applications. Well, actually, you can do just that without a lot of trouble:

1. Open the image you want to work on.

2. Decide which filter you want to apply as a brush.

3. Duplicate the background if it is a flattened image, or create a new layer, move it to the top of the layer stack, and stamp visible. Name it **Source**.

4. Run the filter (or, really, any function or series that makes the change you want to paint in).

5. Create a new layer. Name it **Mask**.

6. Move the layer created in step 5 just below the Source layer.

7. Group the Mask and Source layers.

8. Choose a brush (softness and opacity; it's best to use Normal mode), and paint in your filter by painting on the Mask layer.

This is actually a form of masking, since the Mask layer is creating a layer clipping mask. The functionality is much like the History brush, but perhaps a bit less confusing because you don't have to worry about layers being mismatched between the history source and the current state of the image. You can also apply the brush using a mode that is based on the underlying image content by changing the mode of the Mask layer.

For example, if you want to do some spot changes to color, you can change the Mask layer mode to Color and paint in your source. This keeps the change isolated to a new layer; using the History brush would force you to apply the change directly to a layer to do the same thing (or else the brush mode would not work). In a similar way, you could add spot sharpening by creating your inverted, blurred layer for manual sharpening, changing the Mask layer mode to Overlay, and using the brush to apply sharpening as you need it.

Layered changes can also then be masked, or you can apply Blend If as needed. This gives you broad control over painted filters. The Filter-Paint Mask Layer action included with the Hidden Power Tools will help you set up the masking layer for any history state or filter.

Part III
Creating Objects, Photo-realism, and Illustration

The complexity of a scene captured in your digital images can be almost unfathomable. Objects may have different levels of opacity and different textures; they may cast shadows, give off light, reflect light, reflect other objects, and otherwise interact with other objects in and outside the scene. Creating a realistic scene from scratch is probably not a practical goal for most Photoshop users, and achieving it typically requires huge amounts of time.

However, you may occasionally find that you will need to generate image information from scratch. For example, you may want to add type to an image, or create some artwork for use in an illustration, production art (e.g., a logo), or animation. Sometimes you will just want to replace a pattern or create a texture. In extreme situations, you might have to replace an object in an image. If you don't already own a drawing program, you don't need to buy one for these situations; you can handle them in Photoshop. In the next two chapters, we'll look at both the fundamentals of shaping an object and delve into more advanced techniques of creating realistic objects.

Chapter 5 **Shaping Objects**

Chapter 6 **Vectors and Illustration**

Chapter 5

Shaping Objects

Photoshop obviously doesn't have any buttons or filters for creating things like chairs and bicycles. In fact, it won't, on its own, create a spoke or a spindle. However, it does give you the tools you need to create the parts (spoke and spindles) that add up to the whole (bikes and chairs).

Highlight and shadow (in other words, tone) play the biggest part in creating shape for image objects, as we've seen in handling luminosity and color separations. Changes in tone affect not only the general shape of an object but its texture as well. You can apply building blocks of pattern and texture to shapes to make them appear more realistic—you saw a hint of that when we looked at how to handle noise. You can best understand building objects by reversing the process of dismantling your image, as you have done by separating components of tone and color. This chapter covers the following topics:

Shaping image elements with shadow and light

Creating seamless textures

Tiling backgrounds

Creating objects

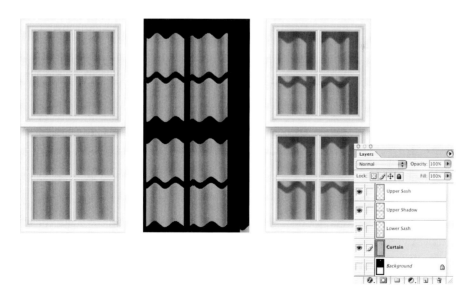

Figure 5.1

The image will still look as it did in step 3 because none of the content in the Highlight and Shadow layers falls over the Button layer.

Shaping Image Elements with Light and Shadow

Light and shadow affect the shape of objects by defining contour and texture, as well as how objects appear relative to one another. A basic use of light and shadow to create shape can be exemplified by creating a raised button, like you might use on a webpage. Try the following steps:

1. Make a new image that is 500×500 pixels.

2. Make a Fixed Size Marquee selection of 300×300 pixels at $100,100$ (x,y) so that the selection is centered on the image.

3. Create a new layer and fill the selection with 50 percent gray. Call the layer `Button`.

4. Create a new layer, group it with Button, set it to Screen, and reduce the Opacity setting to 50 percent. Call the layer `Highlight`.

5. Invert the current selection (it should still be active; if not, choose Select → Reselect) and fill with white.

6. Create a new layer, group it with Highlight, set it to Multiply, fill with black, and reduce the opacity to 50 percent (the selection should still be active). Call the layer `Shadow`. The Layers palette should be set up as shown in Figure 5.1.

7. Deselect and apply a Gaussian Blur to the Highlight and Shadow layers using a 10-pixel radius.

8. Offset the Highlight layer 20 pixels down and to the right. To do this, activate the Highlight layer, choose the Move tool, hold down the Shift key, and press the keyboard right and down arrows two times each.

9. Offset the Shadow layer up 20 pixels and to the left 20 pixels. To do this, activate the Shadow layer, choose the Move tool, hold down the Shift key, and press the up and left arrows twice each.

The blur softens the edge of the shadow and highlight layers, and offsetting the layers moves the effects into place so that they cast their highlight and shadow onto the shape of the button (see Figure 5.2).

Figure 5.2

The effect will give the button a sense of dimension, and it should look raised, and as if light is coming from the upper left.

Certainly highlights and shadows can give an object shape, but they also affect the relationship between objects in a scene. Let's continue from the previous steps:

10. Activate the Background layer, and then create a new layer. Set it to Multiply, 50 percent opacity, and name the new layer Drop Shadow. Creating the new layer after activating the Background layer will insert the Drop Shadow layer behind the Button layer.

11. ⌘/Ctrl-click the Button layer in the Layers palette. Feather the current selection 10 pixels and fill with black.

12. Deselect and offset the layer 20 pixels to the right and down. To offset this time, use the Offset Filter command (Filter → Other → Offset) and enter +20 in the Horizontal and Vertical fields. The result should look like Figure 5.3.

This will leave you with a square button that appears to be slightly raised and separate from the background. The Drop Shadow layer between the Button layer and the Background layer creates a relationship between those objects that suggests depth, similar to the way the Highlight and Shadow layers create object shape. The more extreme the effects, the greater the depth or distance appears.

Simple highlighting and shadow creation of this sort is all that happens when using layer effects. You can achieve the same shaping effect by applying layer styles to the Button layer: a Bevel (Inner, Raised) and Drop Shadow. Handling the highlights and shadows affects the shape of the object. Similar techniques can be used to create and shape more complicated objects. In the larger scheme, your choices for shadows, highlights, and shaping have to show some consistency with the scene and the direction and quality of light in order to portray the desired effect. In other words, you can create some cool effects with light and shadow, but you can't just drop a shadow (or other effect) into an image willy-nilly and have it look right. You've got to take existing lighting into account and make adjustments for angle and direction.

This accounts only for some basic shaping. You also might need to make the shadow fall and adjust it for the landscape. It is possible to do these adjustments either manually or with other functions, such as displacement maps (which we will look at in a moment). You can also paint objects with patterns and texture to give them additional shape, depth, and interest—sometimes by using functions, and at other times by applying adjustments as you might with photographic images. But before we get into making photo-realistic changes, let's look at application of texture and patterns.

Figure 5.3

The Button layer in the layer stack (a) is used as a clipping layer for Highlight and Shadow content, but also masks the Drop Shadow in the result (b).

a   b

Creating Seamless Textures and Tiling Backgrounds

Sample area

Sample used as a pattern

You can apply patterns and textures to objects that exist in the image or objects that you are creating to "paint" them into shape, while manipulating tone and color. Effective application of either patterns or textures will often depend on whether you've created a good source for applying the effect and making it realistic.

One possible solution for filling in texture and patterns is to create a small sample area of the texture or pattern that can effectively be repeated in the image to fill a larger area. Another possibility is to generate patterns to fill the application area. A third method uses a combination of these (or a combination with additional adjustments) to create the result.

No matter what you do, the goal is to create something that is as simple as possible to produce, but at the same time effective in achieving the result.

Creating and Applying Seamless Patterns

You can use a seamless pattern to fill an image area of any size without creating any odd-looking and unnatural effects that make the pattern seem fake. Usually this type of pattern is something that you would naturally want to replicate and repeat, rather than something you want to have appear at all random. For example, a wallpaper pattern, plaid, or bricks might make be a fine choice of something to create as a seamless pattern because repetition in the pattern is expected. Let's take bricks as an example. All you have to do is create or copy a small portion of a brick pattern, be sure it can repeat without obvious seams, and then use that pattern to fill an area. Figure 5.4 shows a sample brick pattern and the same area used as a fill, which effectively repeats and fills an area without giving the feeling that it has been duplicated.

You can see how this works yourself by following these steps:

1. Open the Bricksample.psd image from the CD.

2. Choose Edit → Define Pattern. Name the pattern `Bricks`.

3. Create a new image of any size (2000 × 3000 pixels is used for the example in Figure 5.4).

4. Fill the image with the pattern using the Fill function (Edit → Fill). Choose Pattern from the Use dropdown list, and select Bricks (which you saved in step 2) as the custom pattern.

With a little touchup, you can enhance the patterned fill by changing the color or tone of a few bricks. For example, continuing on:

5. Create two new blank layers and name them `Lighten` and `Darken`. Set the Lighten layer to Screen and the Darken layer to Multiply. Reduce the opacity of both layers to 10 percent.

6. Activate the Lighten layer and make a rough selection of one of the bricks at random. Fill with white, move the selection, and fill again. Fill about 10 bricks.

Figure 5.5

By randomly selecting a few bricks and changing the tone by a few levels, you can make the pattern fill you created appear to be random.

7. Activate the Darken layer and make a rough selection of one of the bricks at random. Fill with black, move the selection, and fill again. Fill about 10 bricks.

You can repeat similar fills with other options. For example, you could use a layer with a different opacity, or with a different color in Color or Color Burn mode. The idea is to add to the effect of randomized bricks in the pattern. When you have finished, your result should look something like Figure 5.5.

Depending on how you use and manipulate patterns, you can make them *seem* random, use them as a base for creating less obviously contrived objects, and avoid flat-out bad, overly predictable, or clunky pattern results.

When you're creating a seamless pattern, keep in mind that the pixels on the right edge of the image have to match those on the left, and the top has to match the bottom as well. If these edges don't match up, you'll get some unnatural-looking patterning, and obvious seams. To correct it, all you do is offset the sample (using the Offset filter) and patch whatever seam there is:

1. Open pattern-sample.psd. This small sample (see Figure 5.6) will be used to construct a tiling pattern.

2. Choose Filter → Other → Offset. The amount you offset (to the right and down) should be about half the height and width of the image. Be sure that the Wrap Around option is checked. You'll see something like Figure 5.7.

3. Adjust the seams of the image. For this sample, it is helpful to first erase the problem areas. When they are gone, draw them back in so that they fit with the image (using a black 95 percent hard paintbrush), and recolor the cells (see Figure 5.8). After erasing badly matched cell walls (a) and replacing them (b), use Blend If (This Layer, set to 0, 165 without splitting the sliders) to drop out the tone within the cells (c). Next,

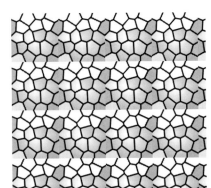

a

b

Figure 5.6

Quickly glancing at the original image (a), you won't see whether it can tile well. If you save it as a pattern, and then use it as a pattern fill in a new 400 × 400 pixel image, you'll see that it fails to tile well (b).

Figure 5.7

Offsetting will shift what would be the seam of the pattern into the center of the image. You can then clean up the transitions to make it seamless.

commit the change by merging the cells to a blank layer (create a new blank layer, move it below, and merge down). Cells are repainted with white or gray (d and e) to leave a single diagonal row of white cells to repeat in the pattern (f).

Depending on the sample and the desired results, you might use many different methods to repair a problem area. The key is to focus on the offset, which lets you see the edges that make the pattern fail to be seamless. You can be sure your correction is complete by offsetting a second time before creating the pattern from the sample.

Using this same technique, you can build many seamless patterns and textures. In some cases, you will want to save them so you can apply your patterns and textures to different images without having to take the time to re-create them.

Patterns can be created with color and may be adjusted to fit the purpose (as we did here with the example of the brick wall) and by recoloring cells in the sample to create a more distinct (rather than less distinct) pattern in the cells when they are applied. Patterns may be applied inside selections and as means to create component objects—usually not as the focus of an image but as a background or fill.

The limitation of making seamless patterns is that they work well where the pattern fill is not likely to call attention to itself as an artificially added pattern. These patterns might work if you are imitating a brick wall, where the viewer expects to see a pattern anyway, but something less defined and even—like the surface of concrete or stucco—might seem to repeat when you really don't want the areas to appear patterned. This is where you can be creative with applying layers and filters to create custom textures for one-time application—entirely from scratch. Depending on what patterning and texture you are trying to match, you can create reusable actions that generate fresh areas to either add to or replace the existing texture. The benefit of working this way is that your result will not look as if it was created by a canned pattern or texture.

As mentioned earlier, working with filters is almost always experimentation. You rarely can just reach into the pile of filters and pull out one that will do exactly what you want without making adjustments or using them in combination. Filters are usually best used to enhance an image rather than change it, which is why it is often wise to use what you already have and adjust it if you can. Re-creating elements is, again, most likely a last resort.

Creating and Applying Seamless Textures

You apply texture in a somewhat different way than you do patterns. Texture is meant to add dimension to the surface of objects (and perhaps to the entire image, as we'll see in the following example). While patterns are generally used to just flatly fill an area, texture creates dimension by manipulating highlight and shadow, in a way similar to what we looked at in the button example. Generally patterns will fill an area, and texture will shape it.

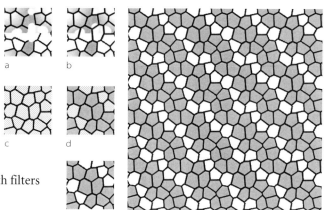

As with patterns, you can use textures to adjust new image objects, or replace or enhance existing elements in an image. The idea of seamless application is important for textures not created with filters for a single application.

There may be instances where you will want to apply a pattern and then texturize the pattern, or vice versa. For example, when creating the bricks for the sample in the last section, a brick texture was created to fill a larger area, and then mortar was added to etch out the shape of the bricks. The same effect might have been achieved the other way around, but that would probably have required additional selection (to keep the texture to the brick face and off the mortar), and would not have been as economical or sensible an approach. There are some components where the reverse will be true: you'll want the texture to apply to the entire image after the pattern. It depends on what you want to accomplish.

In this example we will create a jigsaw puzzle pattern that can be applied as a texture to carve a puzzle imprint into the face of any image, to make it look like… a puzzle. We'll be using the Pen tool to work with some vectors as a warm-up for the next chapter.

1. Check the Preferences for Guides, Grids & Slices. Set the Gridline Every option to 100 pixels and Subdivisions to 4. On the Mac, you'll find the Preferences under the Photoshop menu (Photoshop → Preferences → Guides, Grid & Slices); on Windows the Preferences are under Edit (Edit → Preferences → Guides, Grid & Slices).

2. Open a new image 500 × 500 pixels.

3. Turn on the grid (View → Show → Grid). This will show the gridlines, as shown in Figure 5.9. You may also want to add guides starting at 50 and placed every 100 pixels; create both horizontal and vertical guides in a grid. The guides will be somewhat redundant, but can help you identify where you need to draw tabs.

Figure 5.8

Corrections can take many forms. The idea is to remove the seam so that the image looks continuous.

Figure 5.9

The grid will help you keep in alignment so your result will tile.

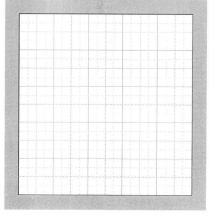

4. Choose the Pen tool. Make sure the Paths option 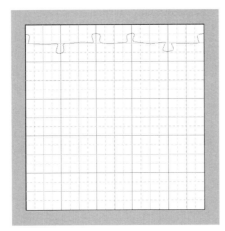 is selected on the options bar.

5. Begin drawing your puzzle shape by creating a path similar to the one in Figure 5.10. There are a few rules to follow here in order to keep things in alignment. You will want to create half-tabs at the edge of the image on either side. While it doesn't matter exactly where you start, you should end in exactly the same vertical place on the other side of the image. So, if you start at 0, 25 (as pictured), you should end at 500, 25. Other tabs for the puzzle pieces should come at approximately the 100-, 200-, 300-, and 400-pixel horizontal lines (though you have some play with these since they don't have to match anything).

6. Choose the Path Selection tool, click on the path you created in step 5, and select the path (so the anchor points are visible). Copy and Paste the path, and then flip it vertically using Flip Vertical (Edit → Transform Path → Flip Vertical). Be sure the paths are active (the anchor points should remain visible). Move the path so that the horizontal line is approximately 250 pixels from the top (see Figure 5.11).

7. Paste in another copy of the path segment. This time flip it horizontally and vertically and move it into position at about 450 pixels from the top, as shown in Figure 5.12.

8. Draw another segment at about 350 pixels from the top, similar to what you did in step 5. Try to vary the tab positions. Your result should look something like Figure 5.13.

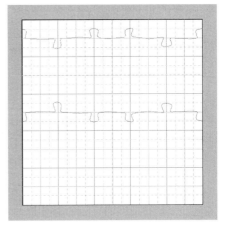

Figure 5.10

Be sure to get this one right; you will be duplicating it a number of times. Vary the tabs up and down instead of all up or all down.

Figure 5.11

The ends of the path component should be aligned to 0 and 500 exactly; the vertical position can vary slightly from 300.

9. Select, copy, and paste the path segment you created in step 8; then move it to about 150 pixels from the top of the image and invert it. See Figure 5.14.

10. Use the Path Selection tool to select the five path segments you have in the image. When the paths are selected (points show as active), copy and paste the path, then rotate it 90 degrees (Edit → Transform Path → Rotate 90° CCW). See Figure 5.15.

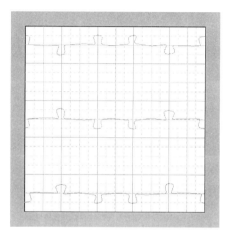

Figure 5.12

Changing the orientation of each of the path segments you paste will help create the illusion of randomness in the pattern. You could draw each one individually, but this will save time.

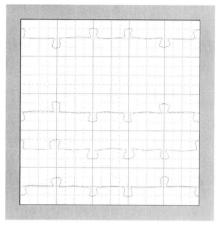

Figure 5.13

Again, be sure the first and last points on the path are perfectly aligned vertically.

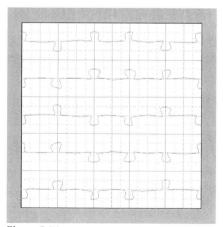

Figure 5.14

This completes the horizontal paths for the puzzle pattern/texture.

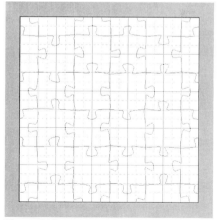

Figure 5.15

You probably will not have to realign the pasted paths if you were careful about creating them.

11. Choose the Paint Brush tool, set the foreground color to black, and change the brush to 90 percent hard and 3 pixels. These settings will be used by the Stroke Path function in the next step.

12. With all the subpaths highlighted, choose Stroke Path from the Paths palette pop-up menu. The Stroke Path dialog box will appear. Choose Brush from the Tool dropdown list, and apply the stroke by clicking OK. The result should look something like Figure 5.16.

13. Save the image as puzzlelines.psd. You may want to save this inside the Photoshop program folder in the Presets\Textures folder to keep it with other Photoshop presets.

To apply the pattern you have just created as a texture, you can use Photoshop's Texturizer or manually apply it. Each method has its advantages. We'll quickly look at both ways.

Applying Textures with Texturizer

The Texturizer filter can be found under Texture on the Filter menu. This filter allows you to apply predefined textures saved as PSD images to your open image:

1. Have an image open that you want to apply a texture to.

2. Choose Texturizer from the Filter menu (Filter → Texture → Texturizer). This opens the Texturizer dialog box.

3. Click the Texture dropdown arrow to open the pop-up menu for this filter.

4. Choose Load Texture, and locate the puzzlelines.psd file you saved in the previous exercise. When the file is loaded, the texture will appear in the image preview window.

Use the Scaling slider to increase/decrease the scaling of the effect, and the Relief to specify the intensity of the effect along the texture edges. Move the direction of the light with the Light dropdown list. Invert will make the effect appear to invert (up for down) by inverting the highlight.

Once you are satisfied, apply the texture by clicking OK. Once you have accepted the changes, you cannot edit the effect.

Applying Textures Manually

It may not be immediately apparent what the Texturizer is doing to create the texture effect. The following manual application will approximate the process so that you can understand the application and take advantage of creating other texture effects. The goal is to create a highlight and shadow based on the puzzle lines, and then apply that like an effect to the image using layer properties to darken and lighten the image below.

1. Have an image open that you want to apply a texture to.

2. Open the puzzlelines.psd file and choose Define Pattern from the Edit menu. Then close puzzlelines.psd.

3. Create a new layer in the image you opened in step 1. Name the layer **Highlight**, and fill it with white.

4. Fill the layer with the puzzlepiece.psd pattern you saved in step 2.

5. To make the effect appear to cut into the puzzle with the settings we will be using, you have to invert the content of the layer (choose Image → Adjust → Invert, or press ⌘/Ctrl+I).

6. Open the Emboss filter (Filter → Stylize → Emboss). The filter preview should show you a highlight/shadow effect. The Height and Amount settings allow you to adjust the depth of the effect, and Angle allows you to adjust the direction of the effect. For this application, be sure the highlight and shadow are distinct—not isolated or indistinguishable. Settings can start with Angle 135°, Height 2, and Amount 100%. The result should look like a puzzle cutout—as if it is cut into the gray of the image. Once you see how it works, you can adjust later applications. Accepting the change will turn most of the image gray, and the outline of the puzzle edges will be black and white.

7. Change the layer mode to Screen.

8. Control the intensity of the Highlight layer using the Layer Styles dialog box (double-click the layer thumbnail). Slide the black This Layer slider to the right until the effect of the gray disappears (128 levels). Split the right of the slider and adjust the blending. This is a judgment call, but try using 191 for the position.

9. Duplicate the Highlight layer and name it **Shadow**. Change the layer mode to Multiply.

10. Control the intensity of the Shadow using Layer Styles. Double-click the Shadow layer thumbnail and slide the black This Layer slider all the way left to reset the blending. Next slide the white This Layer slider to the left until the effect of the gray in the layer disappears (128 levels). Split the left of the slider and adjust the blending. Again, this is a judgment call, but try using 63 for the position.

Figure 5.16

This plain black-and-white image is all you need to apply the puzzle pattern to your images as a texture.

When you're applying this manually to a color image, you may prefer to apply the Highlight and Shadow layers to a merged copy of the image set to Luminosity mode. Just group the Highlight and Shadow layers with the merged copy. This targets the changes to the tone and leaves the color out of the change.

The Blend If sliders allow you to target the impact of the highlight and shadow information that was isolated by the Emboss filter. This highlight and shadow effect is similar to the Button effect we created at the beginning of this chapter. Keeping the highlight and shadow information separate allows you to control these effects individually. For example, you can change the opacity of the Highlight and/or Shadow layers with different settings to control the intensity of the final effect.

You can also adjust the placement of this effect. The edge of the puzzle will probably not fit the puzzle perfectly. It is possible to adjust this effect on an expanded canvas, shift (and even distort) the texture into place, and then erase unwanted tabs by painting them out with gray on the Highlight and Shadow layers, or adjusting the Highlight layer after the fill and before applying the Emboss filter.

The image in Figure 5.17 is made using the pattern created earlier in the chapter and the puzzle texture just completed using the following steps:

1. The cell pattern was applied to a blank layer in a new image.

2. Color was added using Blend If to target the pattern grays.

3. The resulting pattern was shaped with the Spherize filter (Filter → Distort → Spherize), using an amount of 100%.

4. The resulting sphere shape was isolated using a circular selection, reverse and delete (leaving only a ball shape).

5. Layer effects (Inner Shadow; 0 Distance; Bevel) were applied to further shape the ball.

6. The canvas of the image was expanded to allow the background to be shaped and colored.

7. A drop shadow was added to help create a relationship between the ball and the background.

8. The texture was added over the whole image was re-shaped by laying the puzzle texture over it, re-defining the depth.

This is only one simple application of texture to a relatively simple result. However, if you had a scene that begged for a puzzle on a coffee table, it is possible that you might be able to create a realistic effect to place the puzzle in the image as an added element.

But this is only the beginning. Let's take a look at more combinations in the next section.

Figure 5.17

The result rolls together many of the effects you have seen thus far in this chapter.

Making an Object

Creating a viable object from scratch tests everything you've learned so far. You have to make the basic shape of the object using tone and color, and then give it depth and fit it into an image, noting light direction, image quality, and other "intangibles." Be aware that this exercise is challenging, but you can either follow the steps or enhance the approach even more with additions and details if you feel ready.

Keep in mind that if you have worked through the chapter to this point, you have already created a simple, photo-realistic element. There should be nothing to stop you there.

Say you took a picture of a tree, wall, and window and decided the window was the wrong one for your wall (like the image in Figure 5.18, which you'll also find on the CD as tree-and-window.psd). You wanted something a little cuter—a double-hung window, maybe some blue curtains, rather than that black, empty space. You could take a picture of another window and manipulate it to fit it in the space. This might require hours, hunting something down similar to what you were looking for so that you could take a picture of it. Or you could make a window from scratch.

Figure 5.18

The following exercise will go through replacing the window here with something a bit different.

You may think creating a window sounds easy. After all, it's just a rectangle, with maybe a few little crisscross doodads (muntins, they're called). To some extent, it is simple. But to do it you will have to use just about everything you've looked at so far in the book, and learn a few more little tricks.

Making the window will require several minor adjustments, from shaping the molded look of the muntins to dropping the muntin shadows on the wavy curtains. We'll look at those changes in detail here, using a lot of images to keep you in step. Because this exercise is so involved, leave yourself some time to complete it, or save the image in stages as you go:

Make the window Creating the box shape for the window sash is just the beginning. We'll look at adding detail to the woodwork of the sash and muntins using curves to alter gradients. When the first sash is done, it can be duplicated to save you some work, and then shaded to create depth.

Make the curtain Curves can be employed again to create wavy curtain pleats. Then use a transformation effect to make the way they fall seem unique. Once you've created and colored the curtain, you will place it behind the window.

Make shadows for the window and curtain Once the curtain is where it belongs, the image will look a little flat. Adding a shadow from the window falling on the curtain will give it some depth. The angle of the shadow will have to approximate the source in the destination image. The real kick is trying to weave that shadow in and out of the pleats. We'll do that using the Displace Map feature.

Place and fit the window with the wall With the double-hung window complete, you will have to fit it into place where the current window is. This will require more transformation, some feathering, and incorporation of still more shadows.

Making the Window

Here we have to create all the details for the window pieces step by step. As simple as this image may seem, there are a lot of significant details.

Before sizing

After sizing

Figure 5.19

Using Bilinear resampling as you resize adds an evenly stepped gradient.

1. Open a new RGB image at 10 × 10 pixels with a white background.

2. Press D to restore the default color for the foreground and background; then press X to switch black to the background.

3. Change the canvas size to 12 × 12 pixels. This will create a black frame around the image.

4. Resize the image to 400 × 400 pixels using Bilinear resampling. This will increase the size of the image and add an evenly stepped gradient to the edge of the frame, as shown in Figure 5.19.

5. Open the Curves dialog box (⌘/Ctrl+M), and shape the tone of the gradient area by adjusting the curve, as shown in Figure 5.20.

6. Duplicate the background to a layer, hide the background, and clear the center of the image (e.g., select the center of the image with the Magic Wand using a low tolerance and delete). Name the layer `Frame`.

7. Make a selection of a segment on one of the sides of the frame using the Polygonal Lasso . Miter one of the ends to a 45° angle. See Figure 5.21.

8. Copy and paste the segment to a new layer and shut off the view for Frame. Name the layer `Miter`.

9. Position the segment in the Miter layer so that the point of the shape falls exactly in the corner. See Figure 5.22.

10. Duplicate the Miter layer, rotate the duplicate layer (not the canvas) 180°, position the new segment in the opposite corner, and choose Merge Down. See Figure 5.23.

11. Duplicate the Miter layer, rotate the duplicate 90°, and merge down. See Figure 5.24.

12. Duplicate the Miter layer, Flip Horizontal, and merge down. At this point, you see just the corners, but turning on the view for the Frame layer will display the whole frame (see Figure 5.25). Merge the Miter and Frame layers and rename the result `Frame`.

13. Make a new layer, group it with the Frame layer, and fill with yellow (RGB: 255,255,0). Change the mode to Color.

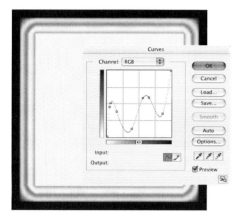

Figure 5.20

The frame is going to give you a rough look at the final bevel. We'll reshape this in the coming steps to sharpen up the corners. Note that the curves are set to percentage, not levels of gray.

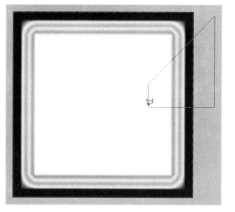

Figure 5.21

Hold the Shift key while creating the angle to make the miter a perfect 45°

Figure 5.22

With Snap To on, the object should snap to the corner readily so you know it is in place.

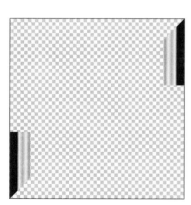

Figure 5.23

The identical segments should be tucked neatly so that the point is right in the corner.

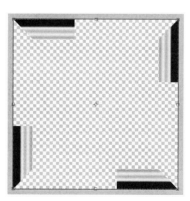

Figure 5.24

Duplicating and rotating will help you create an effective repeating pattern of a different sort than we saw earlier in the chapter.

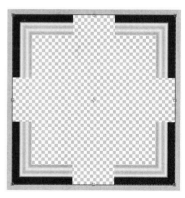

Figure 5.25

Before merging the Miter and Frame layers, you should see these mitered corners.

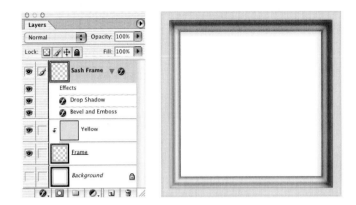

Figure 5.26

Adding Layer Styles will put the bevel edge all around the frame and add a drop shadow on the molded inner area of the sash to give the appearance of depth.

14. Make a new layer, and then make a selection of the black part of the frame (e.g., use the Magic Wand with Use All Layers and Contiguous checked). Expand the selection 2–3 pixels, and fill the selection with yellow. Name the layer `Sash Frame`.

We'll need to add some effects to the frame to give it some shape. For more control, you can create the effects manually.

15. Add a soft Drop Shadow and inner Bevel to the Sash Frame layer using the Layer Styles dialog box. Be sure the Global Angle box is checked and adjust the style to a 45° angle (the approximate direction of light in the image). Use the following settings; keep in mind that your tastes may suggest something different:

    • Drop Shadow: Adjust the Opacity setting to 75%, Distance 15, Spread 5, Size 25

    • Bevel: Style Inner Bevel, Depth 20, Direction Up, Size 5, Soften 0, Highlight and Shadow both black, Multiply 30%

At this point the result should look like Figure 5.26 in the image and in the Layers palette.

There are a lot of other things you could do on your own to further refine the image at this point, such as add effects to give the frame texture if you'd like. The next series of steps moves on to creating the muntins.

16. Make a selection down the center of the image the approximate size of a muntin, create a new layer, and fill the selection with black. Then Copy the layer (you will paste it in the next step).

17. Rotate the layer 90°, then Paste and merge down. You'll end up with a cross over the image, which will turn into your muntins. Name the layer `Original Muntin Shape`.

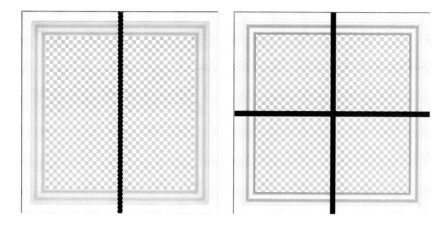

18. Duplicate the layer, then blur with Gaussian Blur (use 3 pixels). Create a new layer below the duplicate layer, name it `Muntins`, fill it with white, and merge the duplicate and Muntins layers. Doing this allows you to shape the muntins in the next step, and then use the Original Muntin Shape layer to reshape the result.

19. Use Curves to shape the beveling on the Muntins layer. Use the curve shown in Figure 5.27. The curve should be applied to the Muntins layer, rather than using an adjustment layer.

If you are not getting the same results as shown by setting your curves, be sure your curves are displaying in percent mode as pictured. Change the orientation using the button on the lower gradient bar ◀▷ in the dialog box.

20. Load the Original Muntin Shape layer as a selection, then Expand the selection (3 pixels), invert it, activate the Muntins layer, and delete it to trim the Muntins layer. Throw out the Original Muntin Shape layer when you are done.

21. Create a Hue/Saturation adjustment layer and group it above the Muntins layer. Check the Colorize box and make adjustments to match the color of the bevel on the frame. Try sliding the Saturation setting all the way up, adjusting the Hue setting until the color seems yellow, and then adjusting the Lightness setting until the shape of the miter reappears.

22. Place guides at 200 horizontally and 200 vertically. Use New Guide (View → New Guide) or just drag these guides out from the ruler. Center the Muntins layer on the guides.

Figure 5.27

You can create far more subtle effects than this with a little patience and a few more curve points.

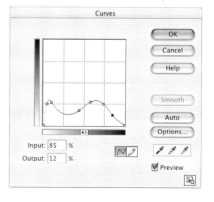

23. Choose the Rectangular Marquee and make a square selection from the center of the image (hold down Shift+Option/Alt). Use Transform Selection (Select → Transform Selection) and rotate 45° using the options bar. Here you see the selection and the rotation.

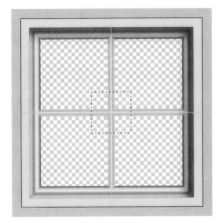 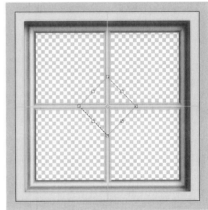

24. Hold down the Shift key and move the selection to the left so it covers only the left part of the muntin. (below left)

25. Be sure the Muntins layer is active, then copy and paste it three times. Name the new layers `Fix 1`, `Fix 2`, and `Fix 3` (as you paste). This will group the new layers with the Muntins layer. You'll use these segments to fix the bevel where the Muntins cross.

26. Activate Fix 1 (it should be the bottom Copy layer), rotate it 90°, and center the segment in the image using the guides. This should align perfectly with the vertical muntin, and will redefine the shape of the vertical at the cross section.

27. Align Fix 2 and Fix 3 to the right and left of the cross section so that the bevels match and the joint looks like it was mitered. (below right)

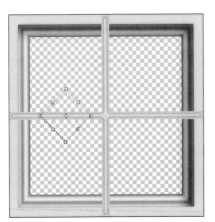 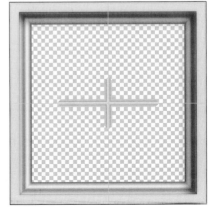

28. Throw out the guides using Clear Guides, and merge the muntin layer copies and the Hue/Saturation layer.

29. Select the Eraser tool, and use a hard, round brush to miter the muntins to the framc. See Figure 28.

30. Move the Muntins layer below the Sash Frame layer, activate the Sash Frame layer, and use the Merge Visible command. See Figure 5.29.

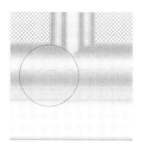

Figure 5.28

A round brush at the right size for the Eraser can create a miter that follows the curve of the frame quickly and convincingly.

You could run through those steps a second time to create a second sash, but duplicating the sash you just created should be good enough. You will paste the duplicate in a new layer above. The upper portion of a double-hung window runs on the outside, and such detail is usually very important in creating realistic effects.

31. Duplicate the Sash Frame layer and change the name to **Upper Sash**. Change the name of the Sash Frame layer to **Lower Sash**.

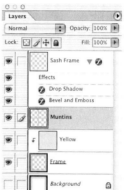

Figure 5.29

This is the layer structure for the window just prior to the merge.

32. Change the height of the canvas from 400 to 800, anchoring the bottom of the image using the Canvas Size function.

33. Choose the Move tool, hold down the Shift key, and slide the Upper Sash layer into place at the top of the image.

34. Create a new layer between the Upper Sash and Lower Sash layers and call it **Upper Shadow**. Choose the Paint Brush tool and a soft brush (about 30 pixels), and then paint a black line right along the bottom edge of the upper sash with the brush centered on the edge of the sash frame. Keep the line straight by clicking at one side, holding down the Shift key, and clicking on the other side to draw the line between the points. Change the Opacity setting of the Upper Shadow layer to lighten the effect. Your result should look like that shown in Figure 5.30.

Figure 5.30

The complete double-hung window as seen from the outside of the house.

You might want to do more than this, but at this point you can stop with the window framing. If nothing else, this exercise should have given you a better appreciation for carpentry. You can still do a number of things to this window frame; additional details are up to you.

Making the Curtain

Now that we have the window frame, we need to add the curtain behind it. The window frame will act as a mask, so there are a lot of details that will be unnecessary, such as the rod and rings.

1. Create a new image that is 400 × 800 pixels. Don't close the Window image; you'll still need it.

2. Create a new layer, fill the layer with a black-to-white gradient from right to left, and call it **Curtain**.

3. Shape the gradient using a curve that looks something like the curve in Figure 5.31. This should not be an adjustment layer—just apply the change.

4. Size the layer to 50 percent width using the Transform function.

5. Move the sized layer to the left, and name it Left Curtain. If you have Snap on (View → Snap should be checked), the content should snap to (align) with the edge of the image.

6. Duplicate the Left Curtain layer, and name it Right Curtain. Flip the new layer horizontally and move the content to the right until it snaps to the right edge of the image; then merge down. Change the merged layer name to Curtain.

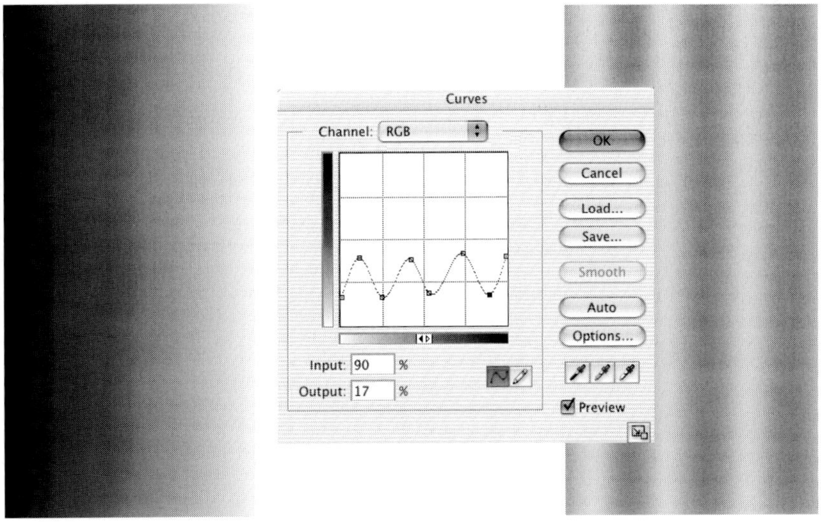

Figure 5.31

The shape of the curve will be similar to the fall of the pleats (looking up from the bottom, or down from the top). Don't bother making the points at exact intervals; "imperfection" will make the pleats look more realistic.

7. Activate the Curtain layer and choose the Perspective Transform tool. Use it to alter the fall of the curtain, as shown in Figure 5.32.

8. Add a Hue/Saturation Adjustment layer, check the Colorize box, and adjust the curtain to an interesting color. The example uses blue, but you can use whatever you like (remember, it will be going with a yellow window, pink wall, and green window frame). Take a snapshot and name it `Step 8`.

9. Shut off the Hue/Saturation layer, flatten, and save the image somewhere as `curtain-map.psd`. You will be using this map later to adjust the way shadows from the window frame fall on the curtain.

10. Step back in the history to unflatten the image by clicking the step 8 snapshot.

11. Merge the Hue/Saturation layer with the Curtain layer and then duplicate the Curtain layer back to the Window image you were working on earlier.

12. Position the Curtain layer below the Sash layers if necessary. The result should look like the image and Layers palette shown in Figure 5.33.

Figure 5.32

This is a simple distortion. Other filters and more complex behaviors (as we'll see with Displace in a moment) can add other touches of realism.

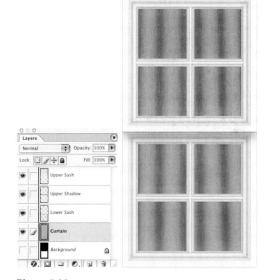

Figure 5.33

This looks a little flat, but we'll add some depth with shadows in the next section.

Making Shadows for the Window and Curtain

The image looks a little flat at this point since the frame is not casting a shadow on the curtain. Adding the shadow will help shape the curtain as well as define the relationship and distance between the objects.

1. Link the Sash layers and Upper Shadow, and then Merge Linked. Change the name of the layer to Window.

2. Load the Window layer as a selection by ⌘/Ctrl-clicking the layer in the Layers palette. Invert the selection.

3. Create a new layer, group above the Window layer, set the mode to Multiply, and fill the selection with black. Call this layer Inner Shadow.

4. Deselect, blur the layer a little (a Radius setting of 5 using Gaussian Blur), and offset it up and right (5 pixels up, 5 pixels to the right).

5. Change the opacity until it looks pleasing. The idea is to give a little depth to the inner portion of the window at the edge of the frame. You may want to turn on the view for the Curtain layer while making this adjustment. Your opacity will probably be between 30 and 50 percent.

6. Load the Window layer as a selection again.

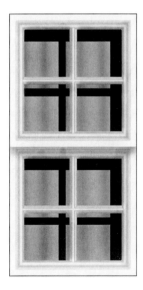 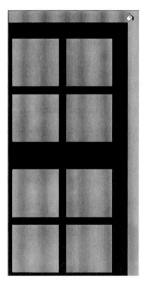 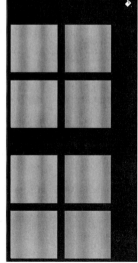

Figure 5.34

This is just a quick positioning for the shadow; we'll soften and shape it in the coming steps.

Figure 5.35

Touching up behind the scenes here ensures that you can reshape the shadow dramatically without having to fill it in later.

7. Create a new layer between the Curtain and the Window and fill it with black. Call it Curtain Shadow.

8. Offset the Curtain Shadow 35 pixels down and left. Your result will look something like that shown in Figure 5.34.

9. Shut off the view for the Window layer and fill the area outside the window shadow frame with black. See Figure 5.35.

10. Choose the Displace filter (Filter → Distort → Displace). Set the Offset setting to 0 Horizontal and 30 Vertical; choose Stretch To Fit and Repeat Edge Pixels. The vertical setting tells Photoshop you want the effect to be adjusted up and down only. Stretch To Fit resizes the map you use—since it was created from the same size file, you could choose either setting and get the same result. Repeat Edge Pixels uses the black border you have if the shadow stretches too far; setting to Wrap Around could send pixels that go off the bottom of the screen to the top. When the Open dialog box appears, choose the `curtainmap.psd` file you created in the last set of steps (step 9 of the previous section). Your result should look like that shown in Figure 5.36.

11. Blur the layer by about 3 pixels and set the opacity to between 30 and 50 percent; then adjust the position of the layer as desired (vertically, that is; moving horizontally will change the alignment of the shadow). When you are all done, it looks like the image shown in Figure 5.37.

Placing and Fitting the Window with the Wall

At this point all that is left to do is flatten the window and copy it to the image with the wall and tree and shimmy it into place (see Figure 5.38). It will be the

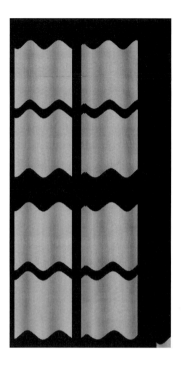

Figure 5.36

This hard dark shadow will be refined by lightening and blurring to complete the shadow effect.

Figure 5.37

With the shadow in place on the curtain, the window has some more realistic depth.

wrong size, and you will have to shape, trim, create a shadow for the window frame, and perhaps alter some color, sharpness, and texture.

As you already know how to do all that other stuff, the details of fitting the window into place are up to you. The sample result (complete with generated wall) can be seen in the color section and in Figure 5.39.

You can spend the good part of a weekend on what is already an interesting image. But hopefully the techniques for shaping and adjustment presented in this chapter have given you the tools you need to make many creative changes.

Figure 5.38

Lower the opacity temporarily to make the initial fit, then transform to shape the space.

Figure 5.39

A new wall, a new shadow, and a new window make a new, less distorted image.

Chapter 6

Vectors and Illustration

Vectors are a powerful means of controlling image content and pixels. Working with vectors is in some ways similar to creating new elements for images using pixels—which we did almost exclusively in the previous chapter—as a way to manipulate and add new content to your images. You can create and control vectors using the Pen, Shape, and Type tools.

The most unique vector property is resolution independence. Unlike pixel content, objects or elements that you create with vectors can be scaled infinitely without losing their shape. Vector shapes corral pixels and other content and can redefine how pixels behave. In addition to introducing another way to create image elements from scratch, resolution independence gives you the ability to create infinitely scalable artwork that you might use in logos or illustrations.

This chapter looks at working with vector art to create image components and covers the following topics:

Producing infinitely scalable art

Building a vector image

Converting pixel images to vectors

Using clipping paths

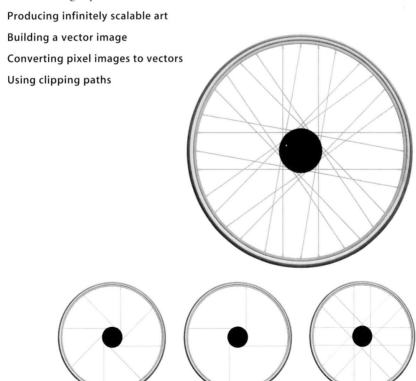

Creating Infinitely Scalable Art

The Shape and Pen tools enable you to develop vector-based artwork in a way that is similar to working with Adobe Illustrator, which has more vector-oriented and layout tools than Photoshop. In Photoshop, you can draw shapes and paths to redefine how pixels work within the image. A key difference between pixels and vectors in your Photoshop images is that vectors *define* image areas, whereas pixels make up the area itself; you never see a vector display as a printable element in an image. All you see is the way the vector affects the pixels it is applied to, as well as the shape of the area it defines. The vector, even at its most complex, is only an outline of a shape.

Vectors can be used like mechanical drawing tools to make fairly precise renderings or intricate freehand shapes. While pixel images are normally trapped by their content, using vectors can help you create art that can be scaled to any size while retaining sharpness. Although you can't turn all elements of a standard photograph into vectors, you can create artwork as vectors so that it can be scaled to suit your needs.

Let's say the owner of the fictitious Captain Hook's Bait & Tackle shop wants a logo and comes to you to make it. He wants to use the logo on his letterhead, business cards, website, and promotional items, such as caps and T-shirts. One other thing the logo will be used for is a little 10 × 16-foot billboard next to the Fishingtown exit from the I-1000 freeway. The only answer you get when you ask how big the logo will be on the billboard is: "Big." It's therefore safe to assume that the logo will run about 9 feet tall.

A 9-foot-tall image in Photoshop at 100 ppi would be almost 11,000 × 11,000 pixels. That's about 333 MB. It isn't a file that you'll want to transfer over the Internet even if you have a fast connection. It also won't work well on a business card; it is way too large and will have to be sized down, or it will take huge amounts of processing time. If you tried to complete this request using pixel-based images, you'd have to deliver multiple versions to satisfy all possible needs.

Figure 6.1

The value of vectors in creating resizable art is clear in this extreme comparison. The benefit can extend to controlling printer dots as well as pixels (see the next chapter).

The logo

Vectors upsized

Pixels upsized

Original Warped Converted to vector

Vector isolated

Warp Text dialog box

Figure 6.2

Even after being distorted with Text Warp, this type can be converted to perfect vector outlines based on the font.

Interestingly, if you are careful about how you use color, shading, and vectors, you can probably create the file you need and make it less than 1000 pixels square, using just one image to get the job done. All you have to do is create exactly what you want to see—with all the detail—using vectors, and apply that vector version of the image at any size.

The benefit of vectors lies not only in the ability to create a single file to get the job done, but in the image result. The difference is also getting good-quality hard edges in type and on shapes you have created. Figure 6.1 shows an approximation of the result of taking a 1000×1000-pixel image and resizing it to $11{,}000 \times 11{,}000$ using pixels and vectors.

Type as Vector Art

Type should be considered, and handled, as a vector art component before rastering. This enables you to use type as shape layers and can allow you to make changes with the Pen tool as you would with other vector art (once the type is converted to vectors). Type is easily converted to vectors; simply choose Layer → Type → Convert To Shape. Treating type like a vector component can give you sharper results in print (as we'll see in the next chapter) and add flexibility to your shape library. For example, type distorted with Text Warp ⌁ (a palette that can be opened from the options bar) can still be converted to vectors. See Figure 6.2.

Figure 6.3

Re-creating this image may look like a challenge. However, many of the components repeat, and patterns are easily replicated.

Creating a Vector Image

To create a vector image, you work with shape layers to create the component bits and pieces you need for your object. Often you build these components in separate layers. This approach can help with positioning, coloring, masking, and adjusting; layer clipping makes it easy to target adjustments, and because of this, it will often be tricky to do everything on a single layer. Whereas using many layers will increase the size of an image if the layers are filled with pixels, using fill layers and vectors can keep file size from getting out of hand.

Here we'll look at a mechanical example of using vectors to render realistic effects. The bike tire in Figure 6.3 was rendered entirely using vectors. We'll

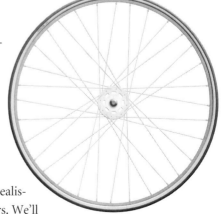

walk through the steps and look at some techniques for creating a few kinds of vector components. We'll also catch some practice using layers, layer sets, and nested layers for organizing image components.

Follow these steps:

1. Open a new image that's 1000 × 1000 pixels in size.

2. Put a guide exactly at 500 vertical and 500 horizontal. You will use the intersection as the center of your wheel. You will also use it as a hub for the components, rotations, and duplication.

3. Choose the Ellipse shape tool and set the foreground color to black. Click on the Shape Layers option for the Ellipse tool. This creates a new shape layer for the ellipse you draw.

4. Click and drag the Ellipse tool on the intersection of the guides you created in step 2. As you drag outward toward the edge of the image, hold down the Shift (to keep the ellipse confined to a perfect circle) and Option/Alt keys (to draw from the center). Make the circle come out nearly to the edge of the image, and then release the mouse button and keyboard keys. This draws a solid circle filled over the entire area; this will be the outer width of the tire. Drawing the circle creates a new layer; name the layer **Rubber**.

> If your Snap To settings are set to Snap To Guides, you can click close to the center rather than right on it and the tool application should snap to the guides as you apply. Otherwise, you may want to use the Info palette to navigate precisely to where you apply the tool before applying it.

Figure 6.4

Creating the two circles in steps 4 and 5 should result in a torus.

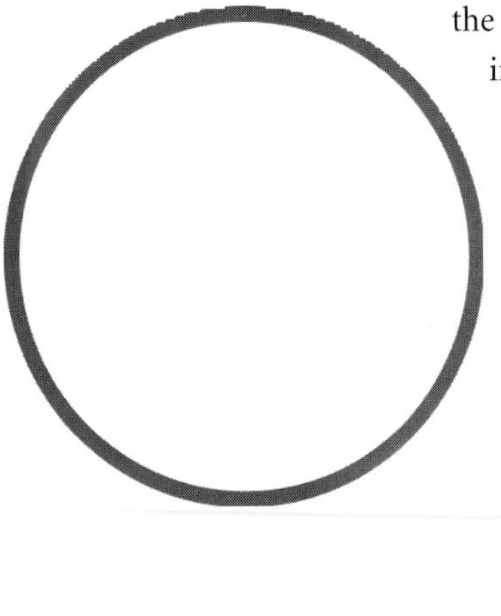

5. Move the cursor back to the center of the image and hold down the Option/Alt key. The cursor for the tool will change from Shape to Subtract. Click on the center of the image again and drag. As you drag, continue to hold down Option/Alt and include the Shift key to confine the shape to a perfect circle. This inner circle defined the inner width of the tire. The result of the last two steps should look something like the image shown in Figure 6.4.

6. Shape the tire with options in the Layer Styles dialog box (choose Layer → Layer Style → Blending Options). Your goal is to make the tire appear to be 3D. Use Bevel (Depth 150 percent, Direction Up, Size 10 pixels, Soften 5 pixels, Angle 60°, Altitude 25°, and Use Global Light enabled), Color Overlay (70 percent gray), and a slight Inner Shadow (Multiply with black, using 1–2 pixels for Size, with 0 Distance and Choke).

7. Repeat steps 4–6 to create the rim for the tire. This goes on the inner side of the rubber and overlaps slightly. Where the tire rubber should look rounded, the rim should probably be flat. After drawing the initial circle, rename the layer **Rim**. The inner shadow setting used in the example was about the same, making the color lighter to approximate the shade of an alloy. Your result should look something like the image shown in Figure 6.5.

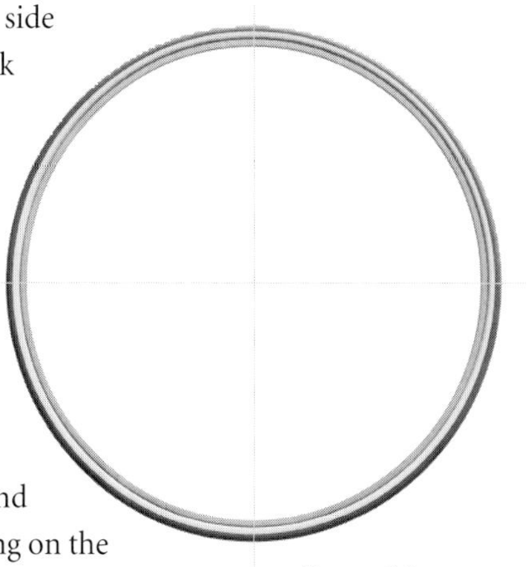

You can add components at this point, such as some noise or streaking in the rubber, and perhaps white walling. You can group these additions to the Rubber layer. To add noise, create a new layer, group it with the Rubber layer, fill it with 50 percent gray, run the Add Noise filter, and then adjust the opacity and layer mode. The percentage will vary depending on the intensity of the noise. Different modes will affect the change in different ways, and the one you use depends on what you feel is realistic or desirable. Overlay is suggested. You might add treads and other details as well, depending on how ambitious you are (and depending on the purpose of the image).

8. When you have finished adjusting the rubber and rim, link all the components and make them a layer set by choosing New Set From Linked from the Layers palette pop-up menu. Name the set **Tire**. The sample layers look like Figure 6.6 after grouping.

Next we'll create the hub. The size of the hub, the angle of the spokes, and other factors can vary in bike designs. We'll work with some simple geometry to create patterns for the final result that look realistic. The goal will be to add 36 spokes—one every 10 degrees on the wheel.

9. Have the Info palette in view and choose the Measure tool. Measure out from the center over the rubber part of the wheel at 100° (watch the Info palette), and then pull a guide down from the top ruler to cross the intersection of the rim and the Measure line.

10. Pull a guide out from the vertical ruler and drag it in to cross the intersection of the Measure line and the rim. This sets a point at the intersection of the two guides that should be 10° left of vertical. See Figure 6.7.

11. Hold down the Option/Alt key, click in the center of the image again, and drag up and right over the rubber part of the tire. The Measure tool forms a V. Move the tool until the Info palette reads 20°. Drag a guide out to intersect where the Measure line and tire rim meet. These guides help you shape the spoke plate (which the

Figure 6.5

The rim component should be thinner than the tire, a lighter color (to suggest metal), and not so heavily beveled.

Figure 6.6

Putting all the elements into a set will help you easily control the position and movement of all the pieces in unison.

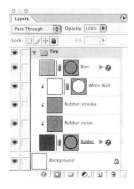

spokes attach to at the center of the image) and place the point where the initial set of spokes will connect, as shown here:

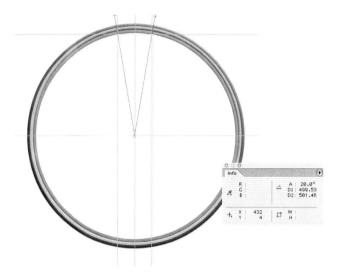

12. Choose the Ellipse tool again and draw a circle from the center of the image just over the guides created in steps 9 and 10, as shown in Figure 6.8. This will act as your hub and the plate that the spokes connect to. Don't worry about the color at this point. Name the layer **Spoke Plate/Hub**.

13. Choose the Measure tool and measure from the center off to the right to 10°. Then pull down a guide to where the Measure line crosses the guide placed in step 10.

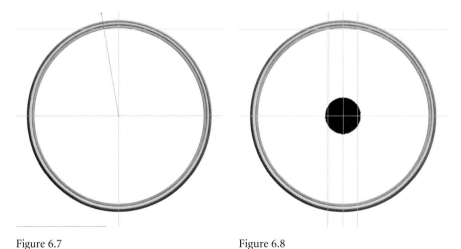

Figure 6.7

The Measure tool and guides help make quick work of creating the right angles.

Figure 6.8

This centered hub will be the inner anchor for the spokes.

14. Choose the Line shape tool, set the weight to 4–5 pixels, and draw a line vertically from the guide intersection created in step 12 to the guide intersection directly vertical from that at the rim. Set the color to 10 percent gray using the Color Picker accessed from the Options bar. Call the new layer **Spoke Rod**.

15. Move the Spoke Rod layer under the Tire layer set in the layers stack. Zoom in to the area where the spoke rod meets the rim, and increase the Line tool Weight setting to 6 or 7 pixels. Draw a line over the end of the rod and into the rim. The line should cover the Spoke Rod and should be masked by the Rim layer. Name the layer **Connector**. Figure 6.9 shows a close-up of this area and the layers stack at this point.

16. Shape the Spoke Rod and Connector layers by assigning layer styles. In the example, a Bevel was assigned to each. For the Spoke Rod layer, the following settings were used: Inner Bevel, Smooth, 100 percent Depth, Up, Size 5, Soften 0, Global Light, and defaults for Highlight and Shadows. For the Connector layer, settings were: Inner Bevel, Smooth, 100 percent Depth, Up, Size 5, Soften 2, Global Light, and defaults for Highlight and Shadows at 25 percent Opacity.

17. Link the Spoke Rod and Connector layers, and then create a new layer set from the linked layers and call it **Spoke**.

Figure 6.9

Note the order of the layers shown here. This will help you clip out and fit the spoke connector.

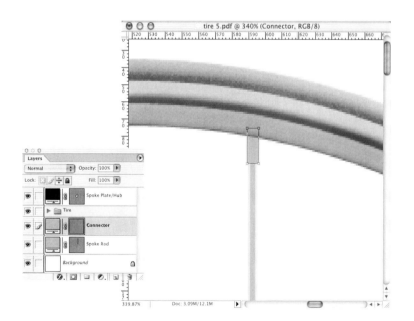

Instead of going through the pain of measuring all 36 spoke sets and drawing individual segments, we'll use layer sets to simplify the work during the next steps.

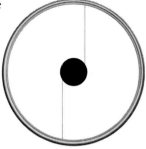

18. Duplicate the Spoke set and call the new set **Spoke 2**. Choose the Move tool, and then choose Edit → Transform → Rotate. Hold down the Option/Alt key and change the position of the Reference Location Point to the center of the image and rotate 180°.

> The Reference Location Point can be found in the center of an area that is active for transforming. To change the position of the rotation center ⌖, you can usually just click on it and drag it into position while holding down the Option/Alt key. A trick for getting it out of tight spaces (like the thin spoke rod) is to move the position using the Reference Point Location ⠿ on the Options bar. Just click one of the corners to move the location, and then move the reference point from that position.

19. Click the Link box on the Layers palette to link the Spoke and Spoke 2 layer sets. Then, choose New Set From Linked from the Layers pop-up menu to create a new set from the spoke pair. Name the new set **Spoke Pair.**

20. Duplicate the Spoke Pair set and name it **Spoke Pair 2**. Choose the Move tool, choose Rotate from the Transform submenu, and rotate the set 90°, as shown in Figure 6.10 (a).

21. Link the Spoke Pair and Spoke 2 sets, choose New Set From Linked, and name the resulting set **Spoke Quad**. Duplicate that set, name it **Spoke Quad 2**, and rotate it 45°, as shown in Figure 6.10 (b).

22. Link the Spoke Quad and Spoke Quad 2 sets and choose New Set From Linked. Name the resulting set **Spokes A**. Duplicate the set, name it **Spokes B**, and flip Spokes B horizontally (Edit → Transform → Flip Horizontal), as shown in Figure 6.10 (c).

Figure 6.10

By duplicating and rotating a single spoke, you can develop spoke pairs and create a realistic array quickly.

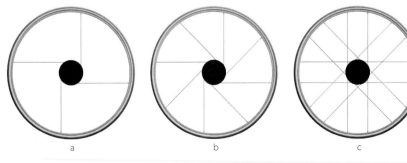
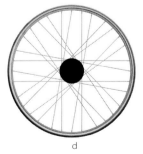

a   b   c   d

23. Link the Spokes A and Spokes B sets, and choose New Set From Linked. Name the resulting set `Spoke Set 1`. Duplicate Spoke Set 1, name the resulting set `Spoke Set 2`, and rotate that 10°. See the current image in Figure 6.10 (d); Figure 6.11 shows the layers stack.

The last set of steps creates the spoke pattern. Once the spokes are created, your image begins to look more like a bike tire. The spoke plate is the next thing on the agenda. We can place it in the proper position in the layers to act as a mask for some content, and then add to it to adjust color and shape, similar to how we created the spokes.

24. Move the Spoke Plate/Hub between the Spokes A and Spokes B layers in Spoke Set 2. This will show only half the spokes in the set above the plate (Figure 6.12).

25. Activate the Spoke Plate/Hub layer and create a new blank layer. Name the layer `Plate Color` and group it with the Spoke Plate/Hub layer. Fill the layer with a Radial gradient from the center of the image to the edge of the plate going from about 3 percent (at center) to 10 percent gray (at the edge of the plate).

26. Apply a bevel style to the Spoke Plate/Hub layer. Use the defaults, but change the Size setting to 1 or 2.

27. Zoom into the plate about two-thirds of the way up from the center. With the Spoke Plate/Hub layer vector mask active, choose the Rounded Rectangle shape tool. Click the Subtract From Shape Area option on the options bar, hold down Option/Alt, and create a hole in the plate by making a rounded rectangle from the center vertical guide, as shown in Figure 6.13. Adjust the shape of the hole to the curve with the Pen tool. Add an anchor point to the top of the hole shape, and then move the anchor with the Up arrow key.

28. Using the Path Selection tool, click on the shape for the hole. This highlights the path component for the hole. Copy and Paste. The hole will be duplicated in the original position. Choose Rotate from the Transform Path submenu, move the reference to the center of the image, then rotate the duplicate hole around the center 180°. This moves a new hole to the other side of the plate.

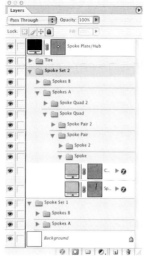

a

b

Figure 6.11

Set duplication leaves you with a host of layers and nested sets (a), but packs them nicely away from view (b).

Figure 6.12

Inserting the hub between sets of spokes makes half of the spokes appear on the near side of the hub.

29. Hold down the Shift key and click the Path Selection tool on the original hole. Copy, paste, and rotate the holes 90°. Two more holes will appear to the left and right.

30. Highlight all four hole shapes, copy, paste, and rotate them 45°. You'll have eight holes in the Spoke Plate/Hub layer.

You can continue with this sort of mechanical patterning to create threads for a thumbnut, sprockets, and additional details, such as manufacturer information on the tires. The point is that you can create realistic components depending on the level of detail you are interested in achieving by creating the element one piece at a time. Working with patterns can speed the process, and by using Photoshop functions for transformation, you can make quick work of it with pretty accurate results. See the biketire.psd file on the CD for examples of a few additional details. You could go even further to duplicate the tire and then create the frame for the bike.

Of course, not all complex objects allow you to depend so heavily on shape tools and simple rotation. Many require more involved custom vectors, which you create either from simple shapes (as we did with the plate holes) or by using the Pen tool. You can create still other and more complex vectors from existing image areas and isolated colors, tones, and components. The latter possibility can sometimes be a good solution for converting pixel-based images to more flexible and expandable vector renderings.

Now that the image has been created, try the following: Press ⌘/Ctrl+0 to view the image, and hide the guides (⌘/Ctrl+;). Go to the Spoke Plate/Hub layer in the Layers palette and click the Effects icon ▶ 𝒇. This opens the Layer Styles dialog box for that layer. Click on the Bevel and Emboss style, and then change the Shading Angle to 160°. You should notice a dramatic shift in all of the lighting effects you applied to the image using the Global Light setting. This can be useful if you need to incorporate a component you have created into another image that has a different lighting angle. Layer Styles allows you to quickly change the lighting direction without reworking the entire image, so you can more closely match the lighting conditions.

Figure 6.13

You can use another vector circle (shown here) as a guide to adjust the curve of the hole so it is consistent with the shape of the hub. If you do, delete it when you are done.

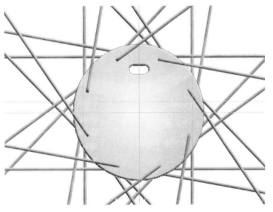
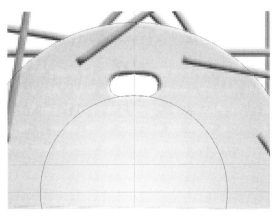

For a quick experiment that demonstrates the power of vectors, open the biketire.psd file from the CD. Look at the type placed on the tire in the upper left of the image by viewing the screen. At the present resolution, it will be quite illegible. The vectors act on this image at the current resolution and show you what the result would be if you rendered the image as is. Choose Save As, and save the image as a PDF retaining the vector information. Open the PDF using Adobe Reader, and zoom in to the type area. This will show you how the information is carried by the file—you should be able to read it perfectly.

Converting Pixel Images to Vectors

At times, it may be tempting to consider the possibility of turning photographic images into vectors. To do that, you would need an infinite amount of time and almost as many layers. You'd need to separate out every color in your image and define it as a vector shape in its own layer to get the result desired.

There are times, however, when it is practical to convert pixel images to vectors to edit, improve, or take advantage of how vectors define images in print. One of the best examples of this is converting a rasterized image back to vectors.

Figure 6.14 shows a line-art drawing of a mask that was scanned from a print. It looks fine on the printed page here because it is small, but if you wanted to blow it up or get even better printed results, you'd want to turn the image into vectors to smooth out any potential pixelation.

Figure 6.14

The mask shown here could be even sharper as a vector image. Note the pixelation in the magnified area.

To convert this to vectors, do the following.

1. Open the image/scan (see jestermask.psd on the CD).

2. Hold down ⌘/Ctrl and click on the composite channel for the image in the Channels palette. For this example, that would be the gray channel.

3. Choose Make Work Path from the Paths palette pop-up menu.

These steps will convert the tone to a selection and the selection to a path. Depending on your Tolerance setting in the Make Work Path dialog box, you will get results like those shown in Figure 6.15. You can now convert the Work Path to a shape layer to use it as vectorized line art by choosing Layer → New Fill Layer → Solid Color. This creates a new layer using the color you select in the color picker and will clip that layer using the active Work Path.

The shapes shown here are not really a very tight fit to the original. It is possible to get much better results—5 or 10 times better! All you have to do is increase the size of the scanned image by 500 or 1000 percent, run through the same process, and reduce the image back to its original size. When you reduce the image again, the vectors will retain the result of the higher resolution sampling. The result is shown in Figure 6.16.

Note the dramatic improvement in contour and the ability of the curve to follow the outline with the Tolerance option set to 1. Using a tolerance of 0.5 is actually overkill; when you increase the size of the image, any jagged edges will be pronounced, so the result will show that. In jagged images, you might want to blur the image somewhat and improve the results. When you blur to smooth out the edges and then load the result as a selection, the selection line will display where the selection is 50 percent or more, and the path will be created along this line. Blur just enough to reduce aliasing, not to obliterate detail.

Figure 6.15

The original (a) can be converted with different settings for the Tolerance option. The results shown here use 0.5 pixels (b) and 1 pixel (c). The fewer pixels, the smoother the result—but also the less accurate.

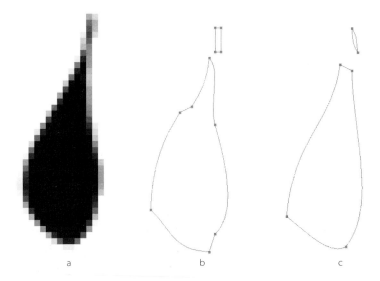

a   b   c

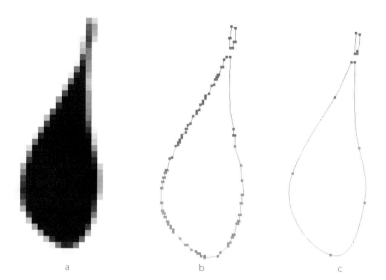

Figure 6.16

The original (a) is converted after resizing the image. The results shown here use 0.5 pixels (b) and 1 pixel (c).

a   b   c

To use this technique to convert color line art, make a selection of each color individually and convert the color in its own layer. In this way, it is possible to re-create high-resolution logos from low-resolution web art, which can sometimes come in handy.

Clipping Paths

Say you want to create an image that isn't constricted to a rectangular shape. The easiest way to do this is to make a selection of what you want to keep, and then invert the selection and delete that area of the image that you don't want. As long as you then set the background color to white, the image shape will appear to be a shape other than rectangular when printed. White areas of images don't print with color (unless you are printing with a spot white ink, and you'd know if you were doing that).

That solution is acceptable if you don't have anything in the background below the image. If you are using the image in layout and print with another image or other content in the background of the digital file, using white won't work. One thing a white background will do in your rectangular image is whitewash anything behind it. You could just re-create the whole image in Photoshop (by bringing in all the image components and reassembling them). But suppose what you really want to do is clip the image out of its background and paste it into the layout—as if you were making a collage. Sometimes you need to reshape the image to make it work the way you want.

Clipping paths do exactly what you need. These are vector shapes that redefine the boundary of your image. They allow you to clip the edge of the image with vector accuracy in shapes other than rectangles and "float" an image over a background in layout (like you'd used scissors). This often works best with images that you create with shapes and type. All you have to do is save a vector in the image as a path, and then assign the path as the image clipping path.

Figure 6.17 and the following steps demonstrate how to use a clipping path to redefine the image shape. Try this out using the trilobite from Chapter 3 (trilobite.psd).

1. Prepare the image by creating the shape that you want to use for the clipping path. Make the shape selection following the color separation technique from Chapter 3.

2. Save the path by clicking Save Path in the Paths palette pop-up menu.

3. Assign the clipping path by choosing Clipping Path from the Paths palette pop-up menu. Leave the Flatness setting blank, and Photoshop will use a default.

> Flatness acts like a tolerance setting during output (device pixels). Higher numbers can cause some variation from the vector while increasing print speed; smaller numbers keep more true to the path. The value can be between .2 and 100.

You can save the file as a TIFF or EPS, and when you place it in layout programs, it will act as if the image is reshaped to the path. Not all layout programs will provide a preview. To test this, you might want to create a PDF and preview the result by viewing it in Acrobat Reader.

Your success in printing (clipping and clipping sharpness) depends on two other things: You've got to save the file in a format that will respect the clipping path, and you've got to print in PostScript. The leap here is that most home printers are not PostScript. It may be possible to approximate the result by using another workflow (such as using PDFs as images, or exporting EPS files from a layout program), but these results will not be optimally sharp. We'll take a better look at printing concerns in the next chapter.

Figure 6.17

Revisit the trilobite (a), create a selection, and then create a path from that selection (b). This path applied as a clipping path will reshape how the image appears in other applications when placed as an image (c).

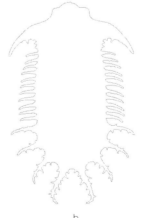
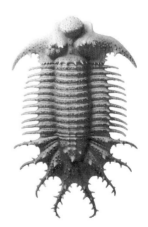

a

b

c

Part IV
Implementing Images

Once you have successfully created an image, you will most likely want to display it in print or on the Web. In many cases, before you even begin, you already have some idea what the image will be used for and how it will be implemented. Knowing where the image is going to end up can often affect how you go about creating it. This part of the book looks at preparing and implementing images for both print and the Web.

The aim of the print discussion (Chapter 7) is not to nail down a one-size-fits-all workflow for getting results. That isn't possible because there is no one *right* way. The goal is to look at options and recommendations, and explore what you need to keep in mind when implementing options.

The web chapter (Chapter 8) deals with some issues that are decidedly oriented toward graphics intended for display. Images intended for use on screen can be animated and swapped, which is mostly lacking in static print. This chapter looks at how to effectively work with display-only techniques.

Chapter 7

Image Output Options

Put simply, printing is rendering your digital image to paper. While that sounds simple, it is a complex action. Granted, you don't have to digest all of that complexity to render images well, but having a good grasp of why things work the way they do can help you decide what devices to use and how to get the best result.

This chapter provides an overview of the wide world of printing options, concepts, and techniques. The goal is to give you the tools to make sense of your color management and workflow, and allow you to get successful proofs and printed images with the results you expect, whether or not you use embedded profiling for color management.

Understanding the printing process

Selecting the right color process

Adjusting print settings

Using profiles

Understanding differences in printers and resolutions

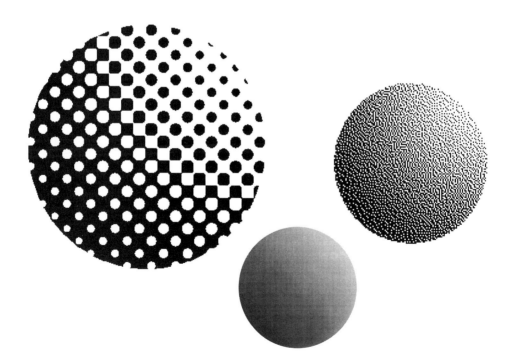

An Overview of Printing

After you've made corrections to your images, you might look at the image on the screen and it will look just fine. When you go to print it, though, the color might not seem as vivid as you remember from the screen. That really isn't unusual, because the process of printing can sap some of the strength from the color. It is partly a result of the necessary conversion from RGB to CMYK and partly because paper and ink, which reflect light, just can't create the bright, rich colors that a computer monitor's phosphors can.

Many printers use a straight CMYK process. By *straight*, I mean the process uses only cyan, magenta, yellow, and black, with no additional inks. CMYK and RGB are not very friendly—or should I say CMYK can often make RGB look bad…or much worse than it has to look. Specifically, vivid red, green, and blue areas of an image can suffer in the conversion to CMYK because there are areas of RGB color that the CMYK process just can't imitate. Getting better results starts with that awareness. Adjusting an image specifically for CMYK results can make a difference. That can mean working with an image that you've converted to CMYK or previewing the image as CMYK.

What goes wrong between your image on screen and the result in print can be hard to track down. Perhaps your monitor isn't calibrated, or it's improperly profiled. Maybe you're having problems with color management in the image, or you should adjust your separations. You might even be having trouble with your printer. To get the best results when printing, you have to know your options and prepare your system and images accordingly. Variables you should keep in mind include:

- Color settings (including preview modes)
- Resolution
- Color process
- Print media

All these factors work together to define the printed result. Once you know how they function within the process, you can make choices or adjustments to achieve the result you want. At the core is your ability to work effectively with your images and process, which means establishing a solid workflow.

A Smart Workflow

A more complex workflow is not necessarily a better one. In fact, a simplified workflow can be easier to maintain. At the same time, a simplified workflow may be hard to develop. If you are constantly fiddling with printer options and customizing image handling, that should set off an alarm that your process needs to change.

The smart workflow begins and ends with knowing what the process requires from your images. The setup for any new workflow can be covered in seven steps:

1. Ask/research what to do with settings.

2. Specify your settings.

3. Print a proof.

4. Adjust your settings.

5. Print a final proof.

6. Confirm your results.

7. Adopt the workflow for future projects.

Ask your printing service and/or research manufacturer settings suggested for the output you want. Set up the image for output according to the standards they set. Proof the output to be sure the settings deliver the results that you expect. Make adjustments if necessary to enhance the result or to compensate for differences between the expected and actual result (depending on the amount of adjustment, you may need to go back to step 3). Then, print a final proof using the modified settings. You can confirm the success of your workflow by comparing the final to the original (if it isn't acceptable, consider possible changes going back to step 1). Once you've settled on a successful workflow, you can reuse those settings whenever you print.

Concentrating on developing a standard workflow for each device that you output to will help you get consistent results whether you're printing at home or with a service, whether or not you're embedding profiles.

Probably the most conspicuous simplification here is step 4. Adjustments can't be willy-nilly renegotiations of your previous corrections. In other words, you don't want to jump in and change monitor settings, attach curves adjustments to your workflow, or grab for a profile to save you from evil output. We'll look at alternatives that make sense, perhaps involving all of these in one form or another. First, let's look at home and service process.

Printing at Home

Printing at home gives you a quick, convenient means of output, without the hassle of going through a service. Printers you use at home tend to be less expensive, and used correctly you can get good results for many purposes—even professional ones—depending on what you need and the equipment you have.

The drawback to home printing is that there is no one to blame but yourself when the color comes out wrong. You need to take the time to learn the equipment, understand how it works, and then test and maintain it on your own. You might also need some technical know-how, such as being able to print to the edge of the paper (bleed).

Processing Color

Selecting the "right" color mode for images destined for print isn't as obvious as it might appear. While it seems sensible to provide images to printers or services in the color mode that will be used for the output, in reality this approach may not always produce the best results. For example, many home printers create their own separations for color, whether you send the image to your printer in CMYK or RGB. If you go out of your way to create a CMYK separation, you may get poor results if your printer treats the information as RGB and separates the CMYK again. In this case, it may be better to send RGB images and allow the device (and drivers) to make their own separation of the original RGB.

> It isn't just devices that may prefer RGB; some services favor RGB so that they can create separations for you—that way, the results are targeted properly to their devices. The waters get muddier with devices that output to variations on the CMYK color scheme (say, CcMmYyK). In addition, you might consider Lab color as a viable intermediary.

First, find out what your printer is doing so you know better how to handle your images—at least with that printer. Run a quick test to see how your printer is handling color. All you have to do is run a rich black (a black that combines black ink with cyan, magenta, and/or yellow ink rather than just using black) to the printer. Once you evaluate the results, consider your options.

Running the Test

The basic test consists of these steps:

1. Open `CMYK.pdf` on the CD using Photoshop. You can also try the same test using Acrobat Reader to see if the two programs give you different results (if they do, the printer settings for the programs are suspect).

2. Print to your usual printer using the settings that you normally use to print.

3. Evaluate the results in a well-lit room.

To evaluate the output, you have to know what you are looking for and what this test print is supposed to be testing. The file is set up with a rich black bar (more than just black ink) across the top. The "black" bar should actually be five different colors—if your printer and driver are printing it as intended. The first three boxes are a rich black with cyan, a rich black with magenta, and a rich black with yellow. The top half of the last box will be black ink only, and the bottom half a rich black using 100 percent of all four inks. The next three bars in the image will be cyan, magenta, and yellow at 100, 75, 50, and 25 percent. The CMYK separation as channels looks like Figure 7.1.

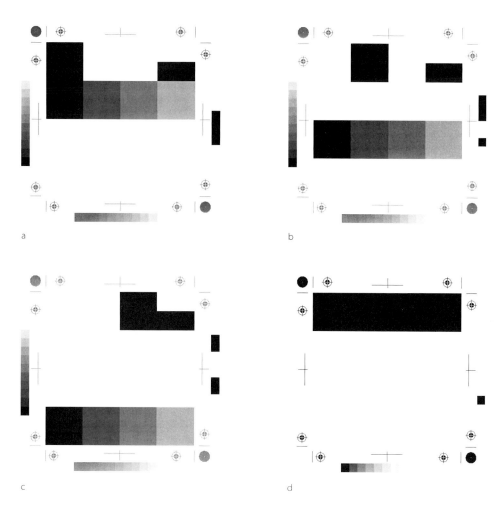

Figure 7.1

The color in your print should use cyan (a), yellow (b), magenta (c), and black (d) in exactly the patterns shown; if not, your printer or driver is getting in the way of your results.

Examining the output in the light should make apparent any differences between what you should have gotten and the actual result. If the black doesn't look like several different blacks but a solid bar, your printer (or the driver) is taking liberty with your CMYK separation. This means that you may not be able to use the printer as a reliable proofing device—unless you can find a solution.

If you want to get the CMYK out that you created by making your separation, you may have to force the printer to accept it. It isn't so much that you want to be a control freak and never want image information to change; you just don't want it to change without you knowing about it so that you can make proper adjustments and not waste your time.

There is more than one solution to controlling the output (including simply living with the result). You could go to the extreme of replacing your printer, but other options don't require making a drastic change in your current setup, and it may be fine to depend on your printer separations. But you need to know what the printer is doing, or you will waste time *and* get even worse results. Your options include:

- Change the output settings for printing.
- Replace your driver or use another method to get the right output.
- Output using a service when pre-separated output is critical (see the section "Using a Printing Service for Output" later in this chapter).
- Work in RGB and accept whatever separation the printer and driver give you.
- Use a combination of these options.

Changing Your Output Settings for Printing

Settings hidden within the interface of your printer driver (and perhaps within the program you are using to do the output) control how the printer handles color. These settings include the obvious ones, such as Convert CMYK Before Printing, as well as the type of option that vaguely mentions something about color management (or profiles). Other options may be more cleverly disguised—or there may be no color control options at all. Regretfully, there are few standards. Depending on how you use the image, you may need to locate these settings in more than one place.

If you look all through your printer dialog box options when you go to print and there are no color options, you will have to consider another solution. Don't give up until you get out the printer manual or check the online documentation of the driver interface and see which settings the driver has and what they affect. The documentation can point you in the direction of the options that you might need to experiment with.

There is no profile in the CMYK.pdf file, which means that the color should not be manipulated by your printer's color settings. However, some printers or drivers may either insist that you have a profile or assume a generic profile, and this can result in a conversion. Again, that will show up most obviously as a change in the black bar. Another option is to use a workaround, and/or replace your driver.

Replacing Your Driver

Printer manufacturers typically have a website for their products where you can download upgrades to system software, and sometimes hardware as well (firmware). New printer software from the website for your printer model can give you functionality that the manufacturer has added either to enhance its product or to address customer complaints. Many websites provide a means for you to offer feedback: don't pass up the opportunity to tell a manufacturer about any problems that you're experiencing.

Third-party drivers that can do what you need may be available. These will usually come at an additional expense. Using third-party drivers can require a lot of trial and error, and is probably impractical for the most part if you try fishing around at random for drivers not specifically made for your system.

One exception where you can find free third-party drivers is on the Adobe website. Adobe makes drivers that are pretty much universal and are intended to help create PDF files. Functionality on the website can help you convert printer files you create to PDF. There are also several ways to get Acrobat Distiller, which is sometimes bundled with other applications and packages. Distiller is a stand-alone converter for turning PostScript files to PDFs.

Creating PDFs to print from is often a good solution for varied application (you'll note that I used this approach for the test file). Using PDFs, you can actually get the near equivalent of PostScript output from non-PostScript printers (some vector qualities can be better imitated using a non-PostScript printer this way). All you have to do is use the driver option to Print to File. This will make a .prn (printer) or .ps (PostScript) file, depending on your settings and the driver used. This file can then be turned into a PDF using a utility (for example, Adobe Acrobat, Adobe's on-line service, third-party PDF creation utilities, or Adobe Distiller), and you can use that file to print. Of course, you can save directly to PDF, but the files created from Photoshop have a different formatting from distilled files and may produce different results.

Exploring other programs to print from can be another solution. For example, layout programs often offer capabilities that can help you get the output you want. For example, Quark, PageMaker, or InDesign all include program-specific options for output. Alternatively, you can convert files to other formats (for example, EPS, or Encapsulated PostScript). Another option may be getting plug-ins designed to control print output within these programs.

Another clever workaround is to print your CMYK process images using multiple passes on the printer by printing one color at a time (the same process that we outlined for making duotone prints in Chapter 2). Although this technique may improve the result, it will probably not work perfectly—only mimicking the desired result—if your driver is ignoring your separations. In other words, this only *masks* the problem rather than fixing it. If you can't control the settings, you still are not controlling the result.

Working in RGB

You may notice that the CMYK test gives you different results from what you get when the printer is using the information you send, but another question you need to answer is whether the results are good enough. In many cases, they might be, and if that's the case, you won't have to make and correct CMYK separations (if this device is your only output). There is nothing wrong with sending an RGB image to your printer to be separated to CMYK if the results are satisfactory. At other critical times (where you are making a specific separation, as I did to create the CMYK test), you may need to explore how you can affect CMYK output through creating and using your own separations.

Using a Combination of Solutions

It should be obvious at this point that not every image will warrant the same process to get the result you need. I might often use several different solutions in a single day, depending on what I need to accomplish. Being aware of the options is half the battle; the other half is realizing that using the right one at the right time saves work, time, frustration, and possibly money as well. Be sensible about your choices, honest in your image evaluations, and flexible enough to change the processes you use most of the time in order to get the right result in the end. The right result will vary, sometimes from image to image.

Selecting Printer Paper

Although there are other processes, you will most often be printing to paper when you print images. Color hits paper in one of four ways: ink, dye, toner, and photo/light process. The type of media you use (either at home or when sending images for processing) determines the way the prints are made, how long they last, and the quality of the result. Knowing the difference between the processes and how they work, as well as knowing the controls that you have to work with, can contribute to your success in output.

While CMYK inks are "standard," the ink's actual color and application can vary, both in a device-dependent and manufacturing sense. That is, one printer manufacturer may use a slightly different hue to its inks to allow for different handling, output, and results. The variation, of course, affects how the image should be separated for optimal results. This same type of variation may be found in pigment or dye, and between one device and the next. The variance can be a reason for deciding to enhance color workflow by embedding color profiles to help translate color for better results.

Paper quality can affect the result as well. The difference between printing the same image to a sheet of flimsy typing paper and to glossy photo paper on the same ink-jet will probably be dramatic, and in some cases it's the difference between a disaster and a decent print—using exactly the same output settings. Using quality paper and using consistent colors and brands can lend consistency to your results. Adjustments for paper on a specific device may require custom profiling if profiles will be used.

Light processes used in film recording and light-emitting diode (LED) print processing may not be as susceptible to change as other processes because the medium is light (which is highly efficient) applied to standard paper. While this advantage may make this type of processing seem like a good choice, limitations include the inability to produce in volume as well as expensive equipment and supplies.

TYPES OF PAPER

Most people tend not to run tissue paper through their printer in hopes of getting a good print. The same goes for toilet paper, paper towels, wax paper, litmus paper, tracing paper, shelving paper (aluminum foil, bubble wrap, plastic wrap), and so forth. What many people never consider is that different papers that look essentially the same have different qualities—and some of these qualities aren't a lot different from some of the sillier suggestions that you would quickly dismiss. Some papers can actually damage printers by melting in heat processes, or a failure to accept the ink or toner can stain, clog, or damage the inside of the printer (and ruin future prints).

Plain old typing paper may be too absorbent, acting more like a paper towel. It might have a texture or coating (for example, easy erase) that impedes ink absorption. It might not be white—or it might be over-whitened (blue). Typing paper isn't made to accept ink from a color ink-jet printer. Paper that works well in one printer (for example, with an ink that dries quickly) may not work as well on another printer (for example, with an ink that is slower to set). You may wind up with a mildly deceiving print to obtuse shifts in color and tone—or a disaster that ruins the printer and voids the warranty.

> While paper can make a difference in quality when you're using a laser printer, it is usually much less of an issue because absorption is not part of the equation.

Photo-quality paper costs more than other paper because it is made specifically to give you the best-quality images from your ink-jet. It is worth the extra money to use photo-quality paper when printing your final images. The paper you should use with your printer is the type recommended by the manufacturer, and sometimes no other flavor will do, depending on the type of printer and the ink application.

You don't have to use special photo-quality paper for every print, but you may need to change printer settings to adjust for the paper type. When you're using plain paper, it should be white. If not, the whites and lighter colors in your image will be influenced by the paper color (usually decreasing the dynamic range of the image). You will find that, even between brands of the fancier photo-quality paper, some brands will work better with your printer than others. This may have little or nothing to do with price.

TESTING PAPERS

If you are going to use a plain paper to proof images before printing on photo-quality paper, or if you will be using different quality papers, be sure to "waste" a few sheets testing your output. Read the manufacturer's recommended settings for photo-quality and plain paper, and run prints on each using the same image. Make a few prints with somewhat different settings; for example, if the manufacturer suggests settings for different grades of photo-quality paper, you might try more than one (especially if the paper you are using is not noted specifically by the manufacturer). Try several prints with the plain paper as well. As you make the prints, note the settings used for each by writing those settings directly on each print you make.

Compare the results of the photo-quality prints to the image on screen first. Choose the result that most closely resembles what you see on screen (it may not be the best print!). Make note of the settings from the print you selected. Next, compare the photo-quality print you selected with the prints made on plain paper side by side. Choose the best match from the plain paper prints to the photo-quality print. These settings will probably be different. Use the settings you determined for each paper type of paper, when making prints to that type of paper. Be sure to retest whenever you switch paper. If you like the quality prints you get with a certain brand of paper, stick with it unless there is a good reason to change (a good reason is not because another brand is slightly cheaper on sale). Using the same paper simplifies your process and guarantees the results you expect without having to retest.

> Photo-quality paper usually has a "right" and a "wrong" side for printing; both are often clearly marked. Check to see which way your sheets run before you print. If you aren't sure which side is up in the paper tray and can't find the answer in your manual (or printed right on the printer tray), put a mark on a piece of plain paper with your best guess and run it in a print as a test. If the printing comes out on the side you guessed, it should have the mark on the same side. Testing like this will save you from wasting more expensive paper.

Testing your paper and noting the settings can ensure that what you see on screen will most closely resemble (as close as it can) what you will finally get in print. Once you make this test, you won't have to make plain-paper proofs for every image you print. You will have essentially completed a form of color management. If you do not change the monitor settings or the paper you use, you'll get similar results to what you see on screen every time.

It is possible (but not necessary) to work with embedded profiles to attempt to improve your print results. The purpose of profiling is to modify your output to enhance your prints using specific paper/printer combinations.

Printing to the Edge

Printing to the edge of the paper, or *bleeding* images, is common in presswork, and it is easy to tell printing services to bleed images off a sheet. All they do is print on a larger sheet (using pages set up to print slightly larger than the final size), and cut off the excess. Printing to the edge at home is similar. There are two solutions to the problem, which are really the same thing: buy perforated paper that you print on and then tear away in the shape of the print, or just do it the old-fashioned way and crop the paper.

Though some printers offer "printing to the edge," it may not work as expected. The tiny gain may not be worth the potential drawbacks; even with the capability, you may still get the best results by cropping.

There should always be an edge area of the sheets you are printing that the printer will not print on—if you use the right paper settings. This is commonly called the "grip edge." It is often a quarter to a half an inch broad, and may vary from edge to edge depending on how paper was designed to go through your printer. You really don't want to print right to the edge of the paper—imagine what would happen if the printer did! You'd end up getting ink on things other than the paper, and it would be bound to muck up the printer or rollers eventually.

So, say you are doing a CD booklet and you want to make your image on the front and back go right to the edge of the booklet. You wouldn't start with paper that was exactly the right size and then use your printer to print the image exactly to the edge; you'd start with a larger sheet, print the cover, and then cut the paper down. Figure 7.2 shows a sample layout.

The image actually prints over the crop edge—say, by an eighth of an inch. This provides a margin of error for the cropping. If the cut doesn't fall precisely on the crop mark, the image should still come to the edge of the paper. In this way, your image comes to the edge even though it was not printed that way.

Figure 7.2

All areas outside the crop hash become waste.

Using a Printing Service for Output

There are two ways to look at printing services: (1) as an expensive place that can be intimidating and inconvenient, and that smells like chemicals, or (2) as a resource for equipment you don't want or can't afford to keep at home. (A third way might be indirectly, through a client that you provide materials to; many of the same concerns apply.) Services will have sophisticated printers that you would probably never buy for home use (or even small business use). Different services may have different equipment, and getting to know what is available—both locally in your area and through the Internet—may give you some good options for other means of output. Options can include color laser, LED, film recorders, offset printing, print-on-demand, and other processes (both high and low tech). For the most part, you'll know whether you need a special service.

If you've never sent a job to a printer or service bureau, you may be a little uncertain about the process the first time. Even if you have submitted jobs many times, you still may not have a set procedure. The following is meant to be a checklist, not only for sending out the files but for getting them in the proper order so you can easily prepare materials for the folks who will be doing the output. These suggestions may go further than your service may require. However, following these steps ensures that what you send produces what you expect. It also gives you some safeguards against incurring extra charges and can speed the project along to completion:

1. Decide on the service.

2. Establish a workflow.

3. Collect the digital files that you need.

4. Copy the collected files and proof.

5. Complete a submission form.

6. Copy the submission media as backup.

7. Submit the files, proofs, and submission form.

With these steps completed, you will have protected your hard work from loss and damage, saved yourself headaches and expense, and done your part to ensure the best results possible from your image-creation efforts.

Deciding on a Service

Always contact any service you will be using before submitting a project. Contact various services about output options and pricing. Describe the job and ask plenty of questions. Know (or find out) what you want to accomplish as a result. Ask about:

- Storage media

- Dot gain (if applicable)

- Total ink (if applicable)

- The pixels per inch (ppi) for the image at final size (or equivalent)

- File type and mode

If it has been a while since you last sent anything to the service, ask about updates on any new equipment they acquired or changes in procedure. Output methods change all the time, and it is not unlikely that the service may frequently update its equipment and/or procedures to keep up with advancements.

The color version of this image was created from the original tones, which were captured before color film was available. Color is reintroduced by combining RGB plates in Photoshop (as shown in Chapter 1).

Red

Green

Blue

Any original image can be separated into its color components (as we do in Chapter 2) by filtering for red, green, and blue light.

Red tone

Red

Green Tone

Green

Blue Tone

Blue

Color information is stored in images as grayscale representations of the red, green, and blue. These tones can be manipulated to adjust image color.

Red

Green

Blue

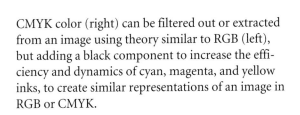

CMYK color (right) can be filtered out or extracted from an image using theory similar to RGB (left), but adding a black component to increase the efficiency and dynamics of cyan, magenta, and yellow inks, to create similar representations of an image in RGB or CMYK.

Cyan

Magenta

Yellow

Black

Cyan component

Photoshop CMYK

Magenta component

Photoshop's separation of an image to CMYK can be created automatically by Photoshop (left) or manually (right), as in the custom separations created in Chapter 2.

Yellow component

Black component

Cyan component

Magenta component

Yellow component

Custom-separated CMYK

Black component

Lilly with gray card—not adjusted

Lilly with gray card—adjusted

Adjusted and enhanced

Color correction with curves (Chapter 3) can be adjusted to gray targets (either placed in or assumed in the image) to adjust for color shifts more accurately.

Original

Luminosity

Color

Color can be separated from tone in an image. This lets you work on the color separately from the tone. A quick color and luminosity separation in layers (Chapter 2) can help you target corrections for better results.

Original color

Converted to grayscale

You can extract color from images to make black-and-white images (Chapter 2)…

Duotone Pantone 472 component

Duotone black component

Duotone result

…and you can convert tone to duotone with either Photoshop duotone mode or one of several manual conversions.

Wagontrain West

Pantone text adjustment

Pantone plate

Wagontrain West

Black text adjustment

Black plate

Control spot colors to limit printing inks, save money, and make the most out of the inks you use without adding extra colors.

Duotone with spot color text

Adding text by controlling the spot colors is something you can't do using Photoshop's standard Duotone mode, but you find out how in Chapter 2.

Make radical improvements by cleaning up your images (and subjects!) using cloning, healing, patching, and manual replacement (Chapter 3).

Original color

Desaturated background

Removing color can help you target areas by
using the absence to make a selection so that
you can isolate the image area…

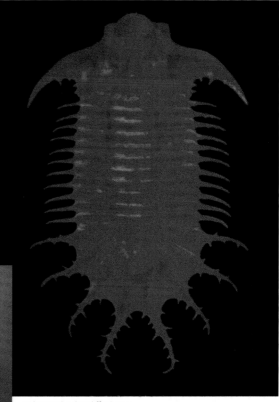

Enhanced color difference

Replaced background

…Once masking is enhanced and the object isolated, image objects and color can be replaced, adjusted, and rebuilt (Chapter 3).

Before

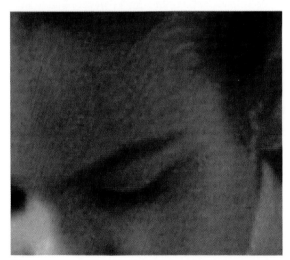

After

Treating color and tone separately and isolating image areas based on color, tone, and edges can help with reducing color noise…

Before

After

…or chromatic noise without losing or distorting details (Chapter 4).

Before

After

Use separations and targeting to find problems that can dull your images. Here, removing cyan from the area of the flames puts fire back in the color…

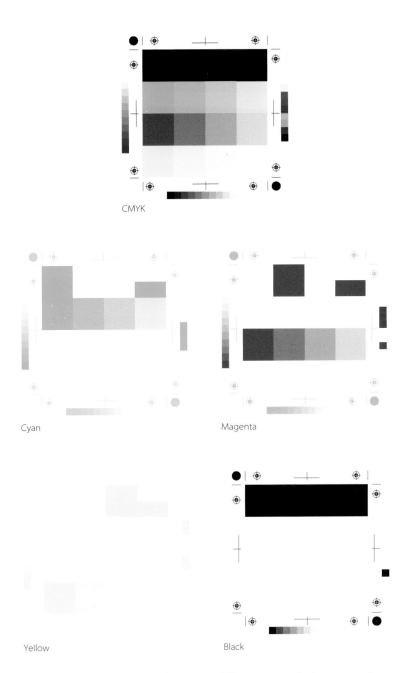

CMYK

Cyan

Magenta

Yellow

Black

…But the result can depend on your ability to control what your printer does and testing that it honors your color separations (as we do with this test pattern in Chapter 7).

Not adjusted

Subjects can fail to stand out from the background because of a lack of sharpness in the image, dot gain on the press, or too much in the image that has a similar focus (Chapter 4).

Adjusted

Sharpening, separating, and blurring components can help an object stand out without much change to the color scheme or the image.

Original

Shifted purple

Shifted blue

In all, the ability to target color and tone from a variety of different means gives you ultimate control not just over general color in an image, but also in specific image areas.

Pattern sample

Pattern fill

Pattern adjusted

Sometimes repairs to images require creating objects and replacements. This can start with creating a basic, repeating pattern to use as a fill and adjusting so that it feels more realistic (Chapter 5).

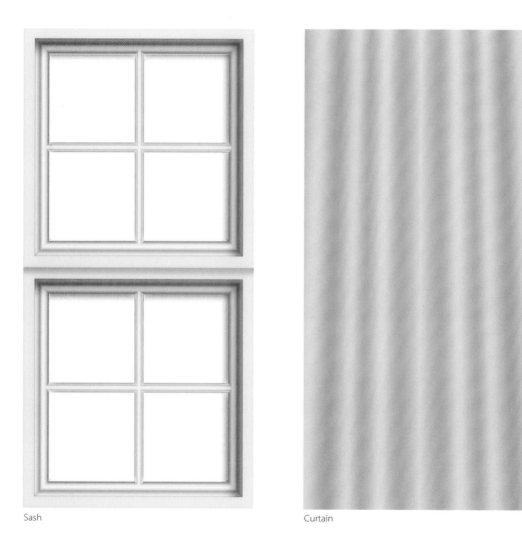

Sash

Curtain

We assembled this window entirely from scratch, using patterns and objects we created in Chapter 5.

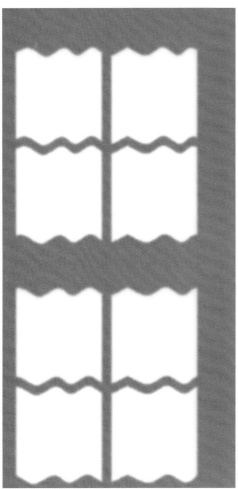

Shadow

Composite

Original image

This image has many smaller flaws in perspective that distort the window, shadow, and sidewalk…

Enhanced result

...The whole image can be rebuilt in pieces to re-create the image and effects at a different angle (Chapter 5).

Vectors can be used in print by saving shape layers with the image, allowing infinite resizing from a single file (Chapter 6).

Using pattern, created objects, and manipulation of color and tone, you can create a whole image, like this bouncing ball puzzle (Chapter 6).

Give the objects you create motion by assembling them in animations (Chapter 8).

Not every service will provide every type of output. It might be a good idea to have several that you use for different projects, or in unison (to compare prices and keep prices down, use the service that is either best or cheapest for what you get).

By the time you have hung up the phone, you should be fairly confident that you can get the service everything it needs so that you can get the job back the right way. If you need to call the service again to clarify, better to do that than to incur another delivery charge, delay the job further, or incur expenses when the job has to be rerun because of something you forgot to include (or included the wrong way).

Printers who don't know what they are doing, how to make things work, or how to satisfy your needs in creating the proper output will not perform well generally and may be showing where their lack of knowledge can impede your results. You need to know what you are doing, in order to avoid charges and delays, but printers need to know their stuff.

Establishing a Workflow

Get sample output from your original files to use for preliminary color matching and proofing. Make adjustments based on the results of the sample if necessary by employing color management, transfer functions (discussed later in this chapter), or other logical changes. Use steps to create a smart workflow (as suggested earlier in the chapter).

Collecting the Digital Files You Need

The files that you include should be all of those used in any layout program, in a file type the service can accept. A service may have different file type requirements for different processes. Making the effort to meet the service's requests will tend to get better results. Printing separations (during proofing) will serve as a check to be sure you have included the correct file type. Duplicate the files to a new folder or directory, including everything that you may need for the job:

- Layout files
- Font files
- Image files

Organize the files that you have collected using subdirectories as required and naming them appropriately.

Copying the Collected Files and Proof

Once you determine what the service needs, collect all files necessary for outputting the project. You may even choose to include a ReadMe file in the folder to help describe the contents. Copy only the files you need for output to the submission media. Test the output by printing proofs directly from the submission set:

- Change the targeting of the layout files. Doing this properly may require backing up and removing (or hiding) originals. You may want to move the output files to a second machine (if possible) for proper testing.
- Print a complete set of page proofs, showing everything that needs to be output.
- Print important color separations and/or separation samples.
- Check the proofs and correct any problems in the layout or image files.

> When you're proofing, print a complete set of document pages as well as separations for the color pages. The procedure will vary somewhat depending on the program you used for the layout, and perhaps the printer driver as well. The goal is to show the plate separations for the color files to be sure that the files separate properly. This can serve as a check to ensure that you assigned colors correctly and that the files are the proper type. For example, if you are using CMYK and you print the separations and get a C, M, Y, K, and Blue spot color plate, this tells you that you have assigned something an RGB blue or spot color in the layout or image files. If the spot color was not added intentionally, you have the opportunity to adjust it.

If you make any changes based on the output:

- Add missing files.
- Resave the corrected files.
- Update the proofed pages if changes have been made.

FONTS

Whenever you use fonts in a Photoshop image, it is recommended that you convert the fonts to outlines when finalizing images, or flatten the image entirely. Flattening the image will reduce the sharpness of the type. Changing the fonts to outline will retain vector sharpness (as long as you include vector information with saves) and won't leave behind potential problems with nested fonts. It's one less thing to worry about.

> To change a font to outlines, just activate the type layer that you want to convert and choose Layer → Type → Convert To Shape.

While it is suggested that you convert fonts, it isn't required. If you don't change fonts to outlines, be sure to collect all fonts for the output of the job. For example, if you use a Dingbat for a bullet, include that in the set of fonts. Be sure you have used quality fonts (such as PostScript) in your layout; some (usually free or inexpensive) fonts are not constructed properly and can fail to render partially, or at all. If your layout program has a collection routine for gathering files for output, it may do much of your work for you.

> Though a service may occasionally suggest that they can substitute their fonts for yours, be sure to include your fonts, and be aware that reflow or other problems with the fonts might be caused by the service being a little lax about using the ones you have supplied. In other words, don't always assume that the problems that arise are your fault—especially if you have provided what you should. Knowing how things work can help you save charges that may not be your fault.

SUBMITTING PDF FILES

You can use PDF files to collect all the images and fonts that you need for output into a single file. To generate the PDF from a layout file, you can use a PDF Writer printer driver, a printer driver of your choice, and Acrobat Distiller, Photoshop (if all the layout is there), or a third-party PDF-creation utility. Be sure to select an option that includes all embedded fonts and generate the file in the proper resolution for the output as suggested by your service. PDF files will generally be small (or smaller than your collection of layout files), will transfer easily, and are widely compatible. They can serve as on-screen proofing (what you see is what you print).

> For more information about PDF files, see the Adobe website (`http://www.adobe.com`).

Reputable services will be pretty flexible: If you have created file types that they don't use specifically, they should be able to give you a means of converting. If they don't accept files from a lesser-known layout program that you use, they should be able to accept a print file you have generated using a PostScript driver or a file you have converted to PDF.

Completing a Submission Form

Have the service fax or e-mail a copy of its project checklist or standard submission form. Fill out the form provided by the service, or write up information telling the service exactly what you want done. Include a listing of files being submitted, highlighting files to be printed, quantities, and other specific information (paper type, number of printed sides, ink colors, and so on). This will help protect you from getting the wrong thing (reflowed type, low-resolution imposition, etc.) and will help avoid mistakes on the service end (wrong number of copies, wrong paper, etc.)—either of which could lead to additional charges.

AVOIDING EXTRA CHARGES

A service may charge extra for a number of things either that you fail to do or that the service performed per your request. For example, if you say, "I need it this afternoon," your service may charge a rush fee. Certainly if it doesn't mention the fee you can probably negotiate it off the bill. However, if you are aware of the potential charge, you should probably ask up front if a charge will apply, and do what you can to avoid it.

Additional items that you can expect to be charged for at a service are broad (including pickup, paper, delivery, press time, binding, folding, storage, and any number of minor fixes). Be sure to go over the bill when you get it and question anything that you don't understand. If charges are applied that you don't think are your fault, let the service know. Your proofs (which the service should make all effort to match) are your verification of what the output should look like. If you are able to show a matching problem between the proofs you provided and the final result (for example, a text reflow), the service will not be able to make too much of a case in their favor.

Don't be afraid to negotiate charges with the service if there are extenuating circumstances, or if you get a lower price from another service for equivalent work. Often a service will meet costs to keep your business.

Finally, make an effort to work with your service. They are providing a needed service and are probably often trying their best. Mistakes will happen, probably just due to the sheer volume of work they have to do. Things will go wrong (both on your end and theirs); your efforts to remain amiable and work with the service (rather than being accusatory or stern) will tend to get you better, more consistent service with less effort.

Copying the Submission Media as a Backup

Never submit your only copy of anything to a service. Back up and archive development files. This is a good time to clear disk space. If you have a copy of exactly what you submitted, you never have to worry about the media you submit getting lost or damaged, and you save the time in collecting and reorganizing the files should that ever happen. Backing up at this point serves as insurance.

Another good option for moving files to the service is File Transfer Protocol (FTP). Many services will have an FTP area where you can upload files. Depending on the files' size, you may be able to submit files via e-mail. FTP is often the better choice; file compression and transport is a little less straightforward when done via e-mail, and more problems tend to occur. A good FTP utility will help you out by treating the FTP upload in the same way as moving files around on your hard drive.

Submitting the Files, Proofs, and Submission Form

Give the package you assembled to the service. You may want to ask for a final proof before going ahead with the whole job if a significant volume involved. It is far worse to find a printing mistake after 5,000 sheets are run than perhaps paying a little more as insurance for a test run. Final proofing may be done on a peripheral machine (laser-jet, IRIS, or other digital output) or right on the machine that you will be printing from (press proofs are a test run on the actual press—accurate and expensive). This will represent the final imposition of elements. You should take the final check very seriously, because you will generally sign off on the result—errors included. Once you have signed for the printer to print "as is," the printer is no longer responsible for anything but matching the proof. If you don't spot an error that was introduced, you will have to live with it, or redo the printing—which is an expensive and demoralizing experience.

What to Expect Back

All of your materials should be returned from the service along with the completed job. Materials should be delivered intact, and that is the responsibility of the service: if you get something on delivery that is damaged, it should be replaced. Anything mailed or sent should be packaged in some form of sturdy container, and perhaps wrapped with cellophane. Damage should never be caused by the packing or packaging. Any missing media should be replaced or deducted as cost. The results in your package should match the final proof, within reason. Whereas you have a case for a reprint when an image appears with different resolution or text reflow between the proof and final, you really can't dispute a slight color shift if the proof was done on a peripheral device. The latter may be an argument for considering more expensive press proofs, which are run on the final device.

Adjusting Color Settings

Adjusting your color settings should start with calibration of your monitor (see the calibration and color management section in the Appendix). Calibrating gives you a base to start from as you make other color decisions and provides a profile for Photoshop to base its screen previews on. What you do from that point on to manage your color workflow should focus on consciously improving your result. In other words, do not make a change from default settings unless you know exactly what the change will affect. Don't change color settings merely because someone else suggested them—unless your service is making the suggestion. All settings pose *options*—which may be available for one or more purposes. Improving your result may or may not include embedding profiles in your images as part of the workflow.

What you see on screen is greatly affected by your calibration and profiling, but you have more tools in your belt for customizing those views. Soft proofing (see the next section), when used correctly, can help you get the best preview using a given output device. Embedding profiles can help devices communicate effectively in color language. However, as you'll learn in the section "Embedding Profiles" later in this chapter, there are pros and cons to forming a dependence on profiles.

Soft Proofing: On-screen Previews

Soft proofing, or on-screen previews, is intended to help the user see what an image will look like without actually running a print or using inks and materials. Previews that show how an image will look on different monitors and platforms can be created as well. Soft proofs can be prepared easily in Photoshop, so long as you have set up your system correctly. This requires an accurate profile and a calibrated monitor (see the section "Monitor Calibration" in the Appendix). Follow these steps:

1. Open the image that you want to preview.

2. Choose View → Proof Colors (or press ⌘/Ctrl+Y).

That is all you have to do to get the preview, but more can be controlled behind the scenes. The Proof Setup dialog box allows you to specify a number of things about the output, enabling you to customize the views without altering the content of the image. The Proof Setup menu (see Figure 7.3) allows you to choose a view and offers a Custom option for customizing that view.

So, say you want to know what your current image will look like when printed or on a different monitor. You can do a soft proof to see the approximate result on screen by selecting the appropriate printer/monitor profile from the Profile drop-down list. Optimally, these profiles will be custom profiles created specifically for your monitor and the particular paper/ink combination you are using, though generic profiles can work. The selection of a profile tells Photoshop what the output device is and how the colors are handled, and the appearance of the image is changed to simulate the result. Do not mistake this for embedding a profile in the image.

Other settings on the preview screen that affects what you see on screen include Preserve Color Numbers, the Intent drop-down list, Use Black Point Compensation, and Simulate (Paper White and Ink Black). Selecting the Preserve Color Numbers check box allows the user to see how the result will look if no profile is embedded for output; it is available only if you're proofing to a like mode (RGB to RGB or CMYK to CMYK).

Intent (available when Preserve Color Numbers is not checked) represents different means of translating the preview from the current color space to the dynamic and color

---

Custom...

✓ Working CMYK
Working Cyan Plate
Working Magenta Plate
Working Yellow Plate
Working Black Plate
Working CMY Plates

Macintosh RGB
Windows RGB
Monitor RGB

Simulate Paper White
Simulate Ink Black

Figure 7.3

You can preview any image (in any mode) in CMYK spaces or other RGB, with or without measuring the effect of profiles, before making a conversion or final save for output.

range of the target. This adjustment simulates four different ways to expand or contract the dynamics of the current image during translation to the target space:

Perceptual Attempts to maintain a view based on the way we perceive color; actual color values may change.

Saturation Attempts to render saturated color in the new space, potentially at the expense of color accuracy.

Relative Colorimetric Attempts to preserve as much of the original color as possible, while adjusting color outside the target space to the closest possible match.

Absolute Colorimetric Does not attempt to preserve or adjust color that is out of range for the target color space.

Selecting the Black Point Compensation check box will adjust the black point in the image for the dynamic range of the target space. This option is available only when Absolute Colormetric is selected as the Intent option.

The Simulate check boxes will adjust the image to represent the white point of paper and the darkness of black ink. Because paper is not pure white and may be shaded, this can affect the color and brightness of the preview. Ink Black will adjust from the pure monitor black to whatever the black point of ink has been determined to be in the target space. This simulates any loss of intensity in the black ink.

These adjustments can be handy for making more reliable previews when you're checking soft proofs. The soft proofs can suggest potential changes you can make to improve the image. For example, if a soft proof seems flat, adjust the image with the proof preview on to see whether the image can be improved for the intended output. When you toggle off the soft proof, your image should appear enhanced. If not, soft proof–induced changes may not be best for the image and you may need to consider reverting. An example of a correction I made to a fire effect appears in the color section of this book. The soft proof suggested the dynamics of the flame flattened out a lot when the image was converted from RGB to CMYK. The conversion enhanced cyan presence in the yellow of the flame, dulling the color in the flame. Removing the cyan cast improved the result of the printed image.

To set up a reliable soft proof of a print image, the correct (or custom) profiles certainly help. Using a physical proof and adjusting the settings to mimic your actual result can help render more reliable soft proofs. Starting with a custom profile selected as the profile (or whatever profile is closest to one for your printer; generic printer, paper, and ink profiles may be available from manufacturer websites), checking Paper White and Black Point Compensation may help render a better preview. These previews may be more reliable if you have selected the color working space as a profile for the current image (choose Image → Mode → Assign Profile).

Do not just accept the settings as they are, and don't be afraid to make adjustments in the testing stage to determine the color settings that are best for your proofs—even if you have to use something other than the manufacturer profile. (Custom profiles, created specifically for your system, are typically the most accurate.)

Once you have a setting that works (for a particular printer/ink/paper combination), you can save the settings as a Proof Setup by clicking Save in the Proof Setup dialog box. Once the settings are saved, you can load them by choosing the setting by name from the Proof Setup menu (newly saved settings appear at the bottom of the list).

Embedding Profiles

Whether to embed profiles is often a subject of great debate and, more often, confusion (depending on the level of the user). Some people are convinced (and will try to convince you) that using profiles embedded with images is the only way to get a good result. This is not true. Others will say that not using profiles is the only way to get a good result. This is also not true. Either method can get good results. The key is testing, and knowing the limitations and benefits of each workflow.

Profiles help describe a theoretical color space (a mapping of color) or how a device will handle color. The goal is an accurate description of how bright and dark the device can print or display (the tonal range) and should include an accurate mapping of potential colors (the color space). This information can be used to help translate color information to attempt to get the most out of a given device, as well as to help with accurate rendering (matching what you see on screen to what you get in print—within reason—between devices). Having the right profile for a given device will not automatically improve your images, and embedding a profile in your image will not wave the magic wand of success. Profiles provide a concrete means of translation between devices. A good profile used incorrectly is no better than a bad profile used correctly. Either can lead to unexpected results at the very least, and terrible results at worst.

It is probably best to avoid embedding profiles until you can get decent results without them. This way, you are building on good results and have something to return to with confidence should the color-managed workflow fail you. Embedding profiles adds a layer of complexity that the user should understand before implementing it in a workflow. While accidents of all sorts can occur—and people with no knowledge of what a profile does can follow some instructions and get a decent result (or even fabulous ones)—the result may be wrongly attributed to embedding a profile (or failing to).

If you choose to embed profiles, make sure that all other steps in your workflow honor the profile. For example, if you embed a profile in an image that will be used in a layout program that you will convert to a PDF before sending it off to the printer, check that your settings for the layout program and PDF creation honor the profile. There is the possibility that settings in intermediate steps can drop or convert profiles and image information. You might check with the printer/service and/or print driver as well to see if they honor profiles. If the decision is made to embed profiles, be sure that the results you are getting can be attributed to your choice to embed. If not, what you thought was a result is really an accident, and can lead to surprises later on.

The proper use of profiles revolves around selecting the right profile for the right purpose, as well as knowing what it means to embed the profile. Proper calibration will help you along in "normalizing" your monitor and describing the measured behavior of your monitor (providing a customized device profile for your monitor). From that point, you have choices to make in selecting color settings to reflect how you prefer to handle color.

Again, a good starting point are the Adobe defaults. You should make assignments under Working Spaces in the Color Settings dialog box for RGB and CMYK. Adobe suggests considering Adobe RGB as your RGB space (because it is a larger space and perhaps a better choice for CMYK conversion), but there are valid reasons for using other spaces. For instance, sRGB is a generic RGB color space that should reflect everything you see on screen. You might also lean toward the monitor color space as being a more accurate description of the editing device. Whichever you choose, this will be the profile that should probably be embedded with your files as an accurate descriptor of the file content when saving as RGB—*if* you choose to embed.

Your CMYK profile should reflect your printer (or better, your specific device/ink/paper combination as a custom profile). This profile is the one you should probably embed—if you choose to embed profiles when saving files for output after CMYK conversion. Embedding at this point may be considered unnecessary, and perhaps even redundant, because the separation is made with consideration of the profile.

> By "larger" color space, we mean that the color mapping goes to a broader range of color. There is still the same, limited number of colors in a color space—no matter how large—depending on the bit depth. An 8-bit image will have 65,536 possible colors; they will just represent different mappings.

Again, the accuracy of profiles is critical for performance. If you are not sure of your profiles or how to deploy them, don't use them for output. Profiles should *not* be used as a substitute for good color correction or as a color-correcting device; far better means of employing color correction are available in the tools within Photoshop. Failing to apply profiles does not prevent you from making a conscious adjustment to the result you are getting on a specific printer, and possibly with better, or more intuitive, control by using transfer functions.

It is impossible to control how color is managed on the receiving end when you're transferring images to another party. The party may ignore profiles (which drops the profile and retains the color numbers of the image without change; this is sometimes the safest route), convert profiles (which converts the image to your chosen and familiar working color space; this should work for the best conversion of the image if color management is doing its job), or retain profiles (which respects the embedded profile and leaves you in the original color space with the option to convert later or retain the color space as delivered). Parties in the color chain need to be in synch for color management to work correctly.

Assigning a Profile

Depending on your setup and purpose, you may want to assign a color profile to an image. Assigning a profile will change the way that the image is previewed, that is, until the profile is changed, dropped, or converted. To assign a profile, use the Assign Profile function by choosing Image → Mode → Assign Profile. This allows you to select from a list of profiles currently available on your machine that are appropriate for the color mode of the image. Usually an assigned profile will reflect the editing space. Changing the profile by reassigning, deleting, or converting can drastically affect the appearance of the image, without changing the content as defined by the pixel values.

Converting a Profile

Converting from one profile to another is possible using the Convert To Profile command. This converts the image and changes the actual content of the image (its pixel values). To convert a profile, choose Image → Mode → Convert To Profile. Usually a conversion reflects what you might expect the output profile to be, though you might use this in conjunction with retained profiles to control conversions.

Color Management Policies

Depending on whether you work in a closed workflow (you always use one device to print to the same printer each time) or you have a more open workflow (you collect or distribute images to a number of sources by a number of paths), your color management policies will be different.

In a closed workflow, you should have a set method of handling profiles. That is, if you always get images from your scanner, you should always handle any profile in the same way, and choices in Color Management Policies should reflect this so that the process can be automated (without annoying pop-up screens). In this case, you would not select the Profile Mismatches and Missing Profile check boxes.

If you receive files from a number of sources in which the workflow may not always be the same, you will be more apt to make a choice depending on the source. This is where the Profile Mismatch and Missing Profile check boxes come in handy. You need to decide whether to accept or reject profiles in an intelligent manner. Being prompted when the image opens alerts you to the opportunity to make a correction, or at least lets you know a file has a profile—or one that doesn't match.

Color management policies will usually reflect your stand on profiles and what they mean. This is a personal philosophy—though it should be tested against real-world results. If you embed profiles, it is more likely that you should respect profiling by other users, and this will be encompassed and handled by selections in the Color Management Policies panel of the Color Management dialog box.

Transfer Functions

Transfer functions are one of the truly hidden features in Photoshop. You can find this option only on the Print With Preview dialog box (choose File → Print With Preview; Show More Options should be checked). Transfer functions are a means of making printer adjustments without affecting the image content and "numbers" in the file, somewhat like assigning a profile. In other words, you can control file output to your printer using adjustments that will not be retained with the image (as a profile can be). If your printer tends to print heavily in magenta, for example, you can use a Transfer Function to create a color curve set to reduce this known behavior and apply the curve set each time you go to print. In this way, you do not affect the previews for the image, you do not have to embed profiles to alter output results, and you can make adjustments for device and paper by simply loading a curve set.

The determination of your curves here is difficult. You can guess and go by eye, but that may be about as reliable as guessing what profile should have been assigned to an image by looking at the code (which is unlikely). It may be better to print your image, scan the print (on a calibrated scanner), and then use curves to correct the image to create a reliable print from a favored proofing device or other standard proof. Be sure to note the settings for the curves and convert them for the transfer curves manually (the dialog box will let you load a curve, but only if the All Same option is checked). Working with transfer functions can help make your home printer a more reliable proofing device. This can be effective if other measures have not provided the desired results.

Printers and Dots per Inch

What is possible in print is defined more by the printer than the image. It is necessary to target image resolution to the capabilities of the device being used for printing. Too little resolution can lead to blocky or blurry printing; too much resolution will result in overkill, increased processing time, and perhaps a failure to print (or additional charges if you send the job out). Maintaining resolution within the target range gives you efficient images that make the most of device resolution.

Image resolution should not be defined by a fixed number used for every image. For a lot of folks, 300 ppi seems to be the long-standing answer to any resolution questions. However, this resolution is too high for some lower-resolution applications and too low for some higher-end processes, such as film recorders.

To achieve the best quality output from the printer, you may have other opportunities to apply the information in your image, such as taking into account your handling of type and vector components. Flattening an image with vectors may not be the best means of handling the vector information in a PostScript environment, but can also be a necessary evil depending on the output and means of incorporating the image.

Differences in Printers and Resolutions

There are essentially three options for buying a printer for your home: photo-quality inkjet, laser, and dye sublimation printers. Inkjets are inexpensive, and not at all a bad choice for getting photo-quality results. They spray tiny dots of ink onto paper in an array (*stochastic* printing) to affect color, tone, and density. Laser printers tend to be more expensive and don't necessarily prove to deliver superior results for photo prints. These printers use toner rather than ink. The advantage of laser printers is that they print using halftone dots, and are more reliable proofing devices for genuine PostScript printing. Dye sublimation printers (similar to thermo autochrome and thermo wax) don't use halftone or stochastic dots like laser or inkjets, but dyes. The dyes are applied by melting or vaporizing color dye sheets so the colors permeate the paper in a continuous tone, more like applying pixels to the page than dots.

The printers handle the same image information in somewhat different ways. Understanding how the resolution works on the printer end can give you clues for preparing an image for output and explains why there is a difference in the result between different types of printers.

Each of these printers has something that represents the absolute resolution of the printer: the smallest representation the printer can make—the finest building block—of the printer's ability to represent an image. The size of this absolute element cannot be altered. In the case of dye sublimation printers, the intensity can differ in the application of the dye (for example, more heat, more color). In laser and ink-jet printing, the dots are either 100 percent on or 100 percent off. Ink or toner applied from the printer is applied with 100 percent of its intensity; it is turned on or off for specific dots to suggest tone. An ink-jet or laser printer printing 50 percent gray would turn on 50 percent of the printer dots in an area, each printing with 100 percent black ink. The dye sublimation printer would apply a continuous tone over the same area with a 50 percent intensity.

Printer elements make up the dpi (dots per inch) for the printer—the maximum resolution noted in the printer specs. The dpi for the printer is the number of these tiny elements that the printer can make in a one-inch increment. The maximum actual resolution of a printer is the *lower* of any two numbers reported by the manufacturer. A 1200×600 dpi rating is really 600 dpi with a half-step for the rows (the half-step allows the dots to overprint). The dpi for a specific printer is always the same; it is the way in which the elements are used that can change.

The pattern that printers use for applying printer elements accounts for the difference in the visible result. The elements used on a laser printer are used to form larger halftone dots in a fixed pattern and shape; elements on an ink-jet form an array or tonal density; elements on a dye sublimation printer are rendered as a solid tone with varying intensity. By definition, halftone screening uses dot shapes (diamonds, circle, and so on) of different sizes in halftone rows to create the tone and color in halftone screens; ink-jets print using randomized printer dots (not shaped dots in halftone rows) to create arrays of tone and color. Instead of being trapped into halftone dot shapes, stochastic (ink-jet) printing randomizes the use of printer dots so that the printing seems smoother and there is little possibility of creating moiré patterning and other potential halftone dot–related trouble. The result is that ink-jets can print with lower resolutions (dpi) than laser printers and appear to create finer results because of the randomized behavior of the dots. Dye sublimation may have larger individual elements, but the continuous nature of the tone can make the resulting prints seem finer than either of the others.

A rough approximation of how laser and ink-jet printing may compare over an area is shown in Figure 7.4.

We'll take a closer look at halftone printing to gain a better understanding of PostScript handling.

A Closer Look at Halftone Resolution

Halftones consist of two types of printer resolution simultaneously: printer dots (also known as printer elements and dpi) and halftone dots (known as screening frequency and lpi, or lines per inch). *Printer dots* are the smallest unit of ink that the printer can print (the "dot" in the dpi of the printer specifications). *Halftone dots* are the screening dot (the size of the halftone dot or "line" in the lpi). The halftone dot is made up of printer dots that create the halftone dot shape (see Figure 7.5).

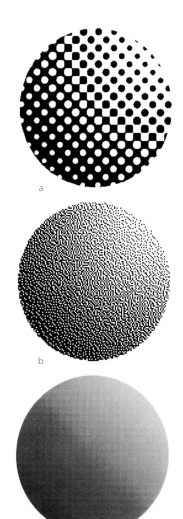

a

b

c

Figure 7.4

Magnified laser (a), ink-jet (b), and dye sublimation (c) representations of an area; printers capable of the same resolution were used. If you squint, the representations should appear to be approximately the same shade.

Figure 7.5

This shows a complete printer dot grid for a 16×16 halftone dot. The black printer dots are on; the gray printer dots are off. The halftone dot uses 60 percent of the printer dots in the grid, so it represents a 60 percent tone.

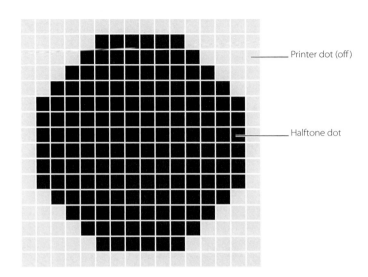

Printer dot (off)

Halftone dot

The halftone dots are made up of smaller printer dots, with a set number of printer dots assigned to each halftone dot, based on the halftone dot size. The printer dots are turned on or off in patterns on a PostScript printer to represent the shape of the halftone dots. Because of this, halftone dots, unlike printer dots, vary in size. The greater the number of tones, the larger the halftone dot size, and the more printer dots are turned on inside. For example, if a halftone dot has 256 printer dots (a 16×16 dot grid), a 50 percent gray will use half the printer dots (128) in the halftone grid.

During the process of describing the image to the printer, the shape, color, and tone of the image is converted into rows of halftone dots with the lpi and screening angles selected (if nothing is selected, the printer will have a default). These dots are arranged in screens for each ink color (like the squares of a window screen in a way) to minimize the visibility of the individual dots and maximize ink coverage on the page so that images appear as continuous tones to the naked eye. The printer is then told which printer dots to print and which to keep off in order to create the halftone pattern and represent the image.

You can set the size of the dot by choosing a line screen (lpi) in the printer settings when you're preparing to print. You can control the size and orientation of the halftone dots by choosing a halftone screen size (lpi) and screening angle. The lpi tells the printer how many halftone dots will be put down in an inch. The screening angle tells the printer how to offset the rows of halftone dots so they don't all land on one another and form less of an obvious patterning. We looked at this briefly when discussing duotone printing in Chapter 2. Knowing what the trade-offs are and how to optimize the use of the printer resolution can help you get the best printed result.

The more printer dots in a halftone dot (the lower the lpi), the more tones it can represent on the printer—and vice versa. But if more printer dots are used to make the halftone dot, the halftone dot gets larger because the printer dots are a fixed size. As you lower the lpi, the halftone dots become larger—the larger the dot, the easier it is to see and the more likely it becomes that the dots will cause dot patterning (moiré patterns). The trick of halftone printing is that halftone dots need to be large enough so that the printer can represent the image tone (by consisting of enough printer dots), but not so large that the halftone dots are easy to see.

Keeping the dots as small as possible while having enough printer dots to represent full image tone requires maintaining a delicate balance. Dot size should be as small as possible while representing the maximal number of tones. In other words, you want to increase the lpi as much as possible to make the halftone dots small, yet you want to keep the dots large enough that they can represent the tone stored in the image.

However, just as with other types of resolution, if you have more information in the halftone dots than you can really use, you just waste it. There is no need to make a halftone dot with more information than you can extract from the image source. So, there are better and worse ways to use up the printer resolution by selecting the right lpi. You have to balance the halftone screen frequency and the size of the dot to get the best result.

Screening can be optimized for printing images that you have created depending on the maximum resolution of the printer you are using. Say you have a printer that has a resolution of 600 dpi. This means that it can print 600 printer dots of information in a linear inch at maximum. At the same time, 8-bit color can store 256 different tones for each pixel color. To be maximally efficient, any halftone dot would have to be able to represent 256 possible variations to present the information correctly (or at least potentially).

A 16×16 element halftone dot can actually have 256 variations (16×16 = 256), and can therefore represent 256 shades of tone. A 20×20 element halftone dot could represent 400 shades of gray—but it would be 25 percent larger—and the source image would still provide only 256 potential variations. You would be printing halftone dots that could potentially represent a lot more information (156 percent) than you have in your image. A 10×10-element halftone dot will be smaller and not as easy to see, but it can have only 100 variations (10×10 = 100), and it will be less likely to show the full potential of your image. The 256 variations in a 16×16 dot allow you to fully represent all the 256 levels of tone possible with 8-bit color. This table shows the size of various halftone dots and the number of shades of gray they can represent:

Elements in Halftone	Shades of Gray
20×20	400
16×16	256
10×10	100
7×7	49
5×5	25
3×3	9

So if the printer has a 600-dpi resolution and you want to run a halftone dot with 256 potential tones, your lpi will have to be 38 (600/16 = 37.5). This is actually a low line-screen frequency and a rather large dot. If you step down to a lesser-size halftone dot with fewer elements—say a 10×10—you can have smaller halftone dots and a higher lpi frequency, and the printed result might actually end up looking better. A 10×10 halftone dot on a 600-dpi printer allows you to run a 60-lpi screen (600/10 = 60).

Regretfully, a halftone dot that can represent all 256 possibilities is not always the best bet with a lower-resolution printer. While a smaller number of elements per halftone dot means that fewer potential colors/tones can be accurately represented by a single halftone dot, this also means the transition between tones won't be smooth. When you step down from a 16×16-element halftone dot to a 10×10, you go from 256 levels of tone representation down to 100. If you decrease the number of elements more, the potential number of tones continues to lower. Each time you lower the number of tones you can create, you increase the potential for color and tonal banding. You have to decide which trade-off to make.

The intertwined concepts of tone, printer dots, and halftones may clarify why you get noticeably better results printing to an image setter (with 2540 dpi+) than you do with even good home laser printers. With 2540 printer dots at your disposal, you can run up to 158-line screen and still get 256 levels of gray. This is compared to the 38 lpi to get 256 levels of gray on a 600-dpi printer as discussed earlier. Running a higher lpi limits the gray levels in output. The only way to get the full gray-level depiction and shrink the screening dots is to have higher resolution in the printer (higher dpi). This is why printer dpi makes a difference in the image result. Printers with greater dpi (resolution) are able to show a greater number of tones using the same size halftone dot.

With the halftone rows defined by the line screen, all that is left to do is convert the image to dots that fit neatly in rows. If you've set up everything correctly, colors are separated into the CMYK components and converted to halftone dots. If only one color (usually black) is involved, screening is fairly simple. All that happens is that the screen is converted to rows of dots at a specific angle. Often this angle is 45° in an attempt to better fool the eye into seeing tone rather than rows of dots (but it can be another angle of your choice).

Color generation is a bit more complicated because the angles of screening for each color are offset so the result doesn't cause the inks to run in parallel. Default settings might be something like C 108°, M 162°, Y 90°, and K 45°. The colors in an area of the image are broken down into their CMYK components and then individually rendered into dot screens at the different angle settings. These are then placed over one another in print to create color and tone.

If you are printing with multiple passes, you may have to adjust screening manually.

Ink-jet and dye sublimation work in similar ways using different schemes of application to create arrays of color and tone that attempt to deceive the eye into seeing a continuous representation of an image. However, due to the nature of application and levels of control, neither ink-jets nor dye-sub printers can affect PostScript halftone results where elements are controlled by vectors.

Using Vectors in PostScript Printing

A most interesting thing about halftone dots and printer dots used in the PostScript environment is that they can be controlled by the presence of vectors. Clipping paths and layer clipping paths can be used to control halftone dots so that they are shaped by vector components. When halftone screening is mixed with vectors, the sharpest results for shapes and type (as printed letters) are possible.

Figure 7.6 shows an example of a shape done with four colors (CMYK) and how that would print using straight halftones or using vectors for the edge. See the example in this book's color section as well.

Vectors can effectively cut a halftone dot into parts, redefining the use of individual elements within the dot. The ability to use vectors to redefine the implementation of halftone dots in fractions affords a level of control that is not available with ink-jets and dye sublimation. Although you can mimic some PostScript results depending on how you handle files before printing (for example, converting clipping path information from files used in layout by printing as a PDF PostScript file to a non-PostScript printer rather than printing directly from a layout program), the sharp lines of type edges and vectors are available only in true PostScript environments.

Figure 7.6

The non-vector edge (a) is softer and far less defined than the vector edge shape (b).

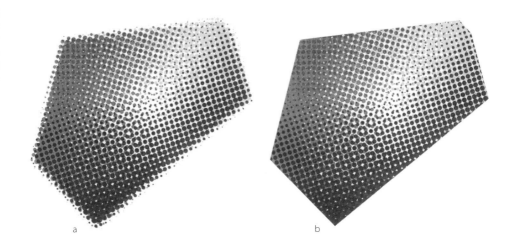

a   b

Custom Picture Packages

Picture Packages (File → Automate → Picture Package) are an easy way to fit multiple copies of an image (and more than one image) onto a printed sheet. Photoshop comes with a bunch of presets, but you aren't stuck with the presets that Adobe assigned. Say you want to print seven images on an 8.5×11 sheet, three images that are 4×5 and four smaller wallet shots at 2×2.5. To create the Picture Package using the measurements from the example, follow these simple steps:

1. Open Picture Package.

2. Click the Edit Layout button. This opens the Picture Package Edit Layout dialog box (Figure 7.7).

3. Enter the name you would like the layout to appear under in the Name text box. Name the layout (7): (3) 4×5, (4) 2×2.5.

4. Select the desired page size from the Page Size drop-down list. If the size does not already appear on the list, add it by choosing Custom and entering the numbers in the Height and Width text boxes, or simply enter the size and the Page Size text box entry will change to Custom automatically.

5. Click the Delete All button to clear the image boxes (called Image Zones).

6. Click the Add Zone button, and click the zone when it appears. Change the size and position to the following: Width 4in, Height 5in, X .25 in, Y .25 in.

7. Duplicate the zone created in step 6 and reposition it. To do this, Ctrl+click/right-click the zone, and then choose Duplicate from the pop-up menu. Change the position to X .25 in, Y 5.5 in.

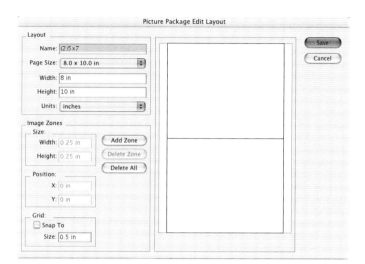

Figure 7.7

This handy dialog box allows you to configure a new layout and save it.

8. Duplicate the zone again, and change the position to X 4.25 in, Y .25 in.

9. Add a new zone that is 2×2.5 inches and position it at X 4.25 in and Y 5.5 in.

10. Duplicate the zone created in step 9 and change the position to X 4.25 in and Y 8 in.

11. Create another duplicate and change the position to X 6.25 in and Y 5.5 in.

12. Create another duplicate and change the position to X 6.25 in and Y 8 in.

13. Save the layout by clicking the Save button. You should store the layout in the Presets/Layouts folder. This returns you to the Picture Package dialog box.

To use your layout, you have to select a file or folder of files to convert to the package. You can change individual images in the layout by clicking them after setup. Each image in a folder will be incorporated into a new package; images will be created for each package at the full layout size. This may take a few moments. Images will be rotated automatically to take best advantage of the layout size. You can then save and/or print the packages.

While there may be many more nuances to explore in printing (for example, setting up printing for objects instead of paper), we have taken what might be a broad approach at implementing your images in print. We looked at the decisions that you need to make not only in selecting a printer for use, but also in making adjustments to images to get optimal results. This section could, of course, fill a book of its own. Please feel free to ask questions on the dedicated website and forum for this book (find links to the forum on these websites: http://photoshopx.com and http://photoshopcs.com).

Chapter 8

Creating Images for the Web with Photoshop and ImageReady

One of the most exciting hidden tools in all of Photoshop is ImageReady. It is a stand-alone program merged with the Photoshop package in version 5.5—mostly intended for helping Photoshop users process web images. Other processing potential and functions add to the power of Photoshop and open new avenues for exploration in image creation and development. Possibilities include creating animated images, Flash movies, and rollovers. These capabilities have been enhanced and the use of ImageReady has become more tightly integrated with Photoshop in the versions since it became part of the release.

This chapter will take a look at getting your images ready for displaying on a monitor in various forms, mostly using ImageReady. This includes creating images for the Web, as well as other applications used mainly for display for example, Microsoft PowerPoint presentations. This chapter covers the following topics:

ImageReady overview

Animated effects

Slicing and rollovers

Image maps

An Overview of ImageReady

ImageReady can be used in a fairly integrated form with Photoshop, though it is a separate application. You can get to ImageReady in one of two ways:

- Open the ImageReady application directly by using the program file located in the Photoshop program folder.

- Open the ImageReady application by swapping an image out to it using the Edit In ImageReady command—the ImageReady button at the bottom of the Photoshop toolbar (see Figure 8.1), or using the ⌘/Ctrl+Shift+M shortcut.

Figure 8.1

This button at the bottom of the Photoshop toolbar launches ImageReady and moves the currently active Photoshop image to Image-Ready for editing when clicked. The same action can be taken by pressing ⌘/Ctrl+Shift+M.

If you choose the second option, the image you are working on effectively moves from being within Photoshop to being within ImageReady. When in ImageReady, you have a similar way to port images back to Photoshop, using the button at the bottom of the ImageReady toolbar. The advantage of moving to ImageReady is you can use the tools and palettes specific to the application. Table 8.1 lists all the unique palettes. Additional differences exist in many areas, however. For example, there are no snapshots in the ImageReady History, and Layer Sets can be changed to layer Groups.

These differences are consistent with the fundamental focus of each of the programs. Photoshop, which is oriented toward image development and enhancing digital photos, shows alignment with creation and editing work-flow; ImageReady, intended to bear most of the bulk of web image development, includes more palettes geared to those modes. We will look at some of the more interesting strengths of ImageReady here, including animation, image maps, slices and rollovers, and web content.

Table 8.1

Palette Comparison Between ImageReady and Photoshop

PALETTES UNIQUE TO PHOTOSHOP	PALETTES UNIQUE TO IMAGEREADY	PALETTES IN COMMON	
Brushes	Animations	Actions*	Options*
Channels	Color Table	Character	Paragraph
File Browser	Image map	Color	Styles*
Histogram	Optimize	History*	Tools*
Navigator	Slice	Info*	
Paths	Table	Layer Comps	
Tool Presets	Web Content	Layers*	

These common palettes show differences between the two applications.

Creating Animated Effects

Animations are an exciting part of digital images because you set your images in motion. Creating animation effects can be as simple as looping two states of an image to create the appearance of a blinking light (see Figure 8.2, and the slightly more complicated version SOS.gif on this book's CD; open it in ImageReady or a browser window). On the other hand, creating even simple animation can be quite involved; you need to consider motion, multiple frames—perhaps multiple images and orchestration of objects in a way quite different than with still images. It can include all that while using all the skills you have developed for manipulating and creating image elements.

> Photoshop is well suited to creating individual frames, effects, and manipulations, but it has no feature for compiling and handling frames and exporting animation, as ImageReady does.

Animations work by displaying a series of stepped movements or other changes in a progressive order, much like frames in a movie or stills in a flipbook. The goal is to create an illusion of movement from static images. The frames are used to control the position of objects and object interaction (shading, reflection, shadows), and to make objects appear to move or change using position and timing. If it takes a cartoon character 3 seconds to walk across the screen at 16 frames per second (fps), 48 separate frames would have to be created, each representing a different state to complete the movement.

When creating animations with ImageReady, you must create a series of sequential movements that accomplish the goals you set for movement. You can have control over the timing of the frames, the series of events, and the speed of the movement. The trick is to plan a smooth motion, create the set of objects that you need to complete the movement, and effectively set up the individual frames. This can be an arduous task, especially if you are building something complicated. More frames makes for more work in development. The more frames, the larger the file, and the longer the animation will take to process (and, for web images, to download).

Figure 8.2

The difference between the initial image (a) and the next (b) makes the light appear to blink. Looping the behavior (c + d) can make the blinking appear to go on indefinitely.

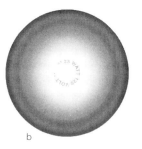

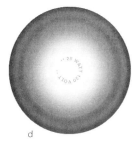

a　　　　　　　　b　　　　　　　　c　　　　　　　　d

Approaching the whole thing tactically is best. Most likely, a bit of work will be involved, so knowing what your goal is from the outset helps save steps. Planning the motion requires deciding how long you want the motion to last, how smooth you want it to be, and what distance or space you want the movement to cover, and allotting the movement to the available frames. At the same time, you want to retain an economy of frames to keep the file small and the process manageable. You'll begin with planning, move on to creating elements and objects, compile the objects into frames, and finally save and display the result. In the sections that follow, we'll look at the stages of planning and development, and then we'll put together an animation.

Planning an Animation

The following steps can help you plan your animation. This stage is useful in determining exactly how to proceed to get to where you want to go, rather than going at the whole thing haphazardly. Once you sit down and plan the movement, you'll have a far better handle on what you have to create, and how it will have to act in the image. Good planning results in economical work time and a simplified process.

1. Decide what you want your animation to look like. It might require making sketches or taking notes to define what you want the animation to do, how long the animation will last (in seconds), and the number of fps that you will use. Table 8.2 lists some frame rates and suggested use. The frame rate can vary for each movement—and even within movements.

> Although using a high number of fps makes the motion smoother, it also increases the file size. More than 32 fps is overkill—especially for the Web. Less than 16 fps might make the action a little blocky and rough, depending on the movement. However, most web applications of animation probably fall in the 8 fps to 12 fps category. Slower speeds not only make the animation chunky, but depending on the activity, they can make it hard to follow.

Table 8.2

Animation Frame Rates and Uses

FRAMES PER SECOND	FRAME SPEED IN SECONDS	USE
Less than 1		Pause in movement or action
1/sec	1 sec/frame	Stop action effects
2/sec	.5 sec/frame	Stop action effects
4/sec	.25 sec/frame	Very chunky web animation
8/sec	.125 sec/frame	Chunky web animation
12/sec	.0833 sec/frame	Minimum smooth web animation
16/sec	.0625 sec/frame	Quality web animation; TV cartoon frame rate
24/sec	.04 sec/frame	Top-quality TV/cinema cartoon animation
32/sec	.03 sec/frame	Maximum move export rate; TV/cinema film quality

2. Make a list of the parts of the scene that need to be animated. This list should be a breakdown of each animated part. Several behaviors in the planned scene may be happening at any one time; the goal here is to identify each individually so that you can tackle the creation of each part one at a time. These parts will be orchestrated later:

   - Make a close approximation of the distances and space that objects will cover. Knowing the distance will define the number of frames.

   - Note how the states, shapes, and/or color will change, and define those changes in finite measures and how many frames each change will cover.

   - If the behavior is repetitive, define the segments that repeat. You will be able to animate the smaller segments and duplicate them.

Planning is pretty much summed up in deciding how many frames each of the movements in the animation will require. This should not be an arbitrary selection, but should be based on the distance of the movement, how smooth you need it to be, and how long you have projected the movement will last, taking into account the finished file size. File size can be important because a web animation that results in a large finished file size may be impractical for loading into a webpage.

Creating the Animation Elements

Once you have planned the animation, you are ready to begin creating the movement. What follows is a rough outline for how to proceed. In some cases, you may want to invert steps or handle objects or movement somewhat differently. These steps may occur in ImageReady and/or Photoshop—and sometimes you may move back and forth between programs to take advantage of different strengths in each program. Later in the chapter, you'll work through a complete example of this process. Here are the basic steps:

1. Create the elements/objects for the image that you will animate. This may include:

   - Isolating image areas that already exist by moving them to their own layer and filling in the background

   - Creating new elements or introducing elements from other images

2. Create the changes in each object you are animating. Depending on the complexity of the scene you are animating, you might have to build many parts, and this can take quite a bit of time. For example, if you create an animation of a man going into a barbershop, you animate the man's right-left stride (which repeats as he walks) and the spinning barber pole, and create the background for the action. This process includes:

   - Duplicating each object once for each change in position and orientation that occurs during the movement/animation.

- Positioning the objects for the movement. This may require aligning and distributing layers.

- Adjusting the elements/objects for any changes in shape, tone, or color that occur in the series.

3. Compile image elements into logical groupings so that you can easily locate components. This might include grouping layers, creating layer sets, or just arranging layers in the stack. Using our barbershop example, you would need to coordinate and group the rotation of the spinning barber pole with the steps of the man as he walks. Grouping can be done in more than one way. For example, you might group the frames (pole and walking man pairs for each progression in the animation) as layer sets, or keep the movement for the barber pole in one set and the character walking in another set. Either method can work and is more a style consideration than a functional one. Constants in the foreground and background do not have to be duplicated for each frame, but should be positioned appropriately at the top (foreground) or bottom (background) of the layer stack.

4. Preview and tidy up the animation. Make alterations and adjustments to image elements and frames. If you want to preview your animation, you can create history states or layer comps. Layer comps (new in Photoshop CS) may be preferable to history states in that they will translate between Photoshop and ImageReady and can be saved with your images. To create layer comps:

   - Open the Layer Comps palette (Windows → Layer Comps).

   - Create a new layer comp by choosing New Layer Comp from the palette pop-up menu, or by clicking the Create New Layer Comp button at the bottom of the palette. (See the palette in Figure 8.3.) This opens the New Layer Comp dialog box.

   - Address the New Layer Comp dialog box.

   - Change the layer settings as desired.

   - Repeat layer comp creations for the subsequent frames.

Layer comps are a new feature shared by Photoshop and ImageReady. They allow you to store image states within the image—somewhat like image histories that can be saved. The difference is that layer comps can remember only layer visibility, layer position (of objects, not layer order), and layer appearance (styles). Remembering these settings is an option for *each comp*. Because of the options, layer comps are not like histories in that they can change. For example, if you change the content of a layer (say, you color-correct), the content will change in all comps where that layer is visible and there is no need to update the comps individually. The ability to save layer comps with images allows you to make some use of Photoshop's more comprehensive tools in setting up frames, a task that required mostly using ImageReady in past releases.

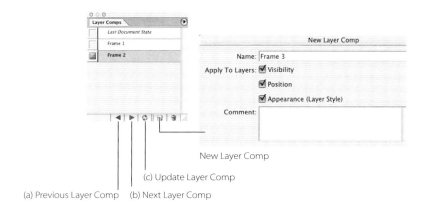

(c) Update Layer Comp

New Layer Comp

(a) Previous Layer Comp   (b) Next Layer Comp

Figure 8.3

Layer comps are much like snapshots, but scroll buttons (a + b) allow you to scroll through sequencing and an update button (c) allows you to change the comp contents, which can then be saved with your image.

5. Save the completed file in Photoshop native format. This will be your backup in case you need to come back and adjust elements in the animation.

Creating the Animation Frames

Up to this point, you may have done most or all of your work in Photoshop (though there may be reasons to jump to ImageReady in between, as we'll see). You should have created all the components you will need for the steps in your animation and then checked them. Now use the following steps to assemble the animation:

1. Create individual animation frames. To do this:

   • Move the image into ImageReady.

   • Open the Animation palette (see Figure 8.4).

Select Frame Delay Time

Frame Number   Frame Thumbnails

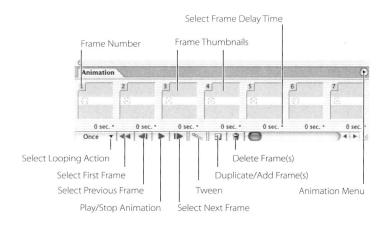

Select Looping Action

Select First Frame

Select Previous Frame

Play/Stop Animation

Tween

Select Next Frame

Delete Frame(s)

Duplicate/Add Frame(s)

Animation Menu

Figure 8.4

The Animation palette is Image-Ready's interface for controlling animation.

- Add frames to the animation. Click the Duplicate/Add Frames button to add frames one at a time. To add several frames, create one new frame, then click the Tween button. As you'll see later in the chapter, Tween allows you to add many frames at one time by calculating and drawing the intermediate stages of a movement.

- Adjust the frame content. Use layer comps if you created them by assigning the comps to each frame sequentially.

2. Preview the animation by clicking the Play button on the Animation palette.

3. Make adjustments to the frame views and settings as desired. This includes adding frames, changing timing, changing layer attributes, editing layer content directly, and setting the looping option.

4. Repeat steps 2 and 3 until you are satisfied with the animation.

You can control frame content over more than one frame at a time in a variety of ways using Unify functions (buttons on the Layers palette), selecting layers for change (on the Layers palette), selecting frames for change (on the Animation palette), and combinations of these. For example, if you left out the background that goes in all the frames, you'll want to turn it on. To do this, you can use the Unify Layer Visibility function: simply activate the Background in the Layers palette, click the Unify Layer Visibility button (see Figure 8.5), and turn on the layer's visibility. To do the same thing with frame selection, choose Select All Frames from the Animation palette pop-up menu and click the visibility for the Background layer in the Layers palette. If you wanted to affect every other frame, hold down the ⌘/Ctrl key and click every other frame, and then turn on the background (the Unify Layer Visibility for the Background layer should be off). Additional controls can be found on the Animation palette pop-up and the Layers palette pop-up.

It is beneficial to keep animation movements simple unless you are interested in spending a lot of time animating. The more frames you use and the more time you spend, the less likely the result will be a usable web animation.

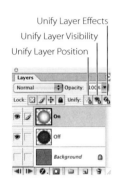

Figure 8.5

These buttons on the Layers palette in ImageReady can help you manage the content of frames by allowing you to unify position, visibility, and effects across frames.

Saving the Finalized Animation

After planning and executing development of the animation, all that is left to do is save it. The way you save will depend on the content and your intended use. You can save the image as a GIF or export as a Flash file (SWF). These files may be readily incorporated to webpages.

SUCCESSFUL ANIMATION HINTS

Following a few basic rules can streamline your animation work considerably:

- Treat all components as separate parts of the animation.

Animate smaller parts of larger moving objects first. Combine the smaller elements with the larger ones rather than re-creating them for each frame. For example, if you're animating a car moving, make the tire rotations for the wheels before adding motion to the car.

- Animate constants or repetitive actions before more complex behavior.

In our earlier example, the barber pole won't change so you can create the repeating set to duplicate. The character's gait might change to walk up steps or turn into the storefront; these changes might be constructed from the repeating behavior you establish in creating the character's regular steps.

- Stack completed frames in layers and layer sets.

Duplicate all the elements you need to complete a frame and compile them in sets, one set or layer per frame. If an element is in the background, leave it as the background and don't bother duplicating it. You can take care of that by displaying the right layers when creating the frames for the animation.

- Simplify, but don't oversimplify.

Simplify to keep animations easy to manage, but keep in mind that oversimplifying can make the effect fake or blocky and diminish the overall result. Even simple movements can be complex. For example, if you show a ball bouncing, you might add a little distortion to the ball in frames where the ball hits the ground. The ball's bounce deteriorates—that is, the height that the ball reaches decreases as it continues to bounce—so each successive impact is different, with less ball distortion and different shadow effects, as shown in frames 1 to 5.

Similarly, you should feel free to repeat frames and copy layers to your advantage, but don't get chintzy with creating new positions and frames as needed.

frame 1   frame 2   frame 3   frame 4   frame 5

Figure 8.6

These nine export options give you some flexibility in saving/exporting your image either as an animation or in single frames.

Another option for saves is to export the animation as a movie or other file. Choose Original Document from the File → Export menu. This will enable a number of different options, as shown in Figure 8.6.

If you choose QuickTime, a number of QuickTime Movie export options become available. These options allow various types of compression and finished quality (and affect the size of the export file accordingly). Photo-JPEG is the default (see Figure 8.7).

When choosing options for saving or exporting your animations, be aware that most options for compression come with a trade-off. For example, increasing JPEG compression introduces more JPEG artifacts, and reducing colors (for GIF) may create posterizing when the colors are remapped. That is, the more you compress, the further you reduce quality. In some instances, more compression is acceptable even if quality is reduced. The value of the trade-off is in reducing file size and reducing download time. The Photoshop and ImageReady Help files cover the particulars on these options. Search for Optimizing Images and Optimizing Animations in Windows → Help for more information.

While the options for saving are important to your result, many options exist for enhancing animation effects. One of the most powerful of these is tweening.

Automating Frame Creation Using Tween

The *Tween* function provides a means for automatically creating intermediate states between two frames of an animation. It can help speed the creation of an animation, fill in for missing frames, and smooth out rough spots.

Figure 8.7

Compression options on this menu affect how the QuickTime movie is exported.

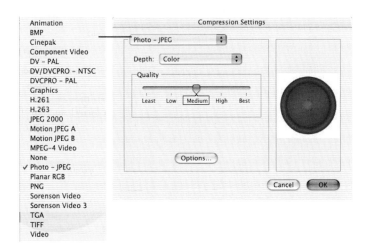

To use Tween, select the contiguous frames between which you want to create intermediate states. Next, click Tween on the Animation palette. The Tween dialog box shown in Figure 8.8 opens.

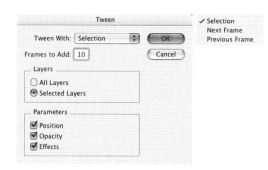

You can choose the target frames (Selection, Next Frame, or Previous Frame), and the number of states you want to create in between. The Tween palette offers Position, Opacity, and Effects options, allowing you specific control of the object qualities that are included in the tweening.

Tweening the position of objects creates intermediate positioning between layer elements rather than intermediate opacities. You tween the position when you want to create movement directly from and to specific states in the image. To do this, select or create frames where the positioning of a layer's content is different from the target. For example, starting with a layer to the left of the image in frame 1, duplicate the frame to create frame 2 and reposition the layer to the right. Applying Tween with the Position check box selected will create frames in equal, intermediate steps between the positions of the layer in the two frames (see Figure 8.9). This can simulate simple movements with minimal effort. Selecting more than two frames lets you orchestrate more complex movements, as long as keyframes are well planned.

Figure 8.8

This palette lets you control the blending that occurs between the states of the image you want tweened.

Figure 8.9

An animated movement between the initial position and end position in one move might be clunky. Adding frames between using Tween can smooth out the motion.

Acceleration, Deceleration, and Constant Speed

Animating elements requires attention to detail and an understanding of how motion is handled. For example, objects can accelerate, decelerate, move at constant speeds, turn, and so on. Acceleration is shown by increasing the distance an object moves between frames (at a set frame rate). This increased movement creates the appearance of enhanced speed, whereas decreasing movement simulates deceleration. (Figure 8.10 illustrates accelerating and decelerating movement.) The effects can be calculated using some plain old good sense, or math if you prefer.

Say you want to give a stationary car an acceleration of 6 pixels per frame over 1 second of movement using 12 frames per second. Over that acceleration period, the movements accelerate in each successive frame by 6, 12, 18, 24, 30, 36, 42, 48, 54, 60, 66, and 72 pixels, when the car reaches maximum speed. By the end of the 12th frame, the car will be moving 72 pixels per second faster than it was in the initial frame.

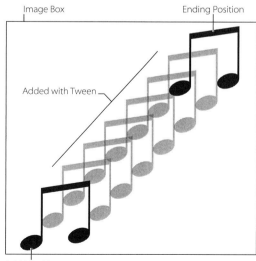

Image Box

Ending Position

Added with Tween

Initial Position

Figure 8.10

This figure shows an acceleration toward the right and a deceleration to the left. The tire steadily accelerates or decelerates by adding or subtracting additional pixels for every frame.

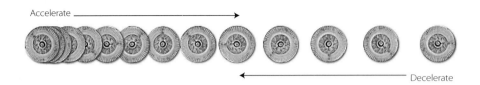

To maintain movement at that point, you keep the incremental movement at 72 pixels per frame. You might notice that this rate of speed becomes impractical on a standard monitor, and this requires a different plan if you are working at final size. Be sure the scale of your acceleration is appropriate to your image and planned result.

You can increase accuracy by applying an acceleration rate according to a bell curve if you have a target. That is, acceleration will gradually become 6 pixels per frame (say .5, 1.5, 3, 4.5, 5.5, and 6 rather than immediately hitting 6). However, as animation is recorded with some limitation (usually frame counts), this type of accuracy may not be possible. To make something move more quickly, ensure that the distance between the position of the object in the current frame (where it is) and the position of the object in the previous frame (where it was) is less than the distance to position it will be in in the next frame (where it is going to be), and vice versa for deceleration. If you want a constant speed, move in even increments.

To simplify spacing in accelerations, you can also use hidden layers to make the calculations for you. For example, say you want to accelerate the movement of an object without using math. Try the following example:

1. Create an image that is 1000×100 pixels in ImageReady.

2. Add a filled circle as a shape layer to the right of the image. To do this, choose the Ellipse tool and be sure the Create New Shape Layer option is selected on the Options bar.

3. Duplicate the object 30 times, putting the duplicate at the bottom of the stack each time, and then delete the original. You can do this by playing the Duplicate 30 Times action included on this book's CD.

4. Move the last duplicate to the left of the image.

5. Link all the layers, and select Edit → Distribute Linked Layers → Horizontal Center. The objects will evenly distribute across the image.

6. Starting at the top of the layer stack, start hiding layers: Activate the top layer, count one layer down, and shut the next layer off. Count one layer down and shut the next two off, count one layer down, and shut the next three off, and so forth. Keep shutting

off layers until you run out. Your Layers palette and image should look something like Figure 8.11.

7. Rotate the canvas 90° CCW (Counter Clockwise).

8. Open or view the Animations palette by choosing Window → Animation. A single frame (1) thumbnail will appear to the left of the palette. Duplicate that frame by clicking the Duplicates Current Frame button at the bottom of the palette. Now two frame thumbnails (1, 2) will appear on the palette.

9. Tween the frames, adding 6 frames between, and select the All Layers, Position, Opacity and Effects options.

10. In the first frame, shut off all but the top layer in the stack and the background (Option/Alt+click the top layer to turn on only the view for that layer, then click the view for the background). In the second frame, shut off all but the second visible layer from the top of the stack and the background. In the third frame, shut off all but the third visible layer from the top of the stack and the background, and so on.

11. Highlight frames 1 to 7, and duplicate them. To highlight the frames, click frame 7 once, then hold the Shift key and click frame 1. Click the Duplicates Current Frame button when the frames are highlighted to complete the duplication.

12. Highlight frames 8 to 14 (the duplicates; these should remain highlighted after the duplication in step 11) and drag them after frame 15; then choose Reverse Frames from the palette menu.

13. Click Play. Figure 8.12 illustrates the results.

Figure 8.11

By shutting off one additional layer in each step, you effectively create acceleration spacing without the math.

This series should animate the ball so that it appears to drop, pick up speed, strike the bottom, and bounce up again—repeating the movement indefinitely. This is actually a complicated movement of the object, showing acceleration in the fall, reverse of the motion, and deceleration toward the top of the bounce. These same techniques are used in developing more complicated animations.

A Complex Animation Example

As suggested in the steps earlier and with the bouncing ball, you will have simple and complex movements in your animations, yet some motions that seem simple are actually complex. For example, tire rotation is a simple form of a complex movement. Not only is the tire

Figure 8.12

This shows all the frames from the bounce you have created from left to right in a progression.

rotating, but it may be moving. Its rotation and movement are two distinct movements in the animation. You would probably want to animate the distinct movements separately.

The idea for this example is to build an animated banner for a fictitious site called Spoken Weal (intended pun of Spoke and Wheel), a company that is essentially an agency for interesting speakers (see Figure 8.13).

The goal of the animation is to enhance the logo—to give some movement to the tire and play with the presentation of the words by having them appear from behind the tire as it rolls into its familiar place in the logo. The entire action consists of fading in the spinning wheel, running the wheel across the logo to reveal the headline, and then fading in the tag line while the wheel continues to turn after it passes the headline. See the whole motion by opening Spoken-weal.gif (on this book's CD) in a web browser.

The process involves all the stages of developing an animation we've discussed so far, so let's take a moment to summarize them:

1. Plan the animation.

2. Create the animation objects and elements (in Photoshop):

    • Create the objects.

    • Create stepped changes.

    • Compile the elements into logical groups.

    • Preview and adjust as necessary.

    • Save the completed parts.

3. Create the frames (in ImageReady):

    • Create the animation frames.

    • Preview the animation in ImageReady.

    • Make adjustments as needed.

    • Repeat preview and make adjustments as necessary

4. Save your final animation.

Figure 8.13

A rather simple static logo for the company was developed using our earlier bike wheel illustration and a simple slogan.

Planning the Animation

We've described the general plan for the animation: The wheel will fade in while rotating, move across to reveal the headline, the tag line will fade in, and the tire will rotate and stop.

The goal is to get the whole motion accomplished in a total of 4 seconds or so, using about 20 fps for fairly smooth motion (and easier calculations than 16 or 24). That is about 80 frames we'll need to build, so there is quite a lot to do, though a lot of the movement will be the repeating rotation of the tire. The first 20 frames will cover a complete rotation of the wheel (18° turn per frame), and fade in (5 percent per frame). The second 20 frames will move the wheel across the screen, revealing the headline while the tire does a second complete rotation. The third set of 20 frames will fade in the tag line as the tire rotates again. The fourth set of 20 frames will continue the rotation of the tire for one more turn, and then the animation will stop, leaving the logo. The wheel will spin at a constant speed throughout.

An acceleration and deceleration of the tire during its movement is possible, and adds some complexity because it affects the rotation of the wheel: the faster it goes, the quicker the rotation. We'll discuss how to add this effect after looking at the simpler execution.

Creating the Objects

We need to create the objects first: the tire, words, and background. We already created the tire in a previous exercise; don't worry if you didn't save yours. If you open biketire-Comp.psd from this book's CD, you can use this as the tire. This version has been somewhat simplified to reduce the number of layers while retaining the vectors. Vectors will help to retain sharpness throughout. Although you can work in either Photoshop or ImageReady, we'll start in Photoshop to create and compile objects.

The size of the background has to be large enough to fit the tire and the words. You will want to figure the approximate size you need for the background and allow some additional room for adjustment and error. The tire is about 260 pixels, and already a bit smaller than the 288 pixels of the canvas. Because none of the motion will be vertical, this should be plenty of room. Horizontally, the words need to fit next to the tire. You want one complete rotation of the tire during its movement, so the words need to fit in that space. The tire will move about 800 pixels (the equation to figure that out is $2\pi r$, or pi times twice the radius). Most of the motion will be horizontal, so you'll want a little extra in that direction—you can always crop it down later. The background will have to be 10% more than the distance the tire will travel (800 pixels), and the width of the tire (about 300 pixels) so that everything will fit. That means the background should be about 1200 pixels wide. It may be easier

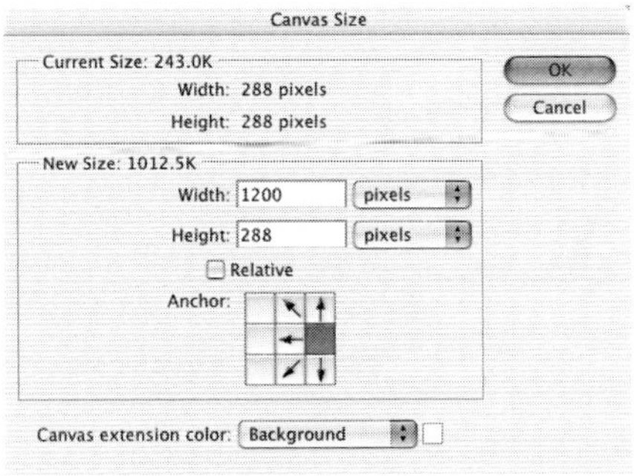

Figure 8.14

Expanding to the left will help create the positions of the final elements. It may be more natural to want to start at the first frame, but this will yield the full size of the image.

to create the background by expanding the canvas of biketire-comp.psd than bothering to create it separately. If you expand to the left (anchor the right box using the settings shown in the Canvas Size dialog box in Figure 8.14), you have room to place the words.

The words can be created in separate layers just above the background to fit the area available. It doesn't matter what font you use. Type the headline and tag on separate layers so you can more easily fit and adjust them as you need to. Keep these as type layers rather than rasterizing.

When you are done, the image should look like the logo shown earlier in Figure 8.13.

Creating Stepped Changes

The mechanics of the motion are taken care of almost entirely by creating the tire rotation. You can also create fade-in/fade-out at this point, but it is easier to control opacity changes at the end of the process, when everything is in place.

The wheel will be turned 20 steps in 18-degree rotations to complete a single revolution (20×18 degrees = 360 degrees). Once the rotation is created, the layer set that makes up the rotation can be duplicated several times, and then positioned, either as a group or distributed.

For this type of motion, the vectors are a distinct advantage because they won't need to resample as rastered components would. A raster version will change shape because the pixels will have to refit to the pixel grid at each step in the rotation. The job of rotating becomes more complex using a rastered object because subsequent rotations will add to distortion: if you just duplicate and rotate the rastered object, the tire might be very different by the time it completes a rotation. To minimize the distortion, duplicate the original each time and rotate in increasing increments (18°, 36°, 54°, etc.). With vectors you can duplicate, rotate 18°, copy the duplicate, and repeat because the vectors will not distort. Once the duplicates are created, you can merge the sets to simplify the image before moving on.

There is an action set on the CD called Tire Actions. If you load this into the Actions palette, you can use these actions to help you speed your way through the duplication. Use Duplicate Set to duplicate the Tire Set 20 times. Just activate Tire Set and click the Play button 20 times on the Action palette, or hold down ⌘/Ctrl and press F2 (wait for the action to complete between runs). The action will hide the current set, duplicate it, show the duplicate, and rotate 18°. Throw out the original Tire Set when you are done. You'll end up with a stack of layers from Tire Set copy to Tire Set copy 20, as shown in Figure 8.15.

Now that you have rotated the wheels, the vectors served most of their purpose. You can simplify the layer sets at this point. Merge the 20 tire copy sets one at a time starting from the top of the layer stack and working down. To merge, click each set in turn and press ⌘/Ctrl+E, or click each set and play the Merge Set action in the Tire Actions. The action helps control views for the sets without having to go through all the clicks. When you get to the bottom of the tire sets, all the tire layers will be rasterized.

As of this writing, some issues with ImageReady and sluggishness in handling large and complex files prevent you from taking full advantage of vectors and exporting large SWF files. These problems may not be fixed for this release of ImageReady.

You will need several copies of the completed tire rotation to make animating a little easier. It is best to duplicate as few times as you can to avoid bulking up the file. Link all the resulting tire layers and choose New Set From Linked from the Layers palette pop-up menu. Duplicate the resulting set two times. Name the new sets `Tire Start`, `Tire Move`, and `Tire End`. Your layers should look like Figure 8.16.

Figure 8.15

You end up with 20 copies of the original set. If you prefer another name for the sets, you can turn on the Select Layer Properties step in the action before you start running it.

Next you will create the movement. You'll use the components in the Tire Move set to position the steps in the tire rotation. Because you have 20 components and need to move about 800 pixels, offsetting each step by 40 pixels will place them in the right positions. Before you start moving, link all the layers in the set (Tire Set copy to Tire Set copy 20), turn on the views, and activate the top layer in the set. Turning on the view for all the layers helps you see if something isn't working quite right as you go. Offset all the layers by –40 pixels horizontally (using the Transform command), and then unlink the top layer that is still linked in the stack and do it again. To help you through these steps, use the Tire Offset action from this book's CD. It will move and unlink the layers as you go.

Shut off the view for the Tire Move layer set and activate the Tire Start set. Use Transform to offset the entire layer set 840 pixels to the left (choose Transform → Scale—any Transform option will do—then click the Relative Position button △ on the Options bar, and change the X value to –**840**). This will reposition the whole set to the starting position.

At this point, all the tires have been moved into position. While you could duplicate the Tire End set, that won't be necessary: You will be able to reuse the one set for both rotations at the end of the animation.

Figure 8.16

The duplicate sets will be moved into position to complete the movement and rotation of the tire

One element we did not yet create was something to hide the headline. We also have not sized the text, which will be easier now that the positions for the tires have been determined. To adjust the type and masking for the type, follow these steps:

1. Turn on the Tire End layer set and the headline layer (it should be named Spoken Weal) in the Layers palette. You should see the beginning and the end position of the tire.

2. Reposition the text for the headline so that it fits between the inside of the left tire and the outside of the right one (see Figure 8.17). Use the Scale function on the Transform menu (Edit → Transform → Scale).

3. Turn on the tag line view and fit the tag line below the headline, as it should look when all is complete. Again, using the Scale function on the Transform menu will probably be easiest. You may want to align the tag line with the beginning and end of the headline text.

4. Create a new shape layer to block the headline. This can be a simple rectangle over the words, or it can be a more complicated shape. For example, you can use a circle slightly larger than the wheel to mask the words under the wheel (rather than the shape of the words) and add a rectangle to the shape layer to block the rest of the headline, as Figure 8.18 shows.

With the mask in place, you have all the elements you need to finish up the animation. Now it is time to compile the elements into positions and frames.

Figure 8.17

Leave a little room in the image below the headline for the tag line. The latter does not have to fit inside the left wheel because it isn't revealed when the tire moves.

Figure 8.18

This mask (shown in white) can travel with the movement of the tire to unmask the headline as the parts of the image move.

Compiling the Elements into Logical Groups

You can move everything to ImageReady at this point and start creating the frames. However, you can also do most of the work in Photoshop (which is what we will do here). To begin, be sure the views are off for the Tire End and Tire Move sets and the Speaking For Your Entertainment layer, and on for the Background, Spoken Weal, and White Mask layers, and the Tire Start set (see Figure 8.19).

1. Expand the Tire Start set by clicking the arrow to the left of the set folder icon (see Figure 8.20).

2. Create a new layer comp by clicking the Create New Layer Comp button  on the Layer Comps palette. If the palette is not open, choose Layer Comp from the Window menu. When the dialog box is open, be sure the Visibility, Position, and Appearance options are checked. Name the comp `Frame1`.

3. Turn off all the layer views in the Tire Start layer set except for Tire Set copy.

4. Update the Layer Comp by clicking the Update Layer Comp button .

5. Repeat steps 2 to 4 a total of 19 times, increasing the frame number and Tire Set copy layer number in each repetition, until you have created 20 frames.

Figure 8.19

The views are on only for the elements that will play into the initial set of frames. These will change as you move through the frames.

Next you want to make frames from the tire movement from left to right. These frames should include revealing the headline.

1. Collapse the Tire Start layer set and shut off the layer set view. Turn on the Tire Move layer set and expand it. Be sure Tire Set copy is the only layer visible in the set.

2. Move the White Mask path 40 pixels to the right. If using Transform, you can use the Relative Position button on the Options bar and change the X value to **40**.

3. Create a new layer comp and call it `Frame21`. It will store the current values and positions.

4. Create a new layer comp and call it `Frame22`.

5. Adjust the views for the Tire Set copy layers (turn off the current layer and turn on the next Tire Set copy layer in the stack).

6. Move the White Mask 40 pixels to the right. You can do this using the Transform Again command (⌘/Ctrl+Shift+T).

7. Update the layer comp.

8. Repeat steps 4 to 7, increasing the frame number each time, until all the Tire Set layers have been used in the Tire Move layer set.

Figure 8.20

You will need to show all the layers in this set to manipulate views and links.

By the end of this set of steps, you should have 40 layer comps for the image. The tire should be almost off the headline (it will move one more time). In the following steps, you will fade in the tag line while keeping the tire spinning.

1. Collapse the Tire Move layer set and shut off the view; turn on the view for the Tire End layer set and expand it. Be sure the Tire Set copy layer is the only layer being viewed in the set.

2. Turn on the view for the tag line (Speaking For Your Entertainment) layer and change the Opacity setting to 5%.

3. Move the White Mask 40 pixels to the right (this will be the final time).

4. Create a new layer comp and call it Frame41.

5. Shut off the White Mask layer view.

6. Create a new layer comp and name it Frame42.

7. Turn off the view for the current layer in the Tire End layer set; turn on the view for the next layer up in the set.

8. Increase the Opacity setting for the tag line layer by 5%.

9. Update the layer comp.

10. Repeat steps 6 to 9, increasing the frame number each time, until all the Tire Set copy layers have been used.

By the time you are done with this sequence, you will have 60 layer comps titled Frame1 to Frame60. The logo will be in full view. To give the tire one last turn, let's wait till we get into ImageReady. Although we could do that here, we'll wait until the final adjustment stage so we can look at some other features.

Previewing and Adjusting

You can check your progress as you go along by clicking the layer comp named Frame1 and clicking the Apply Next Selected Layer Comp button ▶ . This changes the display to the stored value for the comp. Clicking the button again displays Frame2, and so on. Using the button, you can see the frames in order and check to be sure you have correctly completed the steps. If something needs to be changed, you can update the comp by changing the position or views for the layers to what they should be, and then clicking the Update Layer Comp button. Click the Apply Previous Selected Layer Comp button ◀ to play the series backward. All your frames should be in place before the next step, unless you want to use some features in ImageReady to help out—as we'll be doing with the final turn of the wheel, and one or two other adjustments.

Saving the Image

This is definitely a good time to save the image. To retain layer comps, you will want to save in the PSD format (other file types such as TIFF and PDF also support layer comps, but we will use native PSD). This allows you to close the image and open it in subsequent sessions while retaining the comps you have built.

Creating the Animation Frames

With the image saved, you are ready to move to ImageReady. To do this, click the Edit In ImageReady button at the bottom of the toolbox, press ⌘/Ctrl+Shift+M, or just open the file you have saved in ImageReady. Because of the size of the file, you will get a warning letting you know that the file is over 40 MB. It is fine to continue. While this may seem like a lot for a web image (and it is!), the final version of the file will be much smaller—for the Web you will need it to be a fraction of this size.

In ImageReady, be sure the Animation, Layer, and Layer Comp palettes are in view and follow these steps:

1. Change to the layer comp Frame1. To do this, highlight the Frame60 comp and click the Apply Next Layer Comp button. This will bring you from the state where you finished the last set of steps back to Frame1.

2. Create a new animation frame. To do this, click the Duplicate Current Frame button on the Animation palette.

3. Click the Apply Next Layer Comp button to change the content of the frame to the currently selected comp.

4. Repeat steps 2 to 3 until you have created the 60 frames for your animation.

You can also accomplish these steps by loading and playing the Create 60 Frames.isa action included on the CD. When you are done, you have completed the basic animation.

Previewing the Animation

Click Play on the Animation palette to preview the animation to this point. It will probably play back a bit less elegantly than in your browser. You can also preview the animation in your web browser by clicking the browser icon on the toolbar (for example, 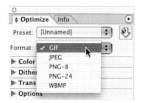 for Microsoft Internet Explorer, or ⬤ for Safari), or press ⌘+Option+P/Ctrl+Alt+P. Be sure you have set the Normal slice (the default) set to GIF in the Optimize palette, because GIF will support the animation (see Figure 8.21).

Figure 8.21

The Optimize palette lets you choose different image types for each slice in an image. Technically this allows you to mix JPEG, GIF, and PNG images in different slices when you choose Save Optimized or preview the result.

For more information on the Optimize palette, consult ImageReady's Help files by searching for Optimization.

Making Adjustments

You can now add in the additional frames for the extra rotation and fade-in at the start. The fade-in is a matter of adjusting the opacity for the layers in the first 20 frames. To adjust the fade-in:

1. Highlight the first 20 frames of the animation. By doing this, you will have to make the frame selection only once, rather than changing frames for each opacity change.

2. In the Layers palette, expand the Tire Start set. Unlink all the layers if they are linked. To do this, activate the Tire Set copy layer at the bottom of the set, and click-drag up the link boxes to remove the link icons.

3. Starting at the bottom of the set, activate the layer and change the Opacity setting to 5%. You can do this by quickly typing **05**.

4. Move to the next layer up in the layer stack (press Option/Alt+]), and type in the percentage of the previous layer plus 5. For the second layer, this would be 5 + 5, or 10. As you type in the values, watch the Opacity value on the Layers palette to be sure the change takes effect.

5. Repeat step 4 until you get to Tire Set copy 20.

These steps create a fade-in for the tire as it is turning in the opening sequence (the first 20 frames). To add the extra turn of the wheel, you can reuse frames 41–60. They already show your tire rotation and the tag line, so all you have to do is duplicate those frames and make the tag line 100 percent opaque. With a few smart moves, as shown in the next set of steps, you can do this far more quickly than creating the frames one at a time:

1. Highlight frames 41 to 60. To do this, click frame 41, then hold down the Shift key and click frame 60.

2. Drag one of the highlighted frames to the Duplicate button. This creates frames 61 to 80, which remain highlighted.

3. With frames 61–80 still highlighted, activate the tag line layer in the Layers palette, then type **100**. This will adjust the Opacity setting for the tag line layer to 100 across all the selected frames.

Make a final preview of the animation after your adjustment. You should see each step of the animation clearly, and it should not appear to hitch or jump. If it does, you may need to discover the reason for the anomaly. In the final build here, you may encounter a slight glitch in frame 61. Give that a good look by clicking frame 58 to activate it and use the Select Next Frame and Select Previous Frame buttons on the Animation palette to scroll through and compare frames 58 to 62.

Saving the Final Animation

At this point you will want to save the animation file again as a PSD, but probably with another name than the one you used for the earlier save. If you made any changes to the layer comps or layers themselves that are not reversible, you can go back to the original file that came from Photoshop either to rebuild or find replacement parts.

Next, save the animation in an animation-compatible file (Export SWF or GIF). You can then check your results in a browser to be sure you've got it right.

The size of the final image is perhaps far too large for a web animation. If web animation were the final target, you would probably want to reduce the file size by reducing the dimensions of the graphic and perhaps the number of frames as well. You can do this by just resizing the image, and perhaps deleting every other frame (as an example). Of course, the result would have been better if you had retained all the original vectors—though this would have added considerably to the complexity of development. The larger image may be more appropriate for a large-screen presentation. Although ImageReady is often thought of as Photoshop's web tool, it has far greater potential.

No matter what the use, by creating a series of controlled movements frame by frame, you develop the elements necessary to make objects appear to be animated. Careful attention to image placement, movement, and timing in frames per second can help you decide where image elements need to be placed and how to control them. Although Photoshop can help do the bulk of the work in the compilation and creation of frames, it cannot save a completed animation, and you will have to depend on ImageReady to compile and save the frames as a unit.

Slicing and Rollovers

Rollovers are often used as graphical buttons placed on a webpage that appear to change or animate depending on the behavior of the mouse or cursor on the viewed page. The term *rollover* comes from the idea that when you roll the mouse pointer over the image, it changes. The image can appear to highlight when the mouse pointer passes over a button area, and can have different actions for clicks and moving out of the rollover area. You can do even more than simple highlighting or basic button actions with rollovers, such as creating complex interactive events, which can be used for simple games or to control the display of page information.

Rollover behaviors are attached to slices, which are areas of the document that you section off using the Slice tool 🔪. Clicking and dragging this tool over the image will form a grid based on where you drag. This grid tells Photoshop or ImageReady to consider the image areas in the slice separately. When your image is exported as slices, the slice areas can be controlled individually (using different optimization settings for each slice and slice state). With a rollover, the behavior can affect the same slice or different (*remote*) slice areas in the same image.

Eight different potential actions exist for any rollover: Over, Down, Click, Selected, Out, Up, Custom, and None (see Table 8.3 for descriptions). When creating a rollover, you don't need to use all the states; in fact, you should use only those you need to create a specific behavior. Each slice can have its own states, and one slice can control the appearance of another (the remote slice).

Table 8.3

Rollover States and Associated Actions

STATE	DESCRIPTION
Normal	The initial rollover state found at the top of the Web Content palette. Normal refers to the state of the image when initially opened or at rest (when no other rollover action is currently active).
Over	The image appears in the browser when the mouse is hovering over the image area.
Down	The image appears in the browser when the mouse button is clicked and held down. This action is used in combination with Up as one of two components in an option, replacing Click. (See Up.)
Selected	The image appears in the browser when the mouse button is clicked. The state remains visible until another Selected state is activated.
Click	The image appears in the browser when the mouse button is clicked. This action is used instead of the Down and Up combination. The image remains visible until the mouse leaves the rollover area.
Out	The image appears in the browser when the mouse exits the image area.
Up	The image appears in the browser when the mouse button is released. This action is used in combination with Down as one of two components in an option, replacing Click. (See Down.)
Custom	For use with additional JavaScript.
None	Never appears. A placeholder; the state is retained with the image but no resulting image file is created based on the slices.

Some rollover behaviors are not compatible with one another. For example, it is best to use either the Down and Up combination or Click on a single slice, not all three together. Also, you would want to use Click or Selected, not both. When you create a slice behavior that conflicts, a warning icon ⚠ will appear in the Web Content palette next to the slice that has the incompatible behavior.

If you haven't created one before, rollovers are really pretty simple. Understanding the difference between the states and what they do is only slightly more complex. To explore some options, create a quick rollover in ImageReady using the following steps:

1. Open ImageReady and create an image that is 300×300 pixels.

2. Change the foreground color to red (RGB: 255, 0, 0) and make a new shape layer using a circle about 200×200 pixels.

3. Duplicate the layer created in step 2, and change the color to green (RGB: 0, 255, 0).

4. Open the Web Content palette, shown in Figure 8.22.

5. Create a new rollover state by selecting New Rollover State from the palette menu, or click the Create Rollover State button at the bottom of the palette. This will insert two items under the Slices area of the Web Content palette, the slice and the Over state for the slice (see Figure 8.23). Rename the slice `First Slice`.

6. Click the Over state in the palette to activate it, and shut off the view for the green layer in the Layers palette.

You have just created a very simple rollover. The image will change from a green circle to a red one when you roll your mouse over it in a browser. You can preview the result right in ImageReady by clicking the Preview Document button on the toolbar (or by pressing **Y** on the keyboard) and rolling your cursor over the image. Preview Document will allow you to preview the behaviors you have set up without leaving ImageReady or exporting. The other way to preview is to choose a browser preview (⌘+Option+P/ Ctrl+Alt+P). You have to roll the cursor out of the slice completely to return the spot to green.

To see just a little more of what rollovers can do, let's continue with the same example:

7. Exit the Preview (press **Y**) and click and drag the First Slice slice that you created in step 5 into the trash. This removes both the slice and rollover state from the Web Content palette.

8. Use the Slice tool (press **K**) , and click and drag outside the image on the upper left to cut a slice that covers the whole left of the image (0, 0 to 150, 300), as shown in Figure 8.24. Name the slice `Left`.

9. Create another slice on the right, from 300, 0 to 150, 300. It is probably easier to slice in this direction than trying to slice to the right from the center. Name the slice `Right`. Figure 8.25 shows how your Web Content palette should look now.

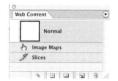

Figure 8.22

The Web Content palette

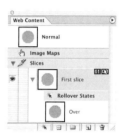

Figure 8.23

When you're creating a new state, ImageReady handles creating the slice and the new state automatically, using defaults.

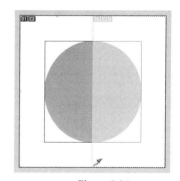

Figure 8.24

This slice sections the images into two equal halves.

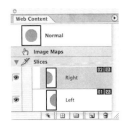

Figure 8.25

At this point you will have two slices in the Web Content palette under Slices, one named Right and the other Left.

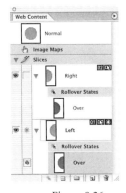

Figure 8.26

This layer stack shows what the layers will look like when you have completed the setup.

10. Create a new rollover state and then turn off the view for the green layer. This turns the spot red on screen and assigns an Over slice state to the current slice (this should be Right).

11. Activate the Left slice (the image will turn green), create a new rollover state, and again shut off the green layer in the Layers palette. Your layout stack should look like Figure 8.26.

When you check the preview and roll over the different slices, the right and left halves of the screen will act differently. When you roll over the right half, only the right will turn red; when you roll over the left half, only the left will turn red. You can also get the right and left to behave differently using remote slices. Remote slices allow you to control the behaviors of slices other than the current one.

12. Activate the Right slice in the Web Content palette, and add a new rollover state.

13. Duplicate the green layer and change the color to blue.

14. Click-drag the pickwhip from the Rollover palette 🔘 to the image, and let it go over the Left slice. A remote-control icon ✥ will appear in the slice display for the Left slice, and a control icon 🔁 appears in the Right slice.

When you preview the rollover now, the rollover will act as it did before: rolling over either side of the image will turn it red. However, clicking the right of the image turns the whole dot blue.

By controlling the views of the layers and creating and targeting rollover states, you can control the behavior of the image in myriad ways and easily create complex rollover behaviors. You can change the views of existing layers to create the view you want to use during a currently viewed state, or create new layers and include additional information that will become part of the slice state. You can also change the positioning of elements on the layers, and ImageReady will remember those changes between states. ImageReady will not allow you to add and remove layers from the stack for different states, nor will it track specific changes to the layer pixels. To add or eliminate a layer from a state, turn the view for the layer on or off: don't delete or add it separately. To change the content of a layer, duplicate it and change it in the new layer, and then shut that view off for states in which it is inappropriate.

Only one image state of each kind can exist in the rollover, and the fewer states you use, the better. Fewer states require less load time because they generate less code and fewer images. To edit image states, highlight the state you want to edit and change the layer views, state type, opacity, or position of elements on the layers. Adding, deleting, or editing layer content can affect other views. Each slice can have its own optimization settings, which gives you a high level of control over saved results and the size of files.

Not every rollover will require a click action. You can use rollovers creatively to change the page contents, and you can even develop simple puzzles and games by hiding and viewing areas of the screen, depending on where the visitor's cursor is. These more complicated rollovers are put together by using different slices to trigger different views.

Saving Rollovers

Once you have successfully created a rollover and have tested it, you will want to save it for use in your webpage. Images can be exported using Save Optimized As, and you can save the image as just the slices, or generate the JavaScript and HTML code needed to run the behaviors.

Before moving on, save your rollover in the PSD format. This will save all the slice, layer, and content behaviors. Next, save the sample you were working on to a new folder named Test Rollover. You should export a rollover to a separate folder so that you can quickly locate all the pieces. Having this separate folder can come in handy when you're putting together sites and pages; it is surely better than having to hunt down slices that you save to a busy folder, and may keep you from inadvertently overwriting other slices and behaviors. In this case, you want to choose options for export HTML And Images, and All Slices. As a result, you will export seven files: one HTML file and six images that will be stored in an Images folder inside the Test Rollover folder you created.

ImageReady generates a complete HTML document ready for loading into a browser. The exported HTML can be opened in a browser and viewed immediately without putting the contents into another page. Doing this enables you to preview the rollover and action(s) to ensure that everything is working the way you want it to before you either combine the code into an existing page or create more of a page around what you have exported. You can use what you exported as is, but if you plan to use the rollover in another page, you must move the code. You can simplify this task by paying attention to the remarks generated in the HTML file during the export. The markings are clear, and you don't have to know a thing about JavaScript to place the code correctly. You barely have to know a thing about HTML.

Moving the code is not that complicated. There are three pieces you need to identify so that you can copy and paste them from the HTML file that you just exported: the JavaScript, the `onload` statement, and the slices. You can edit in a text editor (such as Notepad or SimpleText) or text editing mode in a page design program (for example, Dreamweaver or GoLive). All three of the components have to be successfully placed in a new document or the rollover behavior won't work.

The JavaScript is contained in the source HTML between two tags:

```
<!-- ImageReady Preload Script ([file name]) -->
<!-- End Preload Script -->
```

These tags appear near the beginning of the document. All the text between is the JavaScript. You must copy this script as is and place it between the <head> tags of the target document. You can copy the script with or without the comment lines; keeping the comment lines may help you later if you need to reference the code.

The onload statement is a piece of code that tells the browser to load and store the rollover images. Without this code, the images have to load when a behavior occurs, and that will make the rollovers behave slowly. The whole statement looks like this:

```
onload="preloadImages();"
```

The statement should go in the <body> tag:

```
<body onload="preloadImages();">
```

The last part is the code for the image table. Tables are used to keep all the slices in the positions you sliced them in so they all show up in the right place; without tables, images would just load into the webpage and the positions wouldn't be controlled. The image table is found between two tags:

```
<!-- ImageReady Slices ([file name]) -->
<!-- End ImageReady Slices -->
```

Again, copy all the content between the tags to the new page. Place the table somewhere between the <body> tags. In the target, you need to paste the table into an area where it will fit. While this may sound obvious, that's not always the case. The image table can stand alone, or you can place it inside an existing table on the target page. If you do the latter, be sure the cell you place the table into is already large enough to hold it. If you paste a table into a cell that is too small, the result will probably change the alignment in the target table, and the result can ruin the look of the existing table.

After you move the code, you can save the target file; it is probably a good idea to use another name, or rename the original. When you have saved the file, you need to move or copy the images from where they were saved by ImageReady to a spot where the browser will know where to look for them. Files are saved with relative links: that is, depending on where the HTML file is, the browser will use the position of that file as a starting point and follow the links. It won't know to look for them in the Test Rollover/Images folder where they are stored. All you have to do is move or copy the files to an Images folder inside the folder where your new HTML file is stored.

If you move the code and something doesn't work, chances are you did something wrong during the copy and paste. As long as the original works, you can try again. Using copies of the files to copy from and paste to will ensure that you have originals to return to.

Using Image Maps

A second way to control behaviors is to use image maps. These are something like slices, but instead of cutting up the image to make them "behave," the image maps define areas to serve as hotspots in an image. A distinct difference between using slices for linking and using image maps is that an image map can be created in any shape and can very closely follow the contour of a button, whereas slices have to be rectangular. Image maps can be used in combination with rollovers to create more intricate rollovers behaviors based on both slices and the vector shapes.

There are two ways to create an image map: using the Image Map tool to draw the shape you want, and using the command Layer → New Layer Based Image Map Area to automate shape creation based on the content of specific layers.

The Image Map tool lets you draw shapes to create an image map manually. The tool comes in four variations: the Rectangle Image Map tool, the Circle Image Map tool, the Polygon Image Map tool, and the Image Map Select tool. To create an image map with the Image Map tool, simply click and drag for creating with the shapes, or draw a freehand shape point-to-point with the Polygon tool, similar to the way you would setting anchors for a path. In the Image Map palette, you can control the width, height, and position (x and y coordinates) of the rectangle, or the radius and position (x and y) of the circle.

The New Layer Based Image Map Area command uses the contents of an active layer to determine the image map shape for you. You can choose from three options: Rectangle, Circle, and Polygon. The Rectangle and Circle options draw those shapes for you to encompass the content of the layer. The Polygon option draws a custom shape, based on the content and the selected Quality setting on the Image Map palette. Quality represents how closely the map will follow the layer contents; the greater the number, the closer the shape matches the layer content. The shapes are described in the export HTML, using coordinates for the points that describe the shape. The Quality setting defaults to 80 and can be changed from 1 to 100. Any change to the layer content or the layer-based settings area of the Image Map palette will prompt ImageReady to redraw the related image map.

Changing the Quality option to 100% for the Image Map Area Polygon settings when using complex shapes can generate a lot of coordinates. Be careful to use lower settings when possible so that you don't increase your page loading time by including image maps that describe too much.

Once created, image maps can be assigned to control states and web links just like slices. The maps take precedence over slice-based behaviors, allowing you to use image maps inside a slice to define hot areas of a button.

There are two ways to save an image map: as a client-side or as a server-side image map. Client-side image maps work in the browser window, so they are faster than server-side image maps and are self-contained in the HTML that is generated. Server-side image maps don't work with images that have multiple slices, and you also have to manage the separate image map file. Although there may be specific reasons to use server-side image maps, you will generally use client-side image maps to simplify your process. You specify these options in the Output Settings dialog box.

You can add animation to rollover states to combine images into fluid action on screen. The key is not to go overboard so that you "cool" your website out of existence: if people have to wait a long time for large images and complicated coding to download, they may not hang around to test it out—and your hard work will come to nothing. Plan on keeping it as simple as possible to meet the cool factor and skip what you can.

Part V
Automating Photoshop and Expanding Horizons

One of the most powerful and diverse tools in Photoshop is the ability to customize the program with actions. Actions allow users to take control of the way they work and automate repetitive processes on single or multiple images (called *batch processing*) into a single click that kicks off the process. This can help you complete complex processes with accuracy, duplicate sets of steps on different images, or essentially extend your toolset by allowing you to customize behaviors to fit how you work. Actions can also be used as a teaching and learning tool to repeat processes on specific images in a demonstration.

Actions come in more than one form if you consider actions in Photoshop (.atn files), actions in ImageReady (.isa files), droplets, and the ability to script. At their best, actions recreate a series of events that apply to any image. In other cases, they can act as blueprints to map out processes that take many steps. Actions have been used throughout this book to demonstrate processes, to set up images, and to encourage you to develop an interest in this aspect of Photoshop for yourself. This part looks at what you can do with actions and how you can create and manage them.

Chapter 9 **Creating, Editing, and Using Actions**

Chapter 10 **Exploring Techniques Further**

Chapter 9

Creating, Editing, and Using Actions

In order to use actions, you have to know how to find them (open the Actions palette), load them (use the Load Actions command on the Actions palette pop-up menu), record them (click the Record button on the Actions palette), save them (choose Save Actions from the Actions palette pop-up menu), and play them back (click the Play button). That's about all you need to know; the rest of the basics can be found in the Photoshop help files. The goal here is not to rehash the manual, but to jump right in and create actions as examples that you will find useful as you work.

Actions can be complex, or very simple, sets of events. To get started working with actions, we'll record some functional examples of what they can do for you. The goal is to show you how actions can help you get more out of Photoshop and work more efficiently. We will look at actions in Photoshop first, and examine other options for recording actions in ImageReady and scripting later.

Creating simple actions using custom commands

Recording a more complex action: inserting a copyright

Recording workflow with actions

Prompting users during actions

Batching actions

Using actions in ImageReady

Scripting

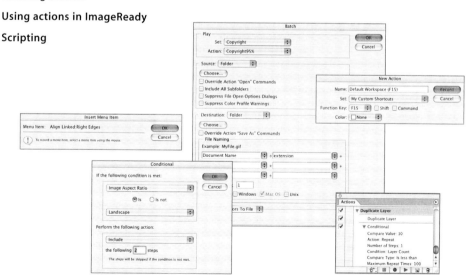

Creating a Simple Action: Custom Commands

Sometimes the simplest actions are the most useful—and the ones you use the most. Part of working with actions is recognizing patterns in the way you work, and then creating an action that simplifies the steps. You can then assign a keystroke to actions you create so that you won't have to hunt through the same menus in the same order, automating the selections and simplifying your process. In doing this, you can assign your own keystroke and personalizing your use of the program.

While you can reassign most keystrokes using the Keyboard Shortcuts editor (⌘+Option+Shift+K/Ctrl+Alt+Shift+K), you can also create useful actions to add shortcuts for custom items that are not set up for keystrokes. For example, you custom-create Tool Preferences or Workspaces that don't have keystrokes. If you record an action to call a specific, basic workspace, you can goof with, resize, and move your palettes all the time and then press a key to set everything on the screen back the way you want it whenever the placements seem to get out of hand. You can then get back to work concentrating on the image rather than the tools.

There are many other occasions where actions may provide an advantage. You might note that you use specific combinations of tools during color correction in the same order every time, or that you often combine a few simple functions. Once you see the patterns in how you work, you can take control and simplify—and speed along—your process.

Recording an action is as simple as clicking the Record button on the Actions palette (see Figure 9.1) and applying whatever it is you want to record. The steps you take will automatically be added to the action you are recording—with few exceptions—and you can then reuse the steps by initiating play of the action at any time.

Figure 9.1

The Actions palette is similar in both Photoshop and ImageReady. The Photoshop palette is shown here.

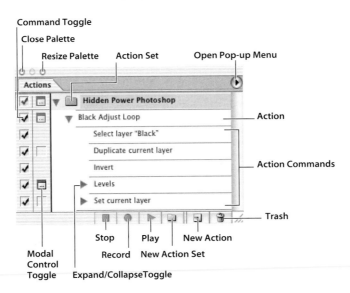

Your basic process for working with an action is as follows:

1. Plan your action.

2. Record the action.

3. Test the action, edit/adjust, and repeat steps 1 and 2 as necessary until the action works as planned.

4. Save the action.

5. Play the action as needed.

Figure 9.2

Make a habit of adding the function keys to action names when you assign them so that you can see what the shortcuts are without opening the Action Options dialog box.

Steps 1 through 3 are where all the work comes in. We'll focus on the basics of recording an action in the next section.

Planning, Recording, Testing, and Saving a Simple Action

The best way to get acquainted with actions is to jump right in and create one. Say you want to set up an action so you can press a key and rearrange all the palettes on your screen. This type of action can be helpful in restoring order to your workspace quickly. Use the following steps to create a workspace and assign a keystroke to the action so you can recall it whenever you want:

1. Set up your palettes in the way you want them to appear when you usually work in Photoshop—in other words, a default setup that you prefer. This need not include the Actions palette.

2. Choose Window → Workspace → Save Workspace. Name the workspace `Default`.

3. Open the Actions palette if it is not already open.

4. Create a new action set by clicking the Create New Set button ⬛ at the bottom of the Actions palette. Name the set `My Custom Shortcuts`.

5. Begin recording by clicking the Create New Action button ⬛ at the bottom of the Actions palette. Name the action `Default Workspace`. Choose a function key from the drop-down list, as shown in Figure 9.2, and assign the Shift and/or Command/Ctrl keys by clicking the appropriate check box.

6. Choose Window → Workspace → Default.

7. Stop the recording by clicking the Stop button ⬛ at the bottom of the Actions palette. Your action set should look like the one shown in Figure 9.3.

Figure 9.3

The single step Select Workspace "Default" is stored in your Default Workspace action in the My Custom Shortcuts set.

Now that your action is recorded and assigned to a keystroke, you can run the action by simply pressing the function key. To test it out, move a palette and press the function key now. The palettes should rearrange to the way they were when you set up the Default workspace. You may want to set up a few workspaces in this way so that you can switch quickly to and from preferred setups for different modes of work. You can assign four setups to the same function key by using Shift, ⌘/Ctrl, and Shift+⌘/Ctrl as combinations with the same function key.

At this point you have created and tested the action. Although it is in the Actions palette, you still have to save it. If you don't save the action, it is possible to lose it—and if you do, you will have to re-record it. If you save the action, it will be stored as a file that you can transfer to other machines or reload as necessary. To save, just highlight the action set name (My Custom Shortcuts, in this case) and choose Save Actions from the Actions palette pop-up menu. You will be prompted to pick a place to save the file. A good place to store actions is in the Presets ➔ Photoshop Actions folder in the Photoshop program folder.

> When you load actions with shortcuts that are already in use, Photoshop will strip the short-cut keys from the action you are loading without letting you know. You will have to assign new keys if they are removed, and possibly rename the action—if you store the function key in the action name.

The action you just recorded is the simplest of actions: playing the action results in running a single step. Actions can include many steps and can be very complex—pretty much without limitation. You can follow these same basic steps to record more complex actions—though you may need to spend more time getting a complex action to behave as you expect. There are different ways to record steps, various controls for dialog views, and ways to make actions more compatible with different image types. Being familiar with the options can help you solve problems during recording and lets you make adjustments more quickly during editing.

Recording a More Complex Action: Inserting a Copyright

If you have followed through to this point in the book and run any actions that were provided, you have seen some fairly complex actions at work. The action that splits CMYK in layers, for example, runs seven subactions with a total of more than 150 steps, each sub-action is a separate action that runs multiple-step actions that were recorded separately. Actions of this type can take hours to conceptualize and build, often with a lot of trial and error. Working with more complex actions requires planning, testing, and editing to be sure you are getting the result you want—one that is flexible enough to run on many images. Complex actions also require more postproduction time for adding prompts or stops to be sure that the process makes sense to you when you come back to use it months later, or when you pass it on to someone else to use.

Complex actions sometimes have many steps, and you may not be 100 percent sure where you are going; you might know *what* you want to do and not *how* you want to do it. If that is the case, it may be best just to turn on the record mode, do whatever it is you think you need to do to record the action, and then go back and edit the action later. During editing you can clear out the steps you don't need to take (or made in error).

To start off working on something more complex, let's tackle creating an action for dropping your personal copyright into an image. The plan is to put the copyright into the current image in the lower right, 5 percent in from the right and 5 percent up from the bottom. For the default we'll just use 12-point white type and some simple text: Copyright©[year] [name of copyright holder]. It would be good if the action allowed the person running the action to change the color, text, and sizing and also prompted for those changes. We'll add these steps to the action during editing.

This plan may seem deceivingly simple. All you have to do is drop in some set type and align it to a specific area in the image. It would be simple if all the images you have are exactly the same size because the type would go in the same spot every time: You'd just have to record the insertion point of the type. The difficulty here is that the type has to be inserted relative to the size of the image, and that is a bit trickier. You don't have a means of telling Photoshop to move your type layer so that the right of the type ends up 95 percent of the way across and down the image.

While there are other ways to solve this problem, what we'll do here is use Align. You'll be able to use the Align functions to adjust the position of the type—by temporarily shrinking the canvas to 95 percent to give us a target for alignment:

1. Open a sample image that you will use to add the copyright.

2. Create a new action set and call it **Copyright**.

3. Begin recording by creating a new action called **Copyright 95%**.

4. Choose the Text tool and enter the copyright text: **Copyright©[year] [name]**.

> To enter the copyright symbol on a PC, hold down the Alt key and type **0169**. On a Mac, hold down the Option key and press G.

5. Activate the Background layer.

6. Duplicate the background layer and name it **Source**. This layer will be used to restore image size.

7. Activate the Background layer.

8. Choose Canvas Size. In the resulting dialog box, change the Width and Height settings to 95% and anchor the upper left of the image (see Figure 9.4).

9. Link the Background layer to the Copyright layer.

10. Choose the Move tool and align the linked layers to the right edges by clicking the alignment button on the Options bar.

11. Align the linked layers on the bottom edges by clicking the alignment button on the Options bar.

12. Choose Image → Reveal All.

13. Delete the Background layer.

14. Change the current layer to the Background by choosing Layer → Background From Layer.

15. Stop recording.

By cutting down the size of the background to 95 percent, you can align the type to the new size of the background and accurately place it 5 percent in from the bottom and right of the image—no matter what the size of the image. The duplicate of the background lets you easily resize the image back to the original shape.

Try playing back the action you just recorded. You'll note that it fails. In looking over the action, a few things should be immediately apparent: The alignments did not record as part of the action because of the way they were executed during the recording. Because the steps weren't recorded, the type won't move when you play the action back. This is a major problem, and it is the type of thing you will need to be able to resolve when recording actions. In addition, the action includes no prompting as we'd originally designed, since we did not try to add the prompts during recording. To correct these things, you will need to edit the action, which we'll look at in the next section.

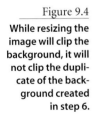

Figure 9.4

While resizing the image will clip the background, it will not clip the duplicate of the background created in step 6.

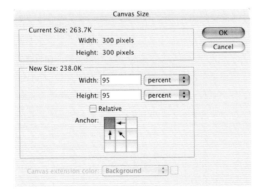

INSERT FUNCTIONS

Insert Menu Item The Insert Menu Item function lets you insert functions into an action by selecting them from menus. This comes in handy when you need to have some function in an action that won't otherwise record, or when you want to launch a dialog box without prerecording settings.

Insert Stop You can add prompts and commentary using stops. Stops can prompt user action; for example, they can let users know what to do in the next dialog box that appears. Other uses include archiving notes about using the action and other comments.

Insert Path Insert Path gives the user an option for pasting in paths. Used creatively, this option lets you make changes based on paths. After a path is created, it can be stroked by recording a Stroke Path command, possibly to play back freehand movements with various painting or toning tools.

Paths can be created in a variety of ways, such as by converting selections or type. After a path is created, the Insert Path command becomes available on the Actions palette pop-up menu. To manipulate several paths in the same action, it may be necessary to record Save Path commands to save the paths separately by name.

When working with paths or freehand strokes, change the Ruler units to Percent. This will scale paths and points relative to the size of the image.

Editing the Action

To adjust this action, we will mostly be looking to insert items to fill in what's missing. There are two ways you can insert steps: temporarily turning on recording, or using the Insert Menu Item, Insert Stop, and Insert Path functions found on the Actions palette pop-up menu. Just clicking the Record button as we did to record the original steps in the example allows you to add more steps at the insertion point. The downside to this method of editing is exactly the same as making a recording: You can get stuck with settings that you choose at the time of the recording, and some items will not be recorded.

Insertions done using the Insert functions are a little different than just recording:

- The action does not have to be in record mode for the steps to be added.

- Some steps can be inserted with these commands that cannot otherwise be recorded.

- Inserted steps will not record specific dialog settings for the functions that they call.

Insertions are all done in basically the same way:

1. Highlight the action and action step that you want the insert to follow.

2. Turn on recording or select the insert function you want to use from the Actions palette pop-up menu.

3. Complete the insertion by running through the additional steps you want to record, by selecting the menu item or path, or by entering text as desired for the stop.

A good practice in editing is to duplicate the original action so that you can go back to it if you have to—just like you should do with images rather than working on an original. This approach lets you keep the original recording in case you have to refer to it or start over. Duplicate the action by dragging it to the Duplicate/New Action button on the Actions palette. Photoshop will rename the action by adding *copy* to the name. Then you just work on the copy.

You might also want to get into the habit of using stops for notation so you know which segments you edited and where you added steps. This type of notation helps you keep track of your editing changes. It is best for when you are changing an approach to a longer segment of events, but we'll use it here so that you can see how it works. When doing this it may be best to use two stops—one that marks the beginning of the insertion or change, and one that marks the end. The initial stop might contain some information about the purpose of the change.

The first thing we'll do is add back the alignments to make the action work; then we'll take a look at adding in some finer details. First, let's duplicate the action and then insert a stop detailing the change:

1. Duplicate the action by dragging it to the Duplicate/New Action button at the bottom of the Actions palette.

2. Activate the step in the action where you linked the Copyright and background layers.

3. Choose Insert Stop from the Actions palette pop-up menu to open the Record Stop window. Type a description of what you plan to do; in this case, it should be something like "Adding the alignment items that did not record."

4. Replay the action from the beginning to get the image to the point where you are adding steps. The stop will automatically pause the action for you.

5. Take a snapshot of the current state of the image. That way, you can return to this point if you have to do some testing for your solution without having to rerun the action. Name the snapshot `Before Alignment.`

6. Shut off the stop item by unchecking the item toggle. This keeps the stop from replaying.

7. Duplicate the stop. You should now have two identical stops in the action following the Link item. You will build your additions between these markers. See Figure 9.5.

8. Activate the first of the two stops (the top one) and choose Insert Menu Item from the Actions palette pop-up. When the Insert menu Item dialog box appears (Figure 9.6, top), choose Layer → Align Linked → Right Edges. When you click OK, Photoshop inserts the item into your action between your stops (Figure 9.6, bottom).

9. Choose Insert Menu Item from the pop-up menu again, and this time add the alignment for bottom edges (Layer → Align Linked → Bottom Edges). This will be inserted into the action after the right edge align item created in step 8.

10. To test, click the Before Alignment snapshot to restore the image to that state, click the first testing stop, and then click Play on the Actions palette.

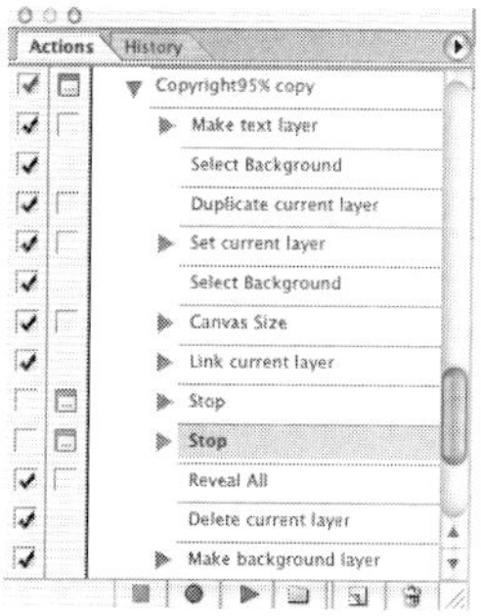

Figure 9.5

Your action should look exactly like this after step 7. The stops mark the spot where you will be inserting steps.

The action should now complete with the copyright aligning exactly where we wanted it: 5 percent from the right and bottom of the image. Had something gone wrong, you would be able to easily locate the segment of the action that you had been editing, and could restore the state of the image at that point to get into further testing and changes.

In testing the action, you will often want to set the Action Playback Speed so that you can watch each step as it occurs. To do so, choose Playback Options from the Actions palette pop-up menu. Setting the action's Playback option to Step By Step allows each step to play and redraw before moving to the next. Setting the Playback option to Pause For allows you to enter a number, which reflects the number of seconds the action will pause after the redraw before moving to the next step.

Figure 9.6

When you're inserting menu items, the Insert Menu Item dialog box will open with no item selected. When you select an item from any menu, the name will be inserted in the dialog box.

To update the action to better fit the purpose of the original plan, add the following items to the action:

1. Add a stop at the beginning of the action describing what it does. First, insert the stop, and then drag it into place in the action as the first step. Be sure to check the Allow Continue box in the Record Stop dialog box.

2. Change the name of the Copyright text layer to `Copyright Text` in the step after adding the text. This will keep any changes that you make to the text from renaming the layer, and can make the action more compatible and easier to handle. To do this:

   · Activate the Copyright Text layer in the Layers palette.

   · Click the Make Text Layer step in the action.

   · Start recording.

   · Change the name of the layer to `Copyright Text.`

   · Stop the recording.

3. Use the Copyright Text layer name to select the type following the step that names the layer. To insert this step:

    - Choose the step that changes the layer name (Set Current Layer).

    - Activate the background (or any layer other than the Copyright Text layer).

    - Begin recording.

    - Click the Copyright Text layer.

    - Stop the recording.

4. Open a stop inviting the user to make changes to the typeface, color, and size. To do this:

    - Activate the Select Layer "Copyright Text" step.

    - Choose Insert Stop from the Actions palette pop-up menu.

    - Enter the text for the stop, and check the Allow Continue box.

5. Offer the option to flatten the image at the end:

    - Activate the final step of the action by clicking on it in the Actions palette.

    - Insert a stop and type the text Click **[Continue]** to flatten. Click **[Stop]** to leave the Copyright text in a separate layer.

    - Record or insert a Flatten Image command.

With all these changes in place, the action will be more versatile and robust. When you are satisfied with the action, you can remove any development stops, return the Action Playback Speed setting to Accelerated, and save the action. After adding the name change to the Copyright layer, you will notice that the Link item no longer works properly. This is because the original recording linked to a layer with a similar name. You need to re-record the Link item to make it work properly. This type of adjustment will often be necessary with more complicated actions as you fine-tune the results. If you use good procedure and are patient with step-by-step viewing of what is going on in the action, the reasons behind any errors like this will often be apparent. To see a copy of the final action, open Copyright 95% in the Hidden Power Tools on the CD.

Naming layers as you create them is often a solution to compatibility issues. If you create an action that depends on Photoshop's default naming of layers, for example, this action may not work in a foreign language version of the product. Renaming the layers immediately—or during creation—is a simple step to take both in making actions more broadly compatible and robust.

LEARNING FROM ACTIONS

The Internet is a great resource for finding actions that you can download and play. Some of these may be of limited utility, but others can be a store of interesting ideas for what can be recorded and methodology—even if you don't like the action. When playing actions you find on the Internet, you should try them out to see if anything interesting happens by playing them at accelerated speed. When you see something that catches your eye ("how'd that happen?"), set the Playback option to Step By Step or Pause For, expand the action, and play. You should get a much better idea of what is going on and why.

If you choose to edit actions that you find on the Internet, you should approach editing in the same way that you would approach editing your original recordings. Be sure you are not violating copyright by editing and then redistributing other action authors' works. While it is fine to edit for your own purposes, distributing lightly edited actions as your own can be considered a copyright violation.

Unless you are going to use the original action for development of other effects, delete the original action that you have edited from the Actions palette and rename the copy by removing *copy* from the name. Save the action to the Actions folder in the Photoshop application folder. This will save your clean, updated action and get rid of the original, which has now become unnecessary. Keeping your Actions palette tidy can help you avoid having many versions of an action. It's better to eliminate the actions you won't need as you develop improvements and replacements.

Edit as You Go

There are times you may choose to edit as you go when working on some actions rather than editing after you have completed the rough draft. Most likely you will use a combination of these techniques: editing as you go along to fix simple problems and doing more formal editing when you have difficulty finding the reason for the result.

To edit as you go, keep the Actions palette visible. When you find yourself wanting to backtrack, simply stop the recording by clicking the Stop button at the bottom of the Actions palette. The action must be stopped before it can be edited, unless you are adding a menu item or other insertion.

Recording Workflow with Actions

Accidents occur in using different combinations of tools and filters that are quite unexpected, and they aren't always a bad thing. These accidents can be used as a creative well—if you record them. It also can be helpful to save some actions to look at later, to see what went right (or wrong) in a series of events. It is possible to use action recording to help document workflow any time you are experimenting with an image or a procedure. This not only lets you create actions for useful effects that you stumble on, but it also helps you backtrack and replay an edited series of events on the same image. It can be an imperfect method because not every item will record, but you can compare between the image histories or the Photoshop History log to determine the missing steps.

> The History log is an option in Photoshop CS that can store the steps you take as you take them, in text form. To turn the option on and locate the file, open the Preferences dialog box and select the History Log check box. In this panel you can choose to write metadata, text, or both to the log. To be sure the steps are written in detail, choose Detailed under Edit Log Items. While this file can't be played back, it can be a very useful reference. It must be cleared or deleted manually.

Reverting with histories will roll back the time on the image clock, and allow you to jump to and from states that have already occurred. You can replay segments of change by clicking through states in order. Histories are limited by the number of states you choose to retain, so the History log can be a means of going back before what is currently logged in the history. Combining the power of histories and the History log with the capability of actions to record steps and events, it is possible to not only revert but also modify a string of events. This can be quite a time-saver, because instead of needing to re-create an entire series of events from the history or log, the reconstruction can occur from essentially any point in your recording.

> You can save actions in a text format by holding down ⌘/Ctrl+Option/Alt before choosing Save Actions from the Actions palette pop-up menu. This will save a listing of the commands as text.

Prompting Users during Actions

Actions can't do everything for you, and there are times you won't want them to. In some instances it will be difficult or impossible to make an action scalable to any image. For example, they may not record certain freehand movements. As with the Copyright 95% action, you can insert prompts in the form of stops to remind the user to select a tool. You can also use stops to tell the user what to do, or use Insert Paths to add a path that can be stroked to repeat the freehand action.

Editing and modifying actions can let you use them on a broad range of images (various sizes and ppi, for example), or share them with other users. For example, it might be helpful to include some information when you insert a stop that will help you when you're

RECORDING ACTIONS FOR ELEMENTS USERS

Photoshop Elements 1 and 2 can run many actions created for Photoshop (versions 6–CS)—if they are recorded and saved correctly. In other words, you can create actions in Photoshop to run with a copy of Elements that you might use as a second Photoshop license.

To make recordings that are Elements compatible usually requires some additional testing, but can often be as simple as following these suggestions:

- Name actions and action sets in small letters with no spaces (underscores can be used in names).

- Record actions in self-contained sets; don't record with references to other action sets. Subactions should be contained in the same set.

- Create components using RGB workarounds. For example, to use luminosity, don't get it from Lab mode, which Elements does not support; create it by loading the RGB channel or using a luminosity layer.

- Insert adjustment layers rather than using menu commands. In this way you can use many functions thought not to be in Elements.

using the action later, or if you're sharing the action with other users. In this way, pertinent notations for the use of actions can be stored and transferred with the actions themselves; this prompts the user without extensive explanation or documentation that might otherwise be necessary to use the action properly (depending on how complex it actually is). Adding steps to modify a procedure after it is recorded can help you refine the process and perfect application of effects.

Batching Actions

Actions are useful for performing a series of commands on a single image. Sometimes you will want to run an action on many images, and Actions can be made to handle those situations, too. By using the Batch command, you can apply an action to a set of images. This allows you to start a batch process and leave while Photoshop completes the process. Batch processing is great for repetitive tasks, such as changing ppi or color mode for hundreds of images at a time—or for dropping your copyright on a group of images without opening each and running the action you have created on each image separately. To run a batch action, simply follow these steps:

1. Record and adjust the action that you want to use for the batch process. You will want to remove stops and prompts if possible so the process can run without intervention. To remove stops, just shut off the items by unchecking them in the Actions palette. Some

actions may require other adjustments. For example, you can set a default color and styling for the copyright text in the Copyright action.

2. Collect the images that you plan to include in the batch in a folder. You can use sub-folders and aliases to group the images, but it may be best to avoid confusion by gathering copies of the images all in one place. For a test run, try collecting just a few images to be sure all is working as it should.

> It is often helpful to copy all the images that you want to process into a particular folder, and to also get in the habit of using a particular folder for batch-process output. Once you have finished processing you can choose to either save over the copies or delete them without worrying about originals. You could create folders called In and Out, for example, to organize the process. Establishing procedures can be especially valuable when you're working in a group. A consistent workflow can help reduce the chance of error, such as overwriting or losing files.

3. Choose File → Automate → Batch. The Batch dialog box will open.

4. In the Batch dialog box (see Figure 9.7), choose the action set and action that you want to apply.

Figure 9.7

This dialog box shows that we've chosen the Copyright 95% action from the Copyright action set to run on the selected images.

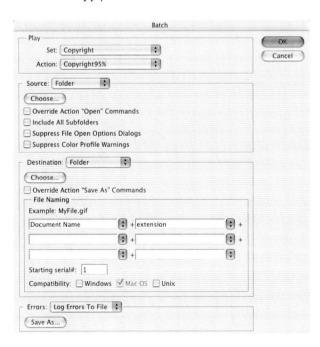

5. Choose the folder where you collected the images in step 2 as the Source for this example, select Folder and then click the Choose button to browse for the folder where you collected the images.

6. Choose the source options:

   • Override Action "Open" Commands overrides and ignores Open commands for specific files that exist in the action.

   • Include All Subfolders processes all images in the target folder as well as images in any subfolders.

   • Suppress File Open Options Dialogs opens files without displaying the Open dialog box. The dialog box will use default or current settings.

   • Suppress Color Profile Warnings will keep color policy messages from displaying.

7. Choose the Destination type where you would like to save images after they are processed:

   • Choose None to keep the files open after running the action.

   • Choose Save And Close to save the files and overwrite the originals.

   • Choose Folder to save the files to a different folder using the naming convention defined in the File Naming panel of the dialog box (see step 8).

In this case choose Folder and create a destination folder outside the folder selected in step 5.

You can choose any folder, local or remote, that you have access to. If you choose a network folder for the destination, make sure that you have permissions to write to the folder.

8. Complete the naming conventions if applicable to your selection. The choices you make here will rename the file. This can keep you from overwriting files and/or make easier work of sorting images (e.g., by date). Using the drop-down lists, you can concatenate up to six filenaming components, including the name of the file in lowercase or uppercase, serial number, various date formats, and extension. You can also choose the operating system compatibility for the output files. Your current operating system will be selected by default.

9. If the action contains a Save command, choose Override Action "Save As" Command—otherwise, every processed image will be saved to the same file (the one named in the action), so you would modify and see only the last image you process. Photoshop does not warn you if original files are being overwritten.

10. Click OK to begin running the batch process.

If everything has been set up correctly, Photoshop will open the images one at a time, apply the action specified, and then save the image according to the parameters you specified, including renaming the result. If you notice that the action is not behaving as planned, you can press the Esc key. You may want to test the batch process with a sample before running it on a large group of images.

Batch processing can be a powerful tool for converting groups of images from one mode to another, for resizing, and for applying copyrights or watermarks. You might want to use it for processing images fresh off your digital camera; you can automate the creation of dated duplicates to work on while saving a second set of images for archiving.

Using Conditional Mode Change with Batch Actions

The Conditional Mode Change command can convert an image mode based on the current mode of the image. These conversions may be less useful for processing single images (where you know the image mode at a glance) than they are in batch (where you may not be sure of the mode of all the images). Conditional mode changes allow you to apply a set of steps in an action or batch without causing an error, and without forcing you to check the mode of the images before running the batch process. The dialog box shown in Figure 9.8 lets you specify which modes you want to change.

The reason you might want to make a conditional change in an action is twofold. First, some filters, tools, and commands work only with images in a specific mode. For example, Indexed Color images do not support the use of any filters or layers. If you want to apply an action that used filters or layers (as the Copyright action does), an Indexed Color image should be converted (most likely to RGB) before attempting to apply the change. Failing to make the conversion first will cause the action to fail. To prevent these errors, you can insert the conditional mode change at a pertinent point in the action that contains mode-specific filters or commands.

Second, you avoid unnecessary mode changes and reduce the potential for damage or changes that will occur to an image during conversions. Inserting the conditional mode change allows you to control the conversions so that they are applied only as necessary, rather than converting every image—whether the conversion is needed or not.

Figure 9.8

The conditions shown here will change a Bitmap, Duotone, Indexed Color, and Multi-channel image to RGB mode before continuing.

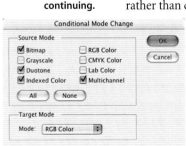

To use a conditional mode change, choose File → Automate → Conditional Mode Change in a step before the mode becomes crucial. This can be the first step of the process, and there can be more than one mode change in an action based on different parameters and needs. Conditional mode changes can also be inserted using Insert Menu Item, but the conditions will be the default or last settings used.

Using Actions in ImageReady

Creating and using actions in ImageReady is similar to Photoshop; however, they are different animals of the same species. Actions can't be traded between the two programs mostly because they are coded differently, but also because commands will not be the same. The difference in coding, however, allows you to do some things with ImageReady actions that you can't do in Photoshop. Two clear distinctions are creating conditional actions and editing actions as text.

Creating Conditional Actions

Conditional actions allow you to create smart actions that can pick between options when processing images. With conditions, you are able to specify such things as the number of times a segment of an action should repeat (known as *looping*), which you can base on qualities of the image.

The basics of conditional actions are covered in the Adobe Help files. To find out more, just open ImageReady Help and search for "Inserting Conditionals." While the descriptions of the options are helpful, they won't give you an example of what you might do with the conditional actions or explain how to use them.

Say, for example, you want to sort a file of images into different folders depending on whether they are portrait (taller than they are wide), landscape (wider than they are tall), or square. You can do this manually by opening each image and viewing image properties, or perhaps by managing the files with the File Browser in Photoshop. However, with conditional actions you can automate the process by having ImageReady determine the orientation of the image and save to a folder based on that orientation. We'll take a look at how to do this in the following steps, incorporating conditional actions and creating a droplet as well.

Droplets are a means of performing actions in a batch process without first opening Photoshop or ImageReady. You create droplets in Photoshop by selecting File → Automate → Create Droplet; in ImageReady, choose Create Droplet from the Actions palette pop-up menu. The result is the creation of a droplet file, which exists wholly outside of Photoshop or ImageReady. You can use the file to process images by dragging images to it. When activated, droplets open the associated program and perform the procedures outlined in the action they were created from.

What we will do is create a series of events that

- Identifies the image orientation
- Sets the output folder based on the orientation
- Saves the image

To do this, we have to use several conditional steps to tell ImageReady what steps to include or skip based on the image orientation:

1. Gather several images of different sizes and shapes into a folder called Sort to use as a test. At least one image in the group should be landscape, at least one square, and at least one portrait. It doesn't matter where you create this folder, and be sure to use image copies, not originals.

2. Create three folders inside the Sort folder and call them **Landscape**, **Portrait**, and **Square**.

3. Launch ImageReady and create a new action called Sort Landscape-Portrait-Square by clicking the Create New Action button at the bottom of the Actions palette. (If the Actions palette is not open, choose Window → Actions.) Creating the action will leave you in record mode.

4. Click the Insert A Step button  at the bottom of the Actions palette. This opens the Insert A Step menu. Choose Insert Conditional from the menu (see Figure 9.9) to open the Conditional dialog box.

5. Choose Image Aspect Ratio from the first drop-down list in the If The Following Condition Is Met panel of the dialog box. Click the Is radio button and choose Landscape from the second drop-down list. In the Perform The Following Action panel, choose Include from the drop-down list and enter **2** for the number of steps. The result should look like Figure 9.10. You are telling ImageReady that if the image is a landscape image, it should include the following two steps but otherwise skip them.

6. For processing the landscape images, you want to set the output folder to the Landscape folder you created in step 2, and then skip the processing steps for Portrait and Square images. To set the output folder, use the Insert Set Output Folder option on the Insert A Step menu. After you select Insert Set Output Folder, a dialog box opens that allows you to specify the output folder. Choose the Landscape folder you created earlier. You will be adding four more steps for processing Portrait and Square images and you will need to skip these steps, so add another conditional that skips the next four steps. You dialog box should look like the one shown in Figure 9.11.

7. For processing portrait images, you will want to include two steps similar to those used for processing landscape images. First, choose Image Aspect Ratio, Is, and Portrait in the top panel of the Conditional dialog box, and then select Include under Perform The Following Action and enter **2** for the number of steps (see Figure 9.12).

8. Next you will set the output folder to Portrait using an inserted Set Output Folder condition. This time, you will skip specifically choosing a behavior for square images, because they are the only images left (see Figure 9.13).

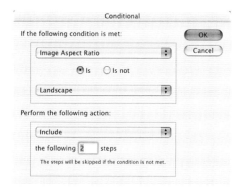

Figure 9.10

In this dialog box, you specify options that will change to reflect the type of image selected. The dialog box will open with the previous options you used by default.

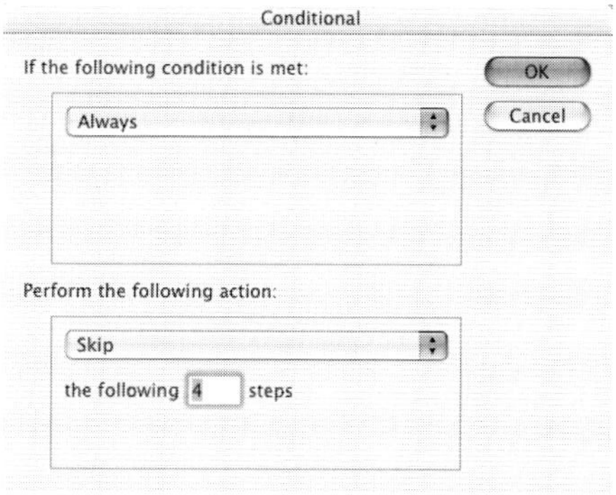

Figure 9.11

Choose Always from the first drop-down list in the upper panel, Skip in the lower panel, and enter 4 for the number of steps to skip.

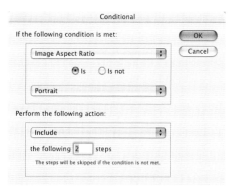

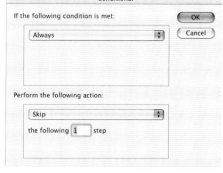

Figure 9.12

The parameters for this condition will be the same as for landscape images, except you will choose Portrait as the type.

Figure 9.13

Because you have eliminated landscape and portrait images, all images that are left will be square. You will not need a condition to identify them.

9. To process square images, you will only need to set the output folder. To do this, insert a Set Output Folder condition and choose the Square folder you created in step 2.

10. At this point, each of the image types has an output folder assigned, so all you have to do is save the image. While this might be more useful if you could record a Save or Save As command, your only option is to record Save Optimized. To do this, you will need to either open or create a new image, and then record saving using Save

Optimized. To begin, stop the recording, create (or open) an image, start the recording, then choose Save Optimized. Do not change the name of the file, make the format Images Only, leave the Setting option at Default, and leave the Slices option set to All (this option will be unavailable if the image is not sliced). The target folder doesn't matter because the action will override that option. When you are done recording the Save Optimized step, stop the recording.

You can test this action by opening any image and playing the action. Photoshop should save the image to the proper folder based on its orientation, and the image will be saved using the last setting used in the Optimize palette (GIF, JPEG, or PNG). It's also possible to add an Insert Set Optimization Settings step using the Insert A Step menu if you want the setting to always be one of these options rather than the last used.

As it stands, this action will work with only one image at a time. If the goal is to process a folder full of images, you have to turn the action into a droplet. To convert the action to a droplet, click once on the action name to activate it, and then choose Create Droplet from the Actions palette pop-up window. The droplet will be created as a separate file wherever you save it. To use the droplet, get the droplet in view (e.g., on the desktop), select all the images you gathered in step 1, and drag them to the droplet. These images should sort automatically into the proper folders. The action and droplet can be found on the CD.

This is only one of the many things that you can accomplish using conditional actions. You may use simple single conditions, or build conditions that are even more complex than the one we've examined here. Feel free to bring up questions about conditionals in the forum for the book (see the additional resources in Chapter 10).

Editing Actions in ImageReady

There are some options for editing actions in ImageReady that are not part of the Photoshop scheme, and these can prove useful in creating variations on recorded actions. ImageReady lets you perform some simple text editing of actions (editing actions as text in Photoshop requires using a hex editor and a lot of patience). You can also use history steps to create action steps. To do this, you just drag a (nonitalicized) command from the History palette to the action in the Actions palette that you want the command in. While that seems pretty straightforward, let's look at an example of editing actions as text, and use the History palette to insert an action step.

Say you want to create an action that duplicates your background a number of times (it may vary). You want the copies to duplicate to the top of the stack. Because of how ImageReady handles recorded steps, and because you can't move layers as you can in

Photoshop using shortcuts, the recording gets a little tricky. We'll work around the problems of straight recording:

1. Open a new image (say 300×300 pixels) and duplicate the background.

2. Create a new action and call it **Dooplicate Layers** (misspelled on purpose). With both the History and the Actions palettes open, click on the Duplicate Layer state in the History palette and drag it under the Duplicate Layers action name in the Actions palette. The step will copy there, complete with the layer name that was duplicated and the position to duplicate to.

3. Insert a conditional step that repeats the action however many times you want it to run. In Figure 9.14, the condition will set the action up to run 10 times.

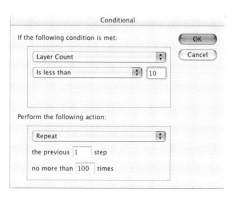

Figure 9.14

The parameter that says No More Than 100 Times doesn't matter because the Layer Count will control the number of times the action repeats.

Your action should have two steps at this point: the Duplicate Layer and the Conditional steps, as shown in Figure 9.15.

If you run this action, it may seem to work, but you will get an inverted layer stack, with the numbers counting down from the top (see Figure 9.16).

To fix this, you need to remove the name of the layer that is duplicated as well as the layer position. Doing this will keep ImageReady from selecting the background each time when duplicating, and will put the copy at the top rather than the bottom of the stack. To make the edit, save the action (e.g., Dooplicate Layer.isa) and open the file in a text editor (using Notepad on a PC or TextEdit on a Mac). This will expose the code for the action. You can get right in here and edit things, resave the action, load it, and play it. For example, if you look at the file, one of the first things you will see is your misspelled action name. Correct it there in the file.

Figure 9.15

Expand the steps to look at the parameters.

Next thing we'll want to do is remove the parts of the action that tell ImageReady to choose the Background layer each time for the duplication and where to place the duplicate. Scroll down and find the following segment of code; then highlight and delete the part shown in bold here:

Figure 9.16

You will not be able to record the Duplicate Layers command without it specifying a layer and layer position. This will lead to ImageReady stacking the layers backward.

```
step1 = new DuplicateLayer;
step1.enabled = true;
step1.doDialog = false;
step1.expanded = true;
step1.layerName = "Background";
step1.layerPosition = 0;
action.AddStep(step1);
```

You should end up with the following:

```
step1 = new DuplicateLayer;
step1.enabled = true;
step1.doDialog = false;
step1.expanded = true;
action.AddStep(step1);
```

Now save the file as a text-only file, and don't add the .txt extension. Name the file **Duplicate Layers.isa** to correct the spelling there as well.

Now that you have saved the action, go back into ImageReady and load the action by choosing Load Actions from the Action palette pop-up menu. Choose the newly saved Duplicate Layers.isa, and it will appear in the palette, spelled correctly (see Figure 9.17). Try the action out on a new image, and you will get the results shown in Figure 9.18. Both of the actions (Dooplicate.isa and Duplicate.isa) are available on the CD.

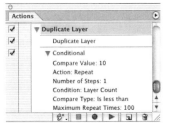

Editing actions like this will probably be something you will only do on occasion, and only when you are having trouble recording actions the way you want. Of course, fiddling with the parameters can lead to unexpected results and failures. You will need some level of confidence and competence in figuring out the code to edit actions via text effectively. This would be another good topic for further discussion on the forum for the book (again, see the additional resources in Chapter 10).

Figure 9.17

Changes to the spelling in the action file change the display spelling. Note that the Duplicate Layers step no longer has additional parameters.

Scripting

Scripting allows you to go beyond some of the limitations of recording actions by using JavaScript, AppleScript, and/or Visual Basic to work with your images, both inside and outside the confines of Photoshop. Because this is more akin to programming than to editing images, it seems to require a separate text. Apparently, Adobe agrees; it has put together fairly extensive introductory texts for using scripting included with the installation of Photoshop CS.

If you look inside the Photoshop CS program folder, there is a Scripting Guide folder. Inside this folder are four guides, totaling 500 or more pages:

Guide	Purpose
Photoshop Scripting Guide.pdf	Introduction to working with scripting in Photoshop CS for Mac and PC users
JavaScript Reference Guide.pdf	Introduction to working with JavaScript commands with Photoshop CS for Mac and PC users
AppleScript Reference Guide.pdf	Code guide for working with AppleScript for Mac users
Visual Basic Reference Guide.pdf	Code guide for working with Visual Basic for PC users

While a good portion of these pages is reference material, it is a good idea to read the Photoshop Scripting Guide.pdf before you start writing scripts. However, even before you do that, it is a good idea to be sure you need scripting at all.

Scripting is usually only necessary when you are trying to do something that an action can't accomplish. Typically this will amount to one of two things:

- You need a condition to make the action work; actions don't work with conditions (excepting conditional mode changes).

- You need to work with an application outside Photoshop; actions are restricted to Photoshop and won't work with external applications (such as a database).

You may want to create a new interface or information display to help you with the way you like to process images. Or you may use scripting as an alternative to actions, or you may just be more comfortable working with scripting.

We'll look at creating and implementing a simple JavaScript so you can see how they work and what's involved in using them.

Figure 9.18

Because the current layer will be copied instead of the Background, and because the copy won't be placed at the bottom of the stack, the copies will stack in number order.

Creating a Simple JavaScript

JavaScript is the most versatile of the three scripting languages offered in Photoshop because it can work between platforms (Mac and PC). At the same time, it is somewhat limited by its inability to converse with other applications. Nevertheless, JavaScript offers you many opportunities to customize your use of Photoshop and the interface itself.

The first script we'll look at does something you can accomplish with actions as well, but it is a simple example of the type of preference you can adjust. We'll look at changing the screen ruler preference between pixels and percent. After that, we'll show you how to do something more unique. To begin:

1. Open a text editor such as Notepad (PC) or TextEdit (Mac). You will need to be able to save the resulting file as plain text only; Microsoft Word or other word processing files often have a lot of other formatting code that will not work.

2. Enter the following text in a new document:

   ```
   // Set the ruler units to pixels.
   app.preferences.rulerUnits = Units.PIXELS
   ```

3. Save the file as **toPixels.js**. If you save to the Presets\Photoshop Actions or Presets\Scripts folder, the script will be available in the File → Scripts menu when you restart Photoshop.

The first line is just a comment: a bit of text following the slashes used to describe what comes next. The next line uses the application (app, or Photoshop) and looks at the preferences (`preferences`), specifically the ruler unit preferences (`rulerUnits`), and sets those units to pixels. The codes are described in the JavaScript type library of the JavaScript guide.

When you restart Photoshop and run the script (by selecting it from the Scripts menu), the preference settings for ruler units will switch to pixels without you having to navigate any screens. Now create the second script:

1. Open a text editor such as Notepad (PC) or TextEdit (Mac).

2. Enter the following text in a new document:

```
// Set the ruler units to percent.
app.preferences.rulerUnits = Units.PERCENT;
```

3. Save the file as **toPercent.js**. If you save to the Presets\Photoshop Actions or Presets\Scripts folder, the script will be available in the File → Scripts menu when you restart Photoshop.

At this point, you can restart Photoshop and switch back and forth between rulers based on percent and rulers based on pixels by choosing what you want from the Scripts menu. However, you can also create actions that run these scripts, just like the one you created earlier for running the workspace action. If you assign a function key (say F13) to toPixel.js in an action called toPixels, and assign Shift+F13 to toPercent.js, you can toggle between rulers with just the F13 and Shift keys without navigating menus. This scripting ability offers a powerful means of customizing commands.

More powerful still is the possibility of building your own interface components. You can create an interface that works right in Photoshop. In the next section, we do this and expand on the ruler switch.

Creating a JavaScript Ruler Switch Interface

The previous section showed a simple type of JavaScript command: a single line of code that is executed when the script is played. It is also possible to combine simple JavaScripts as components of larger scripts that can be controlled through a customized interface. An interface can be a lot of things, but mostly it helps you act on commands in Photoshop by supplying buttons, sliders, and fields that simplify working with the commands. Expanding on the previous exercise, let's build an interface that allows you to click a button to change among one of three choices for ruler units.

To create an interface, we'll do the following:

1. Outline an idea.

2. Create the component commands.

3. Assemble the interface.

4. Assign the commands to the interface.

5. Save the script.

6. Test the script.

7. Make any necessary adjustments to the script.

8. Run the script.

These steps are similar to the steps for creating actions. The difference lies in the ability to customize the commands and create an interface.

Outlining the Idea

We have already outlined much of the idea by deciding what we want to do. In this case, the goal is to develop an interface with three buttons in a single window that will allow you to choose your ruler units with a single click. The click should kick off the component that changes the ruler units as well as close the interface window.

Planning involves sketching out an idea for the interface and how it will work. This is an important step so that you can be sure you are improving on what you have already in Photoshop. The design for the interface will be simple: a window with a single panel and three buttons, one each for ruler units as percent, pixels, and inches (see Figure 9.19).

Creating the Component Commands

The component commands will be the same ones we have already created to change the units along with two additional ones: a command that changes units to inches, and another that closes the interface window. The four commands look like this:

```
app.preferences.rulerUnits = Units.PERCENT;
app.preferences.rulerUnits = Units.PIXELS;
app.preferences.rulerUnits = Units.INCHES;
this.parent.parent.close(0)
```

The first two are from the earlier exercise, and the third is just a variation on these. The possible ruler units are listed in the JavaScript Reference Guide.pdf. Any of these could be listed here and the number of buttons could be increased. However, this is intended as a quick switch interface, and the fewer the choices, the more efficient the example.

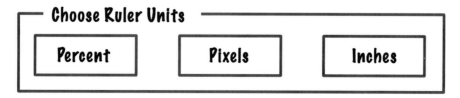

Figure 9.19

A sketch (like this one done in Photoshop) will save you a lot of guesswork. It doesn't have to be a blueprint but should be an outline.

The close command tells Photoshop to close the interface window. The `close(0)` command is preceded by `this.parent.parent`, which tells Photoshop what to close—in this case, the parent of the parent of the current object—the object is a button in a message field in the window. You would think that any window would need a close command, but you can also close a window using the Esc key.

With the components created, let's jump right into creating the interface.

Assembling the Interface

When creating the interface you must first open a new text document in your text editor. Before creating buttons and panels, you will need to create the window they will reside on; you'll create this window in JavaScript as code. In JavaScript this means creating a variable (`var`) and assigning window attributes to the variable that describe the size of the screen in coordinates. Type the following:

```
// Create a dialog and buttons to set rulers to percent, pixels, and inches.
// define variable for the window
var dlg = new Window('dialog', 'Ruler Unit Switch', [150,150,650,280]);
```

The first two lines are comments, which essentially summarize what you plan to do. The way we use comments here is similar to how we placed stops as reminders or guides when we created actions. The variable (`dlg`) could be anything, but you will need to use it when referring to the window you create. `new Window()` is the standard command Photoshop will act on to create a new display element; `'dialog'` is the window type; `'Ruler Unit Switch'` is the name of the window; and the numbers within the brackets define the size and shape of the window box (left, top, right, bottom). The window will open with the top-left corner of the dialog box 150 pixels in from the top and left of the screen. The right side of the dialog box will be 650 pixels from the left, and the bottom will be 280 pixels from the top. This makes the dialog box 500×130 pixels.

Next let's create the message panel that will go inside the window to group the buttons. Type the following code:

```
// create the message panel
dlg.msgPnl = dlg.add('panel',[20,20,480,110],'Choose Ruler Units');
```

Because the message panel is part of the dialog box, you have to attach the components. `dlg` names the window, and `msgPnl` defines the object panel name as an added component for the dialog box using `dlg.add()`. Again the first parameter describes the standard window component type (`'panel'`), the next parameter (the numbers within the brackets) defines the size and shape (in comparison to the parent object, which is the window in this case rather than the screen), and the final parameter represents the title for the panel (`'Choose Ruler Units'`).

Now that we have the message panel, we can create the buttons inside that. Just as you created the panel as a component of the `dlg` window, you will create the buttons as part of the panel using `add()`. The buttons can have any name, but the `add` parameter should specify the object as a button, the button size, and the name on the button. Each button name as a component should be unique; otherwise, the button's behavior will be unpredictable or clicking it will fail. The measurements for the buttons are again relative to the parent component, which in this case is the panel (not the window).

```
// create the Percent button
dlg.msgPnl.perBtn = dlg.msgPnl.add('button', [40,30,140,65],'Percent');

// create the Pixel button
dlg.msgPnl.pixBtn = dlg.msgPnl.add('button', [180,30,280,65],'Pixels');

// create the Inches button
dlg.msgPnl.incBtn = dlg.msgPnl.add('button', [320,30,420,65],'Inches');
```

You are probably itching to see what you've got so far, and you can do that by adding one more line:

```
dlg.show();
```

This line tells Photoshop to show the result. It should look like Figure 9.20. In order to view the result, you have to save the file you are working on as a .js file using text format. If you save to the Photoshop Actions or Scripts folder, you will be able to open the script directly from the File → Scripts menu. If you choose to save elsewhere, you can load the script using the Browse function on that same menu.

Figure 9.20

When you run the action, the interface will take on the attributes of your operating system. The Mac version of the interface window is shown here.

Your code at this point should look like this:

```
// Create a dialog and buttons to set rulers to percent, pixels, and
inches.

// define variable for the window
var dlg = new Window('dialog', 'Ruler Unit Switch', [150,150,650,280]);

// create the message panel
dlg.msgPnl = dlg.add('panel',[20,20,480,110],'Choose Ruler Units');

// create the Percent button
dlg.msgPnl.perBtn = dlg.msgPnl.add('button', [40,30,140,65],'Percent');

// create the Pixel button
dlg.msgPnl.pixBtn = dlg.msgPnl.add('button', [180,30,280,65],'Pixels');
```

```
// create the Inches button
dlg.msgPnl.incBtn = dlg.msgPnl.add('button', [320,30,420,65],'Inches');
```

```
dlg.show();
```

Regretfully, the interface is still just an empty shell. There are no behaviors tied to the buttons. Again, you can exit from the interface by pressing Esc on the keyboard.

Assigning the Commands to the Interface

The next step is to make the buttons apply the commands. The commands themselves will be executed when you click on a button, so each button needs to have an onClick behavior assigned. You incorporate the behavior by adding it to the string in a new line of code associated with the button object (dlg.msgPnl.perBtn becomes dlg.msgPnl.perBtn.onClick). That added command kicks off a function (the unit change) when the button is clicked. The function changes the units when the button is clicked. Add the following lines to the JavaScript:

```
// assign unit
dlg.msgPnl.perBtn.onClick = function () {app.preferences.rulerUnits =
Units.PERCENT};
```

```
// assign unit
dlg.msgPnl.pixBtn.onClick = function () {app.preferences.rulerUnits =
Units.PIXELS};
```

```
// assign unit
dlg.msgPnl.incBtn.onClick = function () {app.preferences.rulerUnits =
Units.INCHES};
```

The onClick behavior is set to the functions we defined earlier, each button with its own unit. Your code should look like this:

```
// Create a dialog and buttons to set rulers to Percent, Pixels, and
inches.
```

```
// define variable for the window
var dlg = new Window('dialog', 'Ruler Unit Switch', [150,150,650,280]);
```

```
// create the message panel
dlg.msgPnl = dlg.add('panel',[20,20,480,110],'Choose Ruler Units');
```

```
// create the Percent button
dlg.msgPnl.perBtn = dlg.msgPnl.add('button', [40,30,140,65],'Percent');
```

```
// assign unit
dlg.msgPnl.perBtn.onClick = function () {app.preferences.rulerUnits =
Units.PERCENT};
```

```
// create the Pixel button
dlg.msgPnl.pixBtn = dlg.msgPnl.add('button', [180,30,280,65],'Pixels');

// assign unit
dlg.msgPnl.pixBtn.onClick = function () {app.preferences.rulerUnits =
Units.PIXELS};

// create the Inches button
dlg.msgPnl.incBtn = dlg.msgPnl.add('button', [320,30,420,65],'Inches');

// assign unit
dlg.msgPnl.incBtn.onClick = function () {app.preferences.rulerUnits =
Units.INCHES};

dlg.show();
```

Test out the script by saving and running it in Photoshop with an image open and the rulers in view.

Adjusting the Results

At this point, if you've written the script properly, the rulers will change as you click a button but the window will not close unless you press Esc. This may not bother you in the slightest, but you may want the interface to behave a little more elegantly. You can take more than one approach here depending on what you want the interface to do. For example, you can add a button to close the window. You can also add the close behavior to each of the buttons so that clicking the button performs the switch and then closes the window. We'll modify the comment and add the close command:

```
// assign unit and close function
dlg.msgPnl.perBtn.onClick = function () {app.preferences.rulerUnits =
Units.PERCENT; {this.parent.parent.close(0)} };
```

We inserted close() as part of the onClick function using an additional set of brackets. You should add it in the same way to each of the buttons so that clicking any of the buttons will make the window close. At this point your code should look like this:

```
// Create a dialog and buttons to set rulers to Percent, Pixels, and inches.

// define variable for the window
var dlg = new Window('dialog', 'Ruler Unit Switch', [150,150,650,280]);

// create the message panel
dlg.msgPnl = dlg.add('panel',[20,20,480,110],'Choose Ruler Units');
```

```
// create the Percent button
dlg.msgPnl.perBtn = dlg.msgPnl.add('button', [40,30,140,65],'Percent');

// assign unit and close function
dlg.msgPnl.perBtn.onClick = function () {app.preferences.rulerUnits =
Units.PERCENT; {this.parent.parent.close(0)} };

// create the Pixel button
dlg.msgPnl.pixBtn = dlg.msgPnl.add('button', [180,30,280,65],'Pixels');

// assign unit and close function
dlg.msgPnl.pixBtn.onClick = function () {app.preferences.rulerUnits =
Units.PIXELS; {this.parent.parent.close(0)} };

// create the Inches button
dlg.msgPnl.incBtn = dlg.msgPnl.add('button', [320,30,420,65],'Inches');

// assign unit and close function
dlg.msgPnl.incBtn.onClick = function () {app.preferences.rulerUnits =
Units.INCHES; {this.parent.parent.close(0)} };

dlg.show();
```

There is, of course, room for even more modifications. For example, you can add a display for the current value of the ruler units (which you won't see if no image is open), or you could add another button just to close the window with no changes. You could change the arrangement and style, perhaps using radio buttons for selection rather than interface buttons. The point is that you can customize the interface to do things and sort behaviors that reflect the way you like to work.

Using the Script

Once you have created and stored your script, you can, as with the earlier example, record an action that references the script and assign the script to a function key. That way, you won't have to have two different functions to change from pixels to percent, and you only have to remember one keystroke.

This type of modification may seem like a lot of trouble to go through to customize behaviors, but it is only the tip of the iceberg when it comes to what you can do with interface modifications and scripting. Taking a few moments (or even hours) to simplify the way you work by creating such enhancements will save you time down the line and allow you to concentrate on images rather than how to access behaviors or change them because they don't work the way you want.

I look forward to more discussion about scripting in my forum, newsletter, and website.

Chapter 10

Exploring Techniques Further

The purpose of this book has been to lay the groundwork so that you can move forward with an advanced perspective on using Photoshop. We have explored the tools you need to make corrections. Most books stop at the end, but in my estimation, this book should be only the beginning for you. The previous nine chapters have set up a framework for using Photoshop to its fullest potential. The problem with books, however, is that they have only so many pages; no matter how many examples, pages, topics, and volumes are included, there is no way to cover every need from every angle. To get the most out of the techniques and examples in this book, you have to explore the implications.

A look back at each chapter

Additional resources

Forward and Back through the Chapters

The purpose of this section is to look at what each chapter covered and expand on the application of the techniques you learned. This section steps through each chapter, summarizing what we did and what you will use the techniques for, what went on while you were working through exercises, why the topic was important, and how the technique is applicable. The hope is to go one step beyond and offer suggestions for additional exercises you might try to make the techniques we discussed more applicable to your everyday work in Photoshop.

You don't really learn anything from just following the steps in a book—you need to explore the opportunities that it places before you and discover some of the landscape on your own. Creativity is limitless, while a book can have only so many pages. With good fundamentals and a strong understanding, you will be better poised to do good creative as well as production work with Photoshop.

Figure 10.1

To create a home-made gray card, you can just try printing a set of swatches on your printer. This set of 10 grays goes in even 10% increments.

Chapter 1: General Tone and Color Correction

The goal of Chapter 1 is to help you grasp and apply color corrections by showing how RGB color works (when you assemble the Prokudin-Gorskii image) and by exploring basic color correction with Photoshop's Levels and Curves tools. Making sure you understand what you see on screen and that it is as accurate as possible is imperative to getting good results. At a minimum, be sure to calibrate your monitor using either the Display System Preferences (Mac) or Adobe Gamma (Windows) tools provided with Photoshop and following the procedure outlined in the Appendix. Once you've done that, the exercises that you try here revolve almost entirely around correcting color in your images.

If you didn't take the opportunity during the chapter, the best thing to follow up on is to experiment with curve corrections using a homemade gray card. Create a 0%, 25%, 50%, 75%, and 100% black card (print it on your printer using black ink only, or toner if you have access to a laser printer). The card need not be large, and can contain more levels of gray if desired (see Figure 10.1).

Simply mount the print on some cardboard or foamcore and place it in your scene when you're shooting the image (preferably at the edge where it will be easy to crop out if necessary). Take several pictures in different lighting situations, and use samples from the card to make your corrections. Follow through with a Color Balance adjustment layer correction to adjust for preference.

In the long run, you will want to make the color correction process your own. The process in the chapter attempts to normalize color and maximize dynamic range to give you a solid base to work from before moving on to other more artistic corrections. You may want to combine development of your personal process for correction with creating actions or scripts that will help lead you through your standard process (see Chapter 9 for more on actions).

Chapter 2: Color Separations

For professional work, understanding color models can help you get more out of an image than it might appear is there at first glance. This chapter starts by taking a look at how you can extract tone from color images, and then shows you how to add it back. We then look at various ways to separate color into components.

The real core of the chapter is that you can adjust images in different ways. Once you are able to separate out the components, you can adjust and recombine them in an infinite number of ways to create color and tone effects. You'll find this helpful in repairing severely damaged images and in restoring lost information that you re-create using separation and adjustment.

Manual CMYK separation is something that relatively few Photoshop users can do (without being familiar with this book). However, if you understand the exercise and have run through it several times, it is time to start experimenting with making improvements to the separations. The action included in the Hidden Power Tools provides levels and curves correction opportunities that you can use to adjust image output and results. You can literally make a study of separation and print process by attempting to create the perfect manual separation using custom curve application and customized black genera-

Figure 10.2
Picture Package can help you quickly assemble your separations consistently on a single sheet before printing.

tion, and printing the result in multiple passes on your ink-jet to view your process color result. Print the images five to a sheet, using half the sheet for the full-color result and the other half to display four equal-sized representations of the color plates (see Figure 10.2). Of course, you may want to automate the process using actions (Chapter 9) and the Picture Package command (Chapter 7).

Chapter 3: Image Change and Repair

Image alteration was probably the original *raison d'etre* for image-editing programs. In this chapter we look at many simple alterations that work together to improve an image a little at a time. Unlike when we're separating images, these changes are targeted to specific areas of an image. Rather than being based on a calculation, they depend on your ability to perceive the needed change and execute the correction. Images can improve significantly with basic adjustments that remove damage and distractions.

Specific work should almost always follow a general correction—explained in the preceding chapters. This way, you're applying specific corrections to corrected tone, color, and landscape. Perhaps the hidden bedfellow here is that targeting image change can take on many forms depending on how the image (or image area) is masked. You'll find opportunities for masking exist in color separations, tones, and color (covered in Chapters 1 and 2).

Moving on from the playground.psd example in this chapter, you might try your hand at working with the gorskiioriginal.psd provided on the CD, to test your ability to spot-correct and make fine adjustments. The parts of the Gorskii image are unique in that the plates were created with separate lenses, and there is a lot to do to adjust for dissimilarity in the optics, let alone the curious flecking and damage to the individual plates. A whole forest of practice work can be had just from the Prokudin-Gorskii archives on the Web: `http://lcweb2.loc.gov/pp/prokquery.html`.

Chapter 4: Filters for Correction

Basic adjustments that you make to remove damage and distractions can help to improve images, but you also need to be careful of removing detail that contributes to sharpness and appearance of reality. Although you will often want to remove undesirable noise, you must do so without harming the natural detail in the image. Selections and masks based on tone and/or color can help you target corrections while defining edge areas to keep them from being affected by changes. This in turn can help you maintain your image's integrity.

Not only will you want to target noise *removal*, but you will also want to target areas to *add* noise in order to re-create natural image and object texture. Combining techniques of removing and then adding back noise in a controlled fashion can give you better, more realistic results in many situations. You can base your targeting on tone and color separations (Chapter 2), or even on corrected areas that you have isolated by techniques used in Chapter 3. Targeting selected areas and objects leads to a natural separation that you can use to enhance an object distinctly from the background—or vice versa.

An interesting exercise to follow up with here is to take a photo and purposely compromise it with JPEG compression. Open any image that you happen to be familiar with, and resave it (by a different name to protect the original) with JPEG compression of 3 or so. Then attempt to resurrect the image. Try making separations that will isolate the damage (hint: take a look at your channels) and try to restore selected areas of tone to make your fixes—perhaps instead of using color.

Chapter 5: Shaping Objects

In Chapter 5 we take a look at creating pixel objects from scratch. The examples include making a button (beveling and drop shadows). That is only the beginning. The chapter goes on to show you how to create seamless patterns that you can apply to fill shapes with color and/or texture—an extension of the process of working with filters described in Chapter 4.

We apply the basics of shaping to creating patterns and texture (the brick wall), and make small changes to patterns so that a generated pattern is made to look more random and realistic.

Finally, we combine techniques that are derivative of separations (creating tone to apply color, as in Chapter 2) and other manipulations to show you how to shape a window to replace an object in an image. In this way, we explore complex ideas of texture and pattern to re-create an image object.

The obvious follow-up to this chapter is to choose images with objects that may be interesting to replace and that may pose interesting challenges in re-creating from scratch. Start with simple, static objects that have rudimentary shapes, and graduate to more complex forms over time. This is one exercise in which you may want to reach forward to the next chapter (Chapter 6) to harness the power of vectors to re-create your shapes.

Chapter 6: Vectors and Illustration

Creating artwork from vectors is a whole different thing from taking a snapshot or making a scan, and is perhaps more challenging because of the blank canvas you start with. However, the techniques you've learned in all the preceding chapters apply: You need to know how to work with color, tone, shading, and blending to give your vectors dimension, color, pattern, and texture. It may take many vector components to create the shapes and objects you need.

Vectors can come in handy when you want to re-create damaged areas of images and other artwork tainted by image processing. A helpful exercise that can also prove valuable is to visit a favorite website, download the company (team, product) logo, and re-create a scalable version of it. This is the type of everyday production work where vectors will prove invaluable. (Of course, once you've done this exercise, you won't be able to use the re-created logo without its owner's authorization.)

In more advanced vector projects you would tend toward creating those things that Adobe Illustrator might be recommended for instead of Photoshop, but they may be worth trying if you can't spend hundreds of dollars on another program. Examples include creating a radio illustration, a cell phone, desk calculator, or other well-defined object. You may need to create many layers and group them with toning, shading, patterning, and noise effects (Chapters 2 and 4) to get the realism that you want in the finished object.

Chapter 7: Image Output Options

This chapter may have felt almost like coming down the slide after having climbed the ladder: You finally get to enjoy the fruits of your labor. While there are some complexities to defining how to handle color, for the most part you will either choose to print or to send your images out to a service once your process and workflow are established.

Certainly you should experiment with working with various workflows, printing with multiple passes, and applying and comparing the differences between vectors and pixels in print. However, pushing yourself beyond your normal workflow will help you learn more about work process, printing processes and image purposing through firsthand experience.

For example, if you always print to your home ink-jet, make plans to send an image out for a digital LED print. If you always print on 8.5 × 11, try a poster print. If you always print a single image at a time, try applying your techniques to finish a project more suited to distribution (such as a holiday card). If you print only from Photoshop, try incorporating your images into a layout program or word processor. Reaching beyond your element can teach you a lot.

Chapter 8: Creating Images for the Web with Photoshop and ImageReady

While Chapter 8 is not entirely focused on ImageReady, certainly the final result in the use of your images is. Here we look at the details involved in creating a complex animation, working with rollovers, and defining image maps. Just as working with vectors and creating objects from scratch draws on all your earlier understanding, so too does working with image actions, but with the added dimension of motion.

Challenges for progressing on your own from this chapter can be many and varied, from simply extending any of the examples to combining them. The most challenging and encompassing of these further explorations is to design a home page. For example, this might be for a product, a service (perhaps your image correction), or just to share your photos and artwork.

Projects can be as simple as creating a single page to display your images in a cycle (using animation to play the frames in a specified order), to creating an animated logo, to creating multiple links to image content areas where you provide additional information about the product or service, to categorizing images for easy browsing.

Chapter 9: Creating, Editing, and Using Actions

Each time you want more from Photoshop—more automation, a simpler process—you need to turn to actions and scripting. In Chapter 9, we look at some simple examples of how to enhance your interaction with the software. But each and every time you say to yourself "Why doesn't this…?" when referring to Photoshop, it may be your cue to consider an automation or customization.

Actions and scripts can both help with your productivity and keep the doldrums at bay by allowing you to automate tedious processes. Building a customized image correction action may be a good place to start. Opportunities to continue, as suggested in the chapter, can be found by becoming aware of your own needs, and "listening" to your process, identifying where it seems to become repetitive or redundant, or function without you. These are places that cry out for automation.

Some of the more challenging, interesting, and rewarding automation projects may actually be those that are not your own. If you visit Photoshop newsgroups and discussion groups (see the short list later in this chapter), you can find all sorts of projects that might warrant a clever action or script to help streamline processes. I hope to see much discussion in the `retouchpro.com` forum along these lines.

Additional Resources

The following list of resources will help you explore, find more information, and discuss ways to use Photoshop—and this book—with other interested users, or its author.

Book Resources

The official listing of book resources here includes URLs to areas meant to help with your use of both this book and Photoshop. In these areas, you will find information not only from the author—who can be found lurking or actively answering questions—but other knowledgeable Photoshop users as well. Please note what kind of resources and interaction you will find in these links. There are better and worse places to get your answers, depending on what your questions are. Also, choose the most appropriate place to post the question instead of posting to all of them. Asking questions in many places at once may seem like a good idea, but it can also sap resources and make discussions difficult to follow.

The Book's Website The website associated with this book will be maintained by the author and dedicated to two things: giving people who don't have the book information about it, and giving people who have the book even *more* information on using Photoshop. Information will be updated periodically, but not as frequently as some of the other sources listed here. These sites will have links to all the items mentioned here (for forums, asking questions, the newsletter) as well as links to additional resources, such as places to find equipment, news, tutorials, and anything added after publishing the book.

Any of these links will direct you to the same information. Multiple sites are provided to make this information easy to access—if you can't access one site, try the next one.

```
http://photoshopx.com

http://photoshopcs.com

http://ps6.com
```

The Forum for the Website A forum is a place where you can post information or questions and read posts by previous visitors. It acts as a rather immediate arena for exchange, and a great way for readers to casually discuss materials with the author. If you have a question about a technique from the book and need a quick answer, this may be the best place to go. Visit regularly to check in on discussions and updates, and to talk with other readers.

> `http://retouchpro.com`

After going to the site, select Forums from the menu to the left of the screen, then scroll down to Tools, click Education, and then click The Hidden Power of Photoshop CS.

Newsletter *The Hidden Power of Photoshop CS* newsletter is a monthly compilation of information that the author believes will be helpful to those reading the book and Photoshop users in general. The newsletter provides a summary of discussions, points of interest, and answers to questions sent directly to the newsletter, forum, or other places that the author frequents. The newsletter is free and is a great source of information and techniques that can help keep you charged up about learning Photoshop long after you have finished reading the book. Send questions that are not of an urgent nature directly to the newsletter. The advantage of posing a question to the newsletter is that often there will be more time for indulging readers and you may get a more polished, complete answer.

> `http://groups.yahoo.com/group/hpps`

You can subscribe to the newsletter by just sending an e-mail to `hpps-subscribe@yahoogroups.com`.

A second option for subscribing is available at the book's website.

Author E-mail Sometimes you won't want to post a question to a forum, or you'll want to contact the author directly, just because…While there is no guarantee that I can get to everything, you can e-mail me directly with notes, questions, problems and concerns. I try to get to everything, but the sheer volume of e-mail may make it impossible. When sending an e-mail, keep the subject short and targeted—a lot of my daily volume of mail is spam and advertisements, and I go through it quickly, and may sometimes delete e-mail with suspicious subject lines. Using simply "Hidden Power" as the subject is recommended.

> `thebookdoc@aol.com`

Other Resources

While it is best to stick to the forum for the book when asking questions related to the book and the techniques it presents, many other forums and resources are available that may prove helpful when you're looking for information about using Photoshop and digital images. These forums range from Adobe's own forum to e-mail discussion lists,

Yahoo-hosted forums, and Usenet services and newsgroups. Several of the more popular groups are listed here as Photoshop specific, or more generally for digital images and photography.

Photoshop Forums

```
http://www.adobeforums.com/
```

You'll find Adobe's forums here. Scroll down the page to Photoshop® & Adobe ImageReady®, then click on the link to your platform. Even though operation of the program is pretty much platform independent, Adobe apparently found there were enough platform-specific issues to maintain separate forums for Mac and Windows. As a result, these forums are largely oriented toward solving platform-specific problems. While there are also issues that are not platform specific, unfortunately you'll see discussion of program-specific information on both forums, so you may want to subscribe to both if you are looking for information on operating the program.

```
http://www.listmoms.net/lists/photoshop/
```

Here you'll find a longstanding and popular e-mail discussion group for Photoshop enthusiasts. This site typically attracts users of widely varied levels.

```
http://groups.yahoo.com/group/colortheory/
```

This group was started by Dan Margulis and is aimed at color professionals. Talk is often highly technical and certainly weighted toward the advanced user.

```
comp.graphics.apps.photoshop and alt.graphics.photoshop
```

These newsgroups can be accessed in a variety of ways, but the easiest may be through Google.com. Just go to the Google search page (http://www.google.com), click the Groups tab, type the group name in the search field, and then click the Google Search button. Caution: Users will widely vary in expertise, and often can get cranky about posting and newsgroup etiquette.

Digital Image and Photography Forums

You can find many more forums on the Web that deal with digital photography and image editing. Here are some popular forums and groups:

```
http://www.photo-forums.com/
```

The forums associated with imaging-resource.com are a good source of information on digital imaging, cameras, and accessories. Photoshop-specific questions fall under the Software forum, but there are many places to explore.

```
http://www.dpreview.com/forums/
```

Digital Photography Review has a forum aimed at those interested in digital photography, as well as dedicated discussion areas for many of the major camera manufacturers. This is only a small niche in the larger website, which provides lots of valuable information.

`http://www.dp-now.com`

Click on the Discussion Forum link to get to the forums. While this may not be the friend-liest forum to navigate, you'll find a lot of serious discussions on a broad range of digital topics.

Appendix

This section collects some information that is important to using Photoshop—mostly technical, and generally a little tedious if you aren't all that interested. Putting it here helps keep it out of the way and lets the rest of the book concentrate on working with images.

This is, however, the place you should come to brush up on a few things that were mentioned in the book that end up mattering when it comes to making the most of your images. If you don't know something about a basic concept, why it is important, and are more-or-less afraid to ask, this appendix will cover it for you—and then some.

This appendix covers the following topics:

Camera RAW files

Resolution 16-bit images

Color management

The image-editing process

Tools you need for corrections

Know your equipment

Know your image

Layer blend modes

Printing options

Camera RAW Files

Camera RAW files are compilations of raw data captured from your digital camera before it is encoded, processed, and turned into a more familiar digital file format (like a TIFF or JPEG). Consider the RAW format as the ultimate archive version of an image; there is no compression, artifacts, or other adjustment made by the camera before delivering the image—all you have is the raw capture data. This lets you make adjustments to the capture, rather than the standard conversion enforced by on-camera processing.

Photoshop CS has the ability to handle the Camera RAW files using the Camera RAW plug-in (included with Photoshop CS instead of being provided as an add-in, as was the case in Photoshop 7). This allows you to open many types of camera raw files from the native data, rather than precompiled files. Setting adjustments include sliders that help you adjust white balance, color temperature, tint, exposure, shadows, brightness, contrast, saturation, smoothness, moiré, color space, size, bit depth, and resolution. These adjustments can help you make the most of the raw camera data. Some of the adjustments may be better deployed during correction stages, so do not feel obligated to use every slider.

Getting the raw camera data is a distinct matter from having the ability to open it with Photoshop. Not all cameras allow you to save files in RAW formats, and will instead convert the raw data into a common file type before storing it. In order to process the RAW data, your camera will have to offer a RAW save option and you will have to change the camera settings to store the data in the camera's RAW format.

When you open the image in Photoshop, you will be presented with a dialog box in which you make adjustments using the on-screen preview as a visual guide. You can save particular settings and use them in actions and batch processes so that you can process your RAW images in bulk. In addition, you can store and archive the camera's RAW files, and at a later date process them differently if a different interface or process becomes available.

The biggest drawback to using RAW format is that the files themselves tend to be much larger than those stored as JPEG. As a result, you will either need to get more storage for image capture or be prepared to fill up your media many times faster. Whether the ability to work with RAW files is a benefit depends on your camera, its processing, and your workflow. An honest evaluation of images you open from RAW against those processed by the camera should give you a good idea whether it is worth the additional space—and the cost of additional storage. In most cases, it is likely that it will be.

Resolution

Put as simply as possible, resolution is a measure of potential detail in your images. High resolution suggests that there will be intricate detail; low resolution suggests detail may be compromised. It would seem, if the description holds, that you would always want high resolution if you consider detail important. But that's not always the case. What you really want is the *right* resolution, and this depends not only on what size you want the result to be but also on what medium you will be using. Output and display can use image resolution in different ways, so the result doesn't depend only on what the resolution of the image is; it depends on how much image information there is as well as how it is used.

In print, if you don't have enough resolution to meet the needs of the output, images won't look as sharp as they could; if you have too much, file sizes are unnecessarily large and processing will take longer than it needs to. On the Web, images without enough resolution will be too small; those with too much will be too large. This carries over into other display-based technologies (such as film recorders). You can't just guess how much image information you need; you have to know and work within those parameters. The key to working with resolution is to target the amount of resolution you need. Understanding what resolution is and how it is used is the only way to use it correctly.

How Image Resolution Is Measured

Image resolution is usually measured in one of several ways: the number of total pixels (image dimension in pixels), the size of the file (number of bytes, kilobytes, or megabytes), or the number of picture elements (pixels) per inch (ppi, or pixels per inch). Different ways of measuring the file size are not necessarily better or worse, so long as you can consistently achieve the desired result—without guesswork.

For most people working in Photoshop, pixels per inch—a measure of output resolution—is more relevant than either total pixel dimensions or file size. Both total pixels and file size describe the source image size, as with scans or images from digital cameras; and while they tell you the quantity of image information in a file, they don't dictate how the information is used. An image with 2100×1500 pixels could be displayed or printed as a 7×5 inch image at 300 dpi, or a 21×15 inch image at 100 dpi—and it can be used that way simultaneously.

File size is even less directly related to output resolution, because the number of bits needed to represent a pixel depends on factors like the color model used. The output dimension of a 12MB image at 300 ppi might be about a third larger in RGB than CMYK. In black-and-white (grayscale), a 12MB image would display much larger still—about 4 times the area of the 12MB CMYK image.

Because there is no single parameter that locks in the output size of the image when you measure pixel dimensions or file size, you can't know exactly what you have and how the image will be applied. File size is probably the least used measure of resolution, and only really makes sense in a workflow where color mode is static (e.g., images are only either RGB or CMYK).

Most Photoshop users will use ppi as a measure of image resolution because it is the most compatible when you're comparing to output resolutions. The measure tells how much of the image pixel information should be applied per inch. Printer resolution is most often a finite measure (based on the printer's dpi: how many printer dots can be made per inch), so the optimal match between digital image information and what the printer will need to produce the best results can be determined.

Using the Correct Image Resolution

Some people generalize and suggest using 300 ppi as a standard resolution for images going to print. For web images, it is usually accepted that images should be 72 ppi. While these are useful as general-purpose guidelines, they don't tell the entire story. For example, 300 ppi may be more than is necessary for all home printers, and may actually be too little for demanding output (such as film recorder output). Because monitor resolutions can vary, your 72-ppi image on a 96-dpi screen would actually be about 75 percent of the intended size. Neither choice is very likely to ruin your output in most cases.

Because output differs, there is no one universal magic formula to determine what resolution to use. Each output type has a target range (minimum and maximum), based on its capability to process and use image information. If you know that range, you simply use that range as a target when working on an image. Find out what your service or printer manufacturer recommends for output on devices you use. This may require reading the manual, or giving a call to the service.

Table A.1 shows approximate resolutions you will want to use for your images depending on how you want to use them. An image sent to a device that uses a specified output resolution should have a specific target ppi. The chart below shows some real-world examples of output resolution and workable ppi ranges. Calculations for the table were based on the formulas shown in the Calculation Used to Get Resolution column; square brackets in the calculations indicate the range of values used to determine the lowest and highest resolution acceptable in the range.

Table A.1

Approximate Resolution for Various Media

MEDIA	OUTPUT RESOLUTION	APPROXIMATE IMAGE FILE RESOLUTION	CALCULATION USED TO GET RESOLUTION
Web	72–96 dpi (monitor)	72–96 ppi	ppi = dpi
Ink-jet (stochastic)	720 dpi	180–234 ppi	ppi = [1 to 1.3] × dpi/4
Ink-jet (stochastic)	1,440 dpi	360–468 ppi	ppi = [1 to 1.3] × dpi/4
Halftone, low resolution	75–100 lpi	116–200 ppi	ppi = [1.55 to 2] × lpi
Halftone, normal	133–150 lpi	233–350 ppi	ppi = [1.55 to 2] × lpi
Halftone, high resolution	175–200 lpi	271–400 ppi	ppi = [1.55 to 2] × lpi
Line art	600–3,000 dpi	600–1,342 ppi	ppi = (dpi/600) $\sqrt{}$ × 600
Film recorder	4K lines (35mm)	2,731×4,096 pixels	Total pixels
Film recorder	8K lines (6×9)	5,461×8,192 pixels	Total pixels

Note that these resolutions are suggested and not absolute. Images will still print and display at other resolutions, but the results may not be predictable or efficient. Actual resolution needs may be somewhat flexible based on circumstances, such as paper and equipment used, original image quality, expected results, and other factors. Be sure to read manufacturer suggestions, and take most of the advice offered by services—they should know how to get the best results from their equipment.

> While dpi is really an output term, it's often used casually as a universal term for resolution (spi, ppi, dpi, and even lpi). It can be confusing if you randomly throw out acronyms when you really mean something specific, but it can also be difficult to use the proper terms consistently. To simplify with better accuracy, use spi when speaking of capture (scanning, sampling), ppi when discussing digital files, dpi when considering output resolution, and lpi in the context of halftone dot size.

Resizing Images

There are essentially two ways to change the size of an area that a group of pixels occupies: one causes you to resample an image (using interpolation), and the other changes the resolution to redistribute pixels over a smaller or larger area. Redistributing pixels does nothing to change the content (mathematics) of the image information that is stored; it just suggests that the content will be applied over a different area. Resampling, on the other hand, actually changes the content of your images, and changes it permanently. The larger the amount of resizing (the greater the percentage of the increase or decrease), the more it affects the image content. One of these two things, redistributing or resampling, has to happen each time you change the size of the whole image (using Image Size, not Canvas Size) or change the size of a selection by stretching or transforming.

When you upsize or downsize an image or image area and retain the resolution (ppi), Photoshop has to interpret and redistribute tonal and color information either creating (upsizing) or removing (downsizing) pixels. It does this through interpolation (or decimation), which is just a fancy name for making an educated guess. Resampling an image larger will never fill in information that is not already there, no matter what you do and which plug-in you use. That trick you've seen on TV, where characters zoom in on an image until it becomes pixelated, and then click a button that lets them zoom in some more as the image gets clearer and clearer, is reverse-engineered: the producers actually start with a clear image, pixelate it, and then show you the result in reverse. The only thing you can do to reclaim image detail that you don't already have is to reshoot an image or rescan (assuming that the detail is present in what you are scanning). Resampling gives you an estimate of the differences between pixels so that you can make a best guess. Details will tend to soften as they are upsized or to be lost as you downsize.

Photoshop has three basic methods of interpolation—that is, of figuring out how to insert new pixels or remove existing ones as you change an image's size:

Nearest Neighbor Nearest Neighbor interpolation picks a representative color from the sample area (whether up- or downsizing). There is no averaging to create new colors or tones. This helps maintain hard color and tone edges but can lead to distortion—perhaps especially noticeable in downsizing. It is useful, for example, for controlled upsampling of screenshots without blurring when used with precision (e.g., changing a 72-ppi screenshot to 288 ppi neatly upsamples every pixel into 4). Keep in mind, however, that if you use an incorrect measure (e.g., upsampling from 72 to 300 ppi, instead of 288), the interpolation is not neat and the result can be distorted. You need to upsize by squares (4, 9, 16,…) so the result of the pixel will be a cube.

Bilinear Bilinear interpolation introduces new tones and colors between existing colors that are not in the original image. This can blur sampling of hard edges, but can provide a smoother transition for tones than Nearest Neighbor. Bilinear upsampling remains true to simple averaging between neighboring tones. It is useful when you want a straightforward averaging and may be valuable when you're downsampling images.

Bicubic The Bicubic resampling process creates new image information by averaging, like Bilinear, but goes one step further to provide some sharpening. This is intended to counteract the blurring result of averaging. It affects change in a greater number of pixels than Bilinear using the same radius setting. Although the affected range is greater, Bicubic can give a better visible result in many cases than Bilinear. Bicubic is the general workhorse for sizing images up or down. New variations (Smoother and Sharper) provide different levels of sharpening for the process.

While making up information and decimating it may sound bad, each has its purpose. Usually you should avoid casual upsampling. However, images can be upsampled with some success—provided the change isn't huge, and depending on the desired quality. Upsampling 10 percent or even 20 percent may not be noticeable if the source image is sharp. Usually you will only upsize to make up small gaps (if necessary) between the resolution you have in an image and what you really need, or to adjust borrowed image components (as when making a composite image).

Downsampling, while certainly damaging and compromising to image content, should be less noticeable in your results. Image information indeed gets averaged or eliminated, but if downsizing is being done for the right reason, any details you lose would have been lost on output or display anyway. Detail loss is inherent in the process of downsizing or outputting images at a smaller size: even if the equipment used could reproduce detail at a smaller size, eventually details will pass the limit of human ability to discern them. In any case, you should always be working on (resampling and resizing) copies of your original; if that is the case, there is no need to worry about permanently losing details.

Multipurpose Images

If you will be making images that you'll use with more than one purpose (e.g., print and web), you're faced with a choice. Optimally, you should work with images so that you maintain the ppi that you need for the final output at final size. This will ensure that you retain all the image detail rather than relying on interpolation or decimation and your choice for sampling type to produce the right results. An image going to print on a high-resolution printer should have more information than one at the same size used on the Web, or you will not optimize detail. If you are working on an image that will be used both in print and on the Web, your only options for working with these dual-purpose images are:

- Create two images, each with a specific purpose.
- Create one image and resize.

Either of these choices poses a trade-off. In creating two images, you sacrifice valuable time to simply try to achieve similar results in two images using the best process. In creating one image and resizing, you have to allow either interpolation of new image information or decimation, which may not be the optimal process.

You can't work on small images and resize up because detail will not be present. It is often self-defeating to work on two images to produce the same results (even using a detailed script) because the difference in size and volume of information in the image will produce different results with the same application of tools.

The best way to go about working with multipurpose images is generally to work with them at the highest resolution and resize them smaller. Working at the higher of two or more resolutions retains the details for the higher-resolution presentations, and resizing will sacrifice only the detail that will not be reproducible at lower resolutions.

Input Resolution

Digital camera resolution is weighted in dimension, total pixels, or both, but that doesn't tell you how big the resulting images will be. Table A.2 offers a brief overview using common camera abilities and maximum output size (in inches).

CAMERA RESOLUTION	TOTAL PIXELS	MAX. FINAL SIZE FOR WEB/MONITOR (96 PPI)	MAX. FINAL SIZE FOR PHOTO-QUALITY (200 PPI)	MAX. NEGATIVE / CHROME OUTPUT (650 PPI)
320×200	64,000	3.3"×2"	1.6"×1"	0.5"×0.3"
640×480	307,200	6.7"×5"	3.2"×2.4"	1"×0.8"
1024×768	786,432	10.7"×8"	5"×3.75"	1.5"×1.1"
1280×960	1,228,800	13.3"×10"	6"×4.8"	1.8"×1.5"
1600×1200	1,920,000	16.7"×12.5"	8"×6"	2.5"×1.8"
2048×1536	3,145,728	21.3"×16"	10"×7.5"	3.1"×2.3"
2400×1800	4,320,000	25"×18.8"	12"×9"	3.7"×2.8"
2500×2000	5,000,000	26"×20.8"	12.5"×10"	3.9"×3.1"
3072×2048	6,291,456	32"×21.3"	15.4"×x10.3"	4.7"×3.1"
4536×3024	13,716,864	47.3"×31.5"	22.7"×15.1"	7"×4.7"

Table A.2

Common Camera Resolutions

With this chart you can look up or approximate the output possibilities for your camera by finding the camera resolution or total pixels. This should give you an idea of the potential for images that come from the camera. This, of course, cannot take cropping or compositing into account.

Monitor resolution

Monitor resolution affects how images appear on screen. Many people will just set monitor resolution to the highest setting suggested by the manufacturer and assume that it is correct—or assume that it doesn't matter. If you set your monitor resolution too high (greater than the monitor was built to handle), you can actually lose detail rather than improve it, and images can appear too small. If you set the resolution too low, images will appear larger but you won't take advantage of the viewing landscape on your monitor. Just as you wouldn't always want to maximize the resolution of your images, it may not be appropriate to go with the highest resolution your monitor is capable of.

The maximum monitor resolution setting is dictated by the monitor's viewing size and dot pitch. Viewing size is simply the monitor area; dot pitch is, essentially, the resolution—the number of image dots that can be represented. The greater the viewing size or the lower the dot pitch, the more the monitor can show. Higher-dot-pitch monitors will tend to look sharper—though this depends on what the dot pitch refers to in the specifications (not all monitor dot pitches are measured in the same way).

There are more complicated means of selecting a monitor display resolution, but a good gauge for choosing the "right" resolution involves choosing the resolution that makes an image appear correctly sized on screen. Choosing the right resolution has the advantage of letting you see things close to the correct size on screen, while pretty much eliminating the chance that your monitor doesn't have enough resolution. Any monitor

DIAGONAL VIEW SIZE	72-PPI RESOLUTION	96-PPI RESOLUTION
23″	1600×1200	1920×1200
21″	1280×1024	1600×1200
19″	1152×870	1280×1024
17″	1024×768	1152×870
15″	870×640	1024×768
13″	800×600	870×640

Table A.3

Common Monitor Sizes and Resolutions

with a dot pitch of less than .28 (about .22 horizontally) should be able to handle the suggested range while maintaining a sharp image. This does not mean that having a higher-resolution monitor is wasted; finer dot pitch almost always translates into finer image display. Using a higher resolution can also have the advantage of making palettes and menus smaller, leaving more space on the screen for you to work.

Table A.3 is a guideline to help you create an accurately sized image on screen, and will give you a target to shoot for. It may not be exact—there are variables in displays—but it should take you closer than just guessing at a size or choosing the maximum suggested resolution willy-nilly (or based on what you think might look good when you have the monitor control panel open). The point is that when you choose View → Print Size, your image will be close to displaying on screen at the size you intend to use it.

Monitor screen size is measured from corner to corner diagonally rather than as height or width. If you are unsure of your monitor size, a quick measure of the diagonal surface area of the screen will tell you approximately what the view size is for your monitor. Choose an available display resolution in the monitor control panel that falls between the range shown in the table (between 72 and 96 ppi) to get the most accurate sizing.

If you prefer to have a very accurate view of print size on screen, you can choose your resolution roughly and make adjustments in the horizontal and vertical projection of the monitor to make the display dimensions nearly exact. To do this, you can match a display ruler (show rulers on an open image displaying at 100 percent) to a household ruler using horizontal and vertical screen controls.

Number of Colors

You may be able to change your color settings to anything between monochrome and 32-bit color in your control panel, and as with resolution, it might be tempting to always pick the maximum. These settings may be presented as the number of bits used to represent color or the number of colors available (depending on the operating system and the utility or control panel you are using for the setting). The more bits used, the more colors; and the more true-to-life color can be. At the same time, the greater volume of data makes color processing more taxing, so this may result in potentially lower refresh rates. Optimally you will want to choose to display the most bits you can, but if you have a less powerful video card and a large monitor, or if you are offered fewer choices for refresh rates, it may be best to choose fewer bits as a trade-off. Your images display 24-bit information (3x8 bits) in Photoshop, so choosing 32-bits for display will not necessarily improve viewing for images.

Refresh Rate

Refresh rate is the frequency at which an image on the screen is updated or refreshed. The rate is measured in hertz (Hz). The higher the frequency (the more Hz), the faster the screen refreshes. The faster it refreshes, the less likely you are to detect flicker, and the more likely that your view of changes and movement on the screen (such as the cursor) will seem smooth. Quick refresh rates can also reduce eyestrain. This can be important if, like some of us, you spend a lot of time staring at your monitor.

Use only suggested refresh rates for your monitor and video card or you can run the risk of damaging your equipment. Refresh rates should generally be as fast as you can make them within the manufacturer's suggested range without cutting into other display properties that reduce performance in other ways.

Bit Depth and "16-Bit" Images

One of the more interesting changes in Photoshop CS is its broader "16-bit" support. Even if you are familiar with what bits are and how they represent information, the terminology can be confusing. So let's start with the basics.

Bits represent how precisely color can be measured. They are the encoded 1s and 0s used in computer language to describe an image. Each pixel in your image (color) is described by the bits. The more bits, the greater the potential accuracy of the color.

Bits themselves are just tiny chunks of information—sometimes described by the term "binary." All that term means is that each bit used in your files can be either on or off. So each bit has only two possible values: either on (1) or off (0). If an image is one-bit, each pixel in the image has one bit that can be on or off. That is pretty much black and white.

The more bits per pixel, the more complex the relationship gets. If your image is a two-bit image, each bit has two potential values, and these values can be paired in any of these combinations: 00, 01, 10, or 11 to define the pixel. Each additional bit per pixel adds a multiple of two combinations, one additional set of combinations for each additional bit. Just to show how quickly this can add up, if a third bit were added to your 2-bit image, this would result in the following set of possibilities for each pixel: 000, 001, 010, 011, 100, 101, 110, 111—a total of eight possible combinations. So each time another bit is added, there are twice as many possible combinations—one additional full set of possibilities for each of the two possible values of the bit.

To get the total number of bit combinations, all you have to do is multiply by two for each bit. Eight bits per channel would be $2\times2\times2\times2\times2\times2\times2\times2$ (or 2^8) totaling 256 combinations. In a 24-bit image, that would be 2^{24}. This could be referred to as 24-bit color or 8-bit per channel RGB. The totals are calculated somewhat differently, though the result is the same. The 24 bits in a 24-bit image are used to describe three tones: R, G, and B. A 24-bit RGB image uses 8 bits for each of the tones: 8 bits red, 8 bits green, and 8 bits blue. These 3 groups of 8 bits describe the 256 tonal possibilities for red, green, and blue. Each of the colors has 256 possibilities that can be combined in any fashion. Whether you multiply 2^{24}, or 256×256×256, you get the same number of bit combinations: 16,777,216. That is how many colors each pixel can represent in 24-bit color. If you add bits, you add potential colors: if you have an image with 30 bits, there would be 10 bits per channel, or 1024 bit combinations per pixel per color, or 1,073,741,824 different potential combinations. That is 64 times as many color combinations, with only a few more bits.

In other words, increased pixel depth exponentially increases the color possibilities, which is why increased color depth is considered by some to be so valuable in color work. The negative effect of increased bit depth (for example, to 16 bits per channel from 8) is increased image size. There is also some question as to the value of increased bit depth. In fact, it seems almost useless for anything but corrections and archiving (the permanent storage of images) for two reasons:

1. If you have 16 million colors, it is not incredibly likely that having even more is going to have a lot of effect on the way you see an image.

2. Output in most cases can't reproduce more than 24-bit color.

Increased bit depth can improve the capture of detail, and may maintain fine discrepancies that can be important during adjustments. For example, in poorly exposed images, you may be better able to salvage information that was captured at 16 bit that would not be distinguishable in 8 bit. While current technology sides with the idea that 8 bit is all you need for output, it is possible that this can very well change in the future; images archived in 16 bit may provide useful detail if this comes to pass. Also, 16 bit may offer additional advantages for working with black-and-white images (which are otherwise limited to only 256 tones). Most users at this stage will find 16 bit suitable for correction and archive only, while 8 bit is all you will need for images in print. Generally your workflow would include working in 16 bit for corrections and converting to 8 bit to finalize the image for print.

Bit terminology can be a bit confusing; bit depth can be referred to either as bits per color/channel or total bits. If used with care, this shouldn't pose a problem. However, it can be confusing when you discover a 16-bit image actually has more image information than a 24-bit color scan. Be sure you are comparing either total bits per pixel or bits per color/channel when looking at specifications or comparing images. Comparing bits per channel to total bits is like comparing grayscale and color images—different representations of the same thing, but they are not equivalent.

Color Management

Color management is the way you handle color in your workflow. To some extent, everyone manages color, even if they choose to ignore their color settings; some people just manage color better or more frugally than others. The goal of managing color no matter what you do should be to enhance your results.

There is no best advice when it comes to color management; there are just learned ways of working and execution. If there were a universally better method of working with color, that model would simply be implemented by Adobe and that would be the end of the issue. The fact is, there are different ways to handle color management because of individual preferences in work style and differing needs. Using broad measures for color management, like embedding profiles, won't tackle your color problems every time, but it also isn't the best idea to always ignore color management totally—either for the potential advantages it can pose or by just curtly dismissing a profile mismatch warning without ever thinking about what it means.

One thing that is crucial to color results is calibrating and normalizing your monitor. Without doing this you are viewing your images on an unknown source. Calibrating is imperative to normalizing the view and letting Photoshop know vital statistics about your display.

Monitor Calibration

Everything you see on screen, whether in Indexed Color, CMYK, RGB, Lab, HSB, or whatever, will be portrayed in RGB. Depending on how you handle color management, even RGB in the image file may be slightly different than what you can see on screen. For example, if you use Adobe RGB as your workspace, there are colors in the color space that you can't see on the monitor: you have digital information that can't accurately be displayed.

Calibrating your monitor is just the first step to avoiding accidents. The simple purpose of calibration is to standardize your monitor view. That is, it helps you make sure your grays look gray and that your monitor is as close as it can be to a "normal" view. A normal view shows the full range of tones and colors possible on a standard RGB monitor. The most frightening thing about calibration is the word itself. Calibration doesn't take days or weeks and doesn't require special equipment (though for serious Photoshop users , hardware calibration is worth considering). If you don't calibrate, your monitor will not be standardized and your previews are less likely to be accurate: you stand little chance of being able to trust what you see on your monitor, and your results will be an accident.

Take your time when calibrating the monitor, and do it as well as you can. Consider that the measurements you make are used to generate previews, and, if you like to embed device profiles, will describe your equipment to other devices. Inaccuracies get compounded as you attempt to correct for an inaccurate preview, causing inaccuracies in previews and descriptions, and the result can be unexpected changes in images when they are used. Run through calibration more than once to be sure you've got it right. The more accurate you are, the more likely you will have a good description of your device and get the results you expect. Experience will tell you when to look closer, when to measure, and when "good enough" really is. A lot of what I am saying here can be summed up as: Don't be fooled by the color you see on screen. Learn to use numbers, measure values, view histograms, check white and black points, and make intelligent use of proofing and profiles.

Whether you are on a Mac or a Windows machine, you will be able to calibrate using either the Displays System Preferences (Mac) or Adobe Gamma (Windows). These utilities will both calibrate and create an ICC profile based on your input. The profile is a description of how your monitor handles color. The profile can be used to describe your monitor to other devices (via embedding in image files) and can be used to help Photoshop generate reasonably accurate previews based on your color settings.

For Windows users, you can locate Adobe Gamma in the Control Panel, or on the Photoshop program CD. Just launch the program. For Mac users, locate Display Calibrator Assistant by opening System Preferences, choosing Display, and clicking the Color tab. Click the Calibrate button to open the initial screen. Once you are on the initial screen, the wizard will lead you step by step through the calibration process. The screens for each utility are about the same.

Here we'll look at the steps for calibrating your monitor. Before you begin, you should know several things about the response and performance of your monitor, including the manufacturer-suggested color temperature, gamma, and phosphor settings. *Color temperature* reflects the monitor display color for the *white point,* which measures the color of white on your monitor. It is usually 5000, 6500, 7500, or 9300 degrees on the Kelvin scale. It is a characteristic of the color balance of your display. *Gamma* is a measure of tonal response, often a number with two decimal places between 1 and 3. *Phosphors* are a set of six numbers with *x* and *y* coordinates for red, green, and blue; these numbers can have up to three decimal places. These settings vary between monitor brands and models, so don't make assumptions about them or copy someone else's; either find the settings in your manual or contact the manufacturer (via the website or technical support).

Monitor manufacturers don't always put monitor specs for phosphors, white point, and gamma in the manuals. When you obtain the information, write it down. I usually write the settings right on the cover of the monitor manual for easy reference.

Before you begin, you should also locate the monitor's brightness, contrast, and color controls. If your monitor has an option for resetting to factory settings, do it now.

1. Turn on your monitor and system, boot up, and let the monitor warm up for at least 30 minutes.

2. If you haven't done it yet, read the owner's manual for the monitor to see if it provides suggestions for calibration.

3. Open Adobe Gamma by double-clicking the icon in the Control Panel folder (Windows), or open Display Calibrator Assistant (Mac) by going to System Preferences, choosing Display, clicking the Color tab, and then clicking the Calibrate button. If you're on a Mac, you'll see the screen in Figure A.1 (Display Calibrator Assistant); you'll see the initial Adobe Gamma screen if you're on a PC.

At this point, you should closely follow the instructions as they appear on screen. You may want to repeat steps as you go more than once—especially if you are not familiar with the process—to be sure you have completed the steps correctly. The options for the screens differ somewhat between the two utilities, but are similar. The following list should cover your options for both. Each selection is crucial to getting the best possible previews and profiles.

Expert Mode or Advanced Options Offers additional options for adjusting the display.

Display Description or Profile Name Type a name for the profile you will be creating. It's best to keep the description short. For example, you might just name the monitor and add the date, so the profiles are easy to identify. This is the first step for Adobe Gamma and the last for Display Calibrator Assistant.

Display Adjustment for Brightness and Contrast Using the monitor controls, set the contrast all the way up and then adjust brightness until the smaller gray area in the center is dark enough that it is just barely discernable from the larger black box surrounding it. Try to maintain the brightness of the monitor white: If you notice the white on your monitor beginning to darken as you darken the center square, stop darkening the screen. As you fine-tune this adjustment, it may help to move the spot you are looking at on screen very frequently (from top to bottom of the center area, for example) to keep your vision from adjusting to the screen.

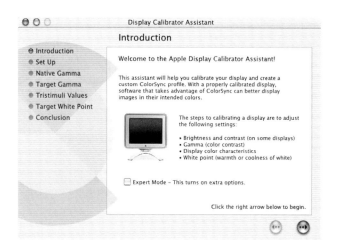

Figure A.1

Adobe Gamma and Display Calibrator Assistant are step-by-step wizards that lead you through the calibration process.

Phosphors, Chromasicities, or Trisimuli Values   Phosphor or Trisimuli values describe the monitor's response to color. It is more accurate to type in the six values obtained from the manufacturer of your monitor in the appropriate fields than to use a preset description. You don't really have to know what each number means, but you do have to place each one correctly as x and y components in the provided fields. If you can't get the values from the manufacturer, you can select a display preset or generic model.

Gamma Adjustment   This will display as either a single grayscale adjustment, or an adjustment for red, green, and blue. Expert Mode or deselecting the View Single Gamma Only check box displays the three sliders. Using the slider, adjust the appearance of the outer area (the alternating lines) so that it matches the tone of the center. Adjust the appearance by squinting at the screen (to blur the box slightly in your vision) while moving the slider. The goal is for the entire square to seem to have a uniform tone.

Monitor or Display White Point   White point is a measure of the "color" of the brightest parts of your monitor, measured in degrees Kelvin. Set the monitor's white point by choosing the value that corresponds with the number you got from the manufacturer. If available, the option to measure the white point is preferable to making a random selection.

Output or Target White Point   Output white point differs from monitor white point. This setting should reflect the color temperature of your output. This may be another monitor, paper, or a projection screen. This selection should be based on the color temperature of the intended output media. If you are unsure, or you are creating images for the Web, use the Same As Hardware setting. You may want to run through setup separately for each target you have to create different profiles.

I never calibrate one time and sit back satisfied—even when using a calibration device. I run through the process a few times. If you change monitors, you will obviously have to build a new profile. Other less-obvious reasons to build a new profile are: monitor aging and changes in response due to use, replacing your system hard drive, and changing room lighting (or computer placement).

When you have finished running through the wizard, you will have calibrated your monitor and created an ICC profile for it. The calibration ensures that the image information you see on screen is reasonably accurate. The ICC profile is a description of your color space and other data that helps describe how color appears on your system. This information can be used by your system to adjust image previews.

After creating your profile, be sure the lighting where you work remains the same as when you calibrated the monitor. The monitor can be calibrated to different light conditions, but it is easier to maintain a consistent room lighting than it is to add lighting as a variable in color corrections. Extremely bright or overly dark rooms might cause some problems with calibrations and monitor viewing. Optimally, room lighting should be bright enough that you can read and view materials that are not on the screen, yet not so bright that it causes glare or washes out the display.

Although Adobe Gamma and Display Calibrator Assistant are adequate tools for visual calibration, calibration devices (see Figure A.2 for an example) can measure more accurately than your eye and can create more accurate profiling. These devices take measurements directly from your screen and create a profile based on those measurements. Using such a device can ensure that your monitor is calibrated properly, and it may actually save some time during calibrations.

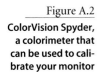

Figure A.2

ColorVision Spyder, a colorimeter that can be used to calibrate your monitor

The Image-Editing Process

Say you are building a house. You get some big power tools and dig a hole for the foundation. The whole time you are digging, you are preoccupied with the bathroom and the wonderful pedestal sink you'll put in. So as soon as you have the hole dug, you start putting in the plumbing for the bathroom to get to the sink, even before you get the foundation poured. Of course, no one would ever build a house that way. You pour the foundation so you have something to build the walls and floor on—and use to help hold the pipes up. The plan that you follow for building the house has to take the whole process into consideration—not just the parts you want to do first.

The same goes for images: it's important to start with the image foundations rather than jump right to the part you think might be the most trouble—or the most interesting and fun to work with. You'll do your best work if you work according to a plan. For image correction, you'll have a general plan for your workflow. Table A.4 shows an overview of the process.

Table A.4

Overview of the Color-Correction Process

PREPARATION STEPS	NOTES
1. Be sure you have calibrated your monitor.	Calibrate your monitor and create an ICC profile. This will ensure that you are looking at the image correctly on screen.
2. Decide how you will handle color management.	Decide how you will handle color management in your workflow, including how you will handle images with profiles and whether or not you will embed profiles. This will determine how you control your results.
3. Decide resolution and color needs for the current image.	Even before you scan or take a picture, it is a good idea to know what your target resolution and use(s) will be. This can help you define targeted capture of your images.
4. Make the best, targeted image capture that you possibly can.	You always want to work with the best possible source. That means taking the best possible image or making the best possible scan. Starting with the best makes for the best result.
5. Store the original scan/image file safely	Work on duplicates of your image so that you do not ever accidentally save over an original. This ensures that you can always go back to the original to start over or use for another purpose.
6. Evaluate the image.	Look at the image and make a list of things you want to change or fix.
CORRECTION STEPS	
7. Crop and size the image so that you are working with the image areas you really need.	Cut out extra stuff to focus on the parts of the image you need. This will keep processing to a minimum. In some cases, you may want to flip-flop this step with the next if cropping will affect color corrections.
8. Make general color and tonal corrections.	Make levels and curve correction to adjust tone and color overall, as discussed later in this chapter. Corrections may also include Color Balance, Variations, and other general color corrections. This step may be flip-flopped with the previous step if cropping will remove information that is critical to color correction.

continues

9. Correct general abrasions and damage.	Clear dust, scratches, and other debris from an image that will obviously need to be removed. View the image at 200% or more to see all the damage. This will ensure that the image or parts you will be using else-where are clear of damage.
10. Make selective compositional and color changes and corrections.	Make local changes in composition, tone, and color. These changes will require selection and masking or other means of targeting change.
11. Simplify the image as appropriate.	Remove unused and test layers, commit acceptable changes, and remove unnecessary additional paths and channels. Rename layers for clarity of purpose. This simplifies the image and content, saves space, and helps with any edits or adjustments made in the future.

PURPOSING AND STORAGE STEPS

12. Save the layered RGB version of the image.	Storing the image with corrections allows you recall and adjust corrections as needed.
13. Optimize the image for output and use.	Make color and tonal adjustments or conversions, cor-rect white and black points for printing, sharpen, adjust local or global contrast, adjust final brightness, etc. This ensures that the image works optimally for the purpose it was created for.
14. Save the file in output file format with a new name.	This steps ensures that you have saved the targeted image with adjustments for its specific purpose and use.

Keep in mind that this is a general floor plan. You may have to spend a lot of time in any one area depending on your image, or you might be able to skip some steps (for example, a conversion may not apply).

Tools You Need for Corrections

In each step of the image-editing process, you can usually use a small subset of tools to accomplish your goals. Having these smaller sets in mind will streamline your image pro-cessing and keep you on target. It doesn't mean the other tools are useless, or that you'll never need them, or that you don't have to learn them at all. However, it does suggest where you need to be strongest—or at least where to start.

The tool sets in Table A.5 are based on the steps in the preceding section. The tools mentioned are standard Photoshop tools, but may include other hardware and software—notably during image capture. You may, occasionally, reach outside these suggested toolsets for a special purposes, but this table offers a good general guideline to simplifying the tools you need to get excellent and consistent results. The choices are based not on which tool is the easiest to use, but on which will get the best results.

STEP	TOOLS TO USE	
1. Be sure you have calibrated your monitor.	Adobe Gamma, Display Calibrator Assistant, calibration device	**Table A.5** **Toolsets**
2. Decide how you will handle color management.	Color Settings, Previews	
3. Decide resolution and color needs for the current image.	Know output needs for resolution and color	
4. Make the best, targeted image capture that you possibly can.	Scanner, digital camera	
5. Store the original scan/image file safely.	Save, or duplicate original image files.	
6. Evaluate the image.	Eyedropper, Info palette, Histograms	
7. Crop and size the image so that you are working with the image areas you really need.	Crop, Marquee	
8. Make general color and tonal corrections.	Levels, Curves, Color Balance	
9. Correct general abrasions and damage.	Clone Stamp, Healing, masking, Copy/Paste	
10. Make selective compositional and color changes and corrections.	Hue Saturation, layers (masking, modes, clipping, adjustment layers), channels, filters (Add Noise, Gaussian Blur, Unsharp Mask), History Brush, Gradient Maps, Blend If, Selection (Quick Mask, alpha channels)	
11. Simplify the image as appropriate.	Color modes, layers, vector properties, Merge functions	
12. Save the layered RGB version of the image.	Save	
13. Optimize the image for output and use.	Color modes, layers, vector properties, Merge functions, Unsharp Mask	
14. Save the file in output file format by a new name.	Save	

This table cuts out many tools, most of which provide redundant (and sometimes inferior) means of completing tasks. The list leaves off a few tools, but if you follow the methods in this book, you will find they are seldom necessary.

A few tools don't really fit any category in particular, but they can be very useful. These include histories, actions, workspaces, and tool presets. When doing serious correction and experimentation, histories and actions are valuable for navigating steps and automating processes. Workspaces and tool presets can keep you focused on working with the image, rather than manipulating the interface.

Know Your Equipment

Because all computers and systems are not alike, it is impossible to cover every nuance of every system in every situation in one book. There are innumerable digital cameras on the market, a plethora of ways to get the images off the cameras, and hundreds of home printers to print the result to. If you have trouble getting the images off your camera, or have trouble with your printer or computer, the place to find answers is in the user manual for these devices and through technical support from manufacturers. What may not always be obvious is that other software, hardware, and peripherals can affect the way Photoshop performs.

The following is a short checklist of maintenance items you should recognize and understand for your computer, peripherals, and software.

Scanners (and optical-based equipment):

- Calibrate, per manufacturer suggestions, if available. Third-party calibration tools may prove useful if the manufacturer offers no solution.

- Maintain a regimen for cleaning the optical components and objects (scanned or photographed).

- Be sure to use proper connections, connection settings, and accessories.

- Consider services for outsourcing; they may have equipment designed for a specific job.

Digital cameras:

- Choose appropriate settings per manufacturer recommendations, and don't change settings if you don't know what they do.

- Learn about special features and settings by reading the manual.

- Understand image control and exposure.

- Understand how to format camera storage.

- Know how to properly connect a camera to your computer and download images from the camera.

Printers:

- Use appropriate paper and inks as suggested by the manufacturer.

- Read maintenance and cleaning suggestions and follow these practices rigorously.

- Don't expect RGB results from a CMYK printer. CMYK is a smaller color space, meaning there are simply fewer colors available.

Computer software and hardware:

- Maintain a firewall if you are using an open Internet connection (e.g., cable or DSL).

- Use virus-protection software to identify infected digital files, especially if you trade a lot of files. Never open a file from an outside source (even a known source) if it has not been scanned for viruses.

- Maintain a schedule of maintenance for data backup, disk error scanning, and associated digital maintenance (such as defragmenting).

- Check manufacturer websites regularly for software updates, bug fixes, and compatibility notices.

- Keep a log of program installations to help locate software conflicts.

- Note when multiple problems occur in the operation of your system. If you have problems with more than one program or device, there may be a common link to the real cause.

- Simplify your system whenever possible by detaching chronically unused peripherals and uninstalling unnecessary software.

Know Your Image

Some matters involved in repairing and compositing images are not judgment calls, and some are. One thing no book or manual can tell you is exactly what you want to do with an image. While I can suggest proven ways of getting good results, learning to evaluate an image's composition and deciding what to do to improve it will be a judgment call you must make.

Don't ever say it is good enough if it isn't good enough. Give up on an image only when it is not worth the effort to improve it. There is almost nothing you can't do with an image if you have the desire. You can also correct the same image from now until doomsday, improving it in increments all the time. Sometimes putting an image aside for a day or two can give you a new perspective: when you come back to it, you may see solutions you hadn't previously considered. Solutions won't always jump out at you, and sometimes you'll have to manufacture them. In trying to stretch your limitations, no matter what you are attempting to do to an image, chances are you will learn from each solution you attempt.

The more you work with images, the easier and quicker the manipulations will become. Feel free to ask questions through the website and forum (`http://photoshopcs.com`, `http://retouchpro.com`).

Layer Blend Modes

Blending modes calculate a result based on the interplay of image information. The original information is altered either physically (with direct application of the mode via a brush mode) or as a visible result (with indirect application applied via layer mode). Different modes combine the information in different ways. A blending mode used in a layer will look at the pixel qualities in the top layer and display a result based on how those combine. When a mode is used with a painting tool, Photoshop looks at the quality of the color being applied (foreground color) as if the color were being applied in a layer, using the selected brush dynamics. The more significant difference is that brush application changes the content of the layer you are painting on to achieve the result.

Modes can create effects using calculations based on select color components. For example, the result might be a calculation of red, green, and blue components (tone and color together), a calculation of luminosity, a calculation of color, and so forth. Table A.6 describes the blending modes available in Photoshop.

Adobe is pretty stingy with the exact calculations. Adobe's descriptions of the modes are actually obfuscated by the language used to describe them. To simplify: the more obscure and difficult to calculate, the less useful the mode will tend to be.

Table A.6

Photoshop Blending Modes

BLEND MODE	QUICK KEY	EFFECT
Normal	Shift+Alt+N/Shift+Option+N	Plain overlay of content. The result takes on the color/tone of the pixels in the upper layer.
Dissolve	Shift+Alt+I/Shift+Option+I	The result takes on the color/tone of the pixels in the upper layer, but the result is dithered (randomized) according to the opacity of the application. The greater the opacity, the more the selection is weighted to the upper layer. 100% opacity will produce a 0% dissolve effect; 50% opacity will produce a result where 50% of the result has the applied color.
Darken	Shift+Alt+K/Shift+Option+K	Chooses the darker color value set for each pixel in comparing the two layers. Uses either the applied color or the original. No portion of the image gets lighter.
Multiply	Shift+Alt+M/Shift+Option+M	Darkens the result by darkening the lower layer based on the darkness of the upper layer. Any applied tone darker than white darkens the result. No portion of the image can get lighter.
Color Burn	Shift+Alt+B/Shift+Option+B	Burns in (darkens) the color of the underlying layer with the upper layer, darkening the result. No portion of the image gets lighter. The greater the difference between pixel colors, the greater the change.
Linear Burn	Shift+Alt+A/Shift+Option+A	Similar to Multiply but somewhat more extreme.
Lighten	Shift+Alt+G/Shift+Option+G	Chooses the lighter color value set for each pixel in comparing the two layers. Uses either the applied color or the original. No portion of the image gets darker.
Screen	Shift+Alt+S/Shift+Option+S	Brightens the result by lightening the lower layer based on the lightness of the upper layer. Any color lighter than black lightens the result. No portion of the image can get darker.
Color Dodge	Shift+Alt+D/Shift+Option+D	Dodges (lightens) the color of the underlying layer with the upper layer, lightening the result. No portion of the image gets darker. The greater the difference between pixel colors, the greater the change.
Linear Dodge	Shift+Alt+W/Shift+Option+W	Similar to Screen but the result is more extreme.

continues

BLEND MODE	QUICK KEY	EFFECT
Overlay	Shift+Alt+O/Shift+Option+O	Multiplies (darkens) the light colors and screens (lightens) the dark ones. Colors at light and dark extremes are less affected than quartertones.
Soft Light	Shift+Alt+F/Shift+Option+F	Multiplies (darkens) the dark colors and screens (lightens) the light ones depending on the applied color. If the applied color is light, the pixel lightens; if dark, it darkens. Soft, or 50% application of the upper layer.
Hard Light	Shift+Alt+H/Shift+Option+H	Multiplies (darkens) the dark colors and screens (lightens) the light ones. 100% application of the upper layer.
Vivid Light	Shift+Alt+V/Shift+Option+V	Similar to Color Burn when the applied color is darker than 50% gray; similar to Color Dodge when the applied color is lighter than 50% gray.
Linear Light	Shift+Alt+J/Shift+Option+J	Similar to Linear Burn when the applied color is darker than 50% gray; similar to Linear Dodge when the applied color is lighter than 50% gray.
Pin Light	Shift+Alt+Z/Shift+Option+Z	Similar to Multiply when the applied color is darker than 50% gray; similar to Screen when the applied color is lighter than 50% gray.
Hard Mix	Shift+Alt+L/ Shift+Option+L	Posterizes the image to one of 8 pure colors: red, green, blue, cyan, magenta, yellow, black and white based on a comparison of layers.
Difference	Shift+Alt+E/Shift+Option+E	Reacts to the difference between pixel values: A large difference yields a bright result; a small difference yields a dark result (no difference yields black).
Exclusion	Shift+Alt+X/Shift+Option+X	Uses the darkness of the applied layer to mask the Difference effect (described previously). If the original value is dark, there is little change as the result; if the original color is black, there is no change. The lighter the original color, the more intense the Difference effect.
Hue	Shift+Alt+U/Shift+Option+U	Changes the hue to the applied layer while leaving the saturation and luminosity unchanged.
Saturation	Shift+Alt+T/Shift+Option+T	Changes the saturation of the applied layer while leaving the hue and luminosity unchanged.
Color	Shift+Alt+C/Shift+Option+C	Changes the hue and saturation of the applied layer while leaving the luminosity unchanged.
Luminosity	Shift+Alt+Y/Shift+Option+Y	Changes the luminosity of the applied layer while leaving the saturation and hue unchanged.

High-End Printing Options

When the book discusses printing, it is usually in the context of printing at home with ink-jet printers. There are actually a number of other printing options for your images, and what we will focus on here are the higher-end possibilities. You can turn your images into negatives or slides for use in photo printing or projection, and you can use other printing processes, like offset printing and LED. You will have many more options than those mentioned here, but in dealing with digital images and photography these will be common and useful. Check with your local services and on the Internet for more ideas.

Film Recorders

A film recorder is a means of generating film exposure using a digital image. Film recorders can be used to re-create slides and negatives, which can then be used for slide presentations and print exposures.

Within the film recorder, a cathode ray tube (CRT) is employed to project a thin beam of light through a filter and onto film to expose it. Film is then processed and developed using conventional photo processing, resulting in an image on traditional analog film.

Film recorders come in varying resolution and quality based both on the number of lines of resolution possible and the quality (and size) of the CRT. Cost for processing can vary based on the quality of the film recorder and the available resolution. Usually it is not cheap, but when you need slides or film and have an image with enough resolution, the quality can be unsurpassed. Resolution can be 650–1000 ppi at the final size.

Generally, 35-mm film is used with 2000- and 4000-line recorders. While 8000-line recorders can be used with 35-mm film, this resolution begins to surpass the limitation of the film grain. Typically, 8000-line recorders are used with larger film stocks (2.25 inch), and 16,000-line recorders with 4×5 inch and larger.

A list of exactly what to use as far as resolution would be meaningless because the varying quality of these devices may require different sources. You'll have to contact services both to see if they have film recorders available and what they require for output.

Offset Printing

Offset printing is standard CMYK printing on printing presses. This may come in handy for producing such things as cards, business cards, books (and covers), CD inserts, calendars, posters, and the like—top quality in both black-and-white and color printing. Presses can be of varying quality. The better quality presses will run upward of 133 lpi and 2540 dpi. All will use PostScript and halftone approaches.

The only real reason to consider offset printing would be for multiple prints—usually numbering in the thousands rather than hundreds. While shorter runs may be available, this type of printing is almost exclusively effective in volume.

LED

Light-emitting diode (LED) printers generate photographic results from RGB digital files. Somewhat like film recorders, your files can be printed without the conversion to CMYK because the process used is light based. Exposure is created on photographic paper in up to poster size directly from digital files. Exposures are then processed (often right in the same machine).

Whereas prints may be somewhat more expensive than traditional photo prints, the gap isn't very wide. The advantage is that you will use this process selectively with images that you have had the opportunity to correct and improve and still get photographic results. Unlike using a film recorder, which would require two steps (record to film and then print) to get results, an LED is a single step. Because it cuts out having to pay for film and photo, it can end up being much less expensive to process.

Again, quality can vary, but the color results will often be superior to home printing. Files often only require about 250 ppi at final size. Check with your service to be sure, and ask to see samples of prints before you buy.

Index

Note to the Reader: Throughout this index **boldfaced** page numbers indicate primary discussions of a topic. *Italicized* page numbers indicate illustrations.

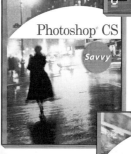